J. P. Whittet

PORTRAIT AND PAGEANT

BOOK
PRODUCTION
WAR ECONOMY
STANDARD

THIS BOOK IS PRODUCED
IN COMPLETE CONFORMITY WITH
THE AUTHORIZED ECONOMY STANDARDS

THE RT. HON. WINSTON S. CHURCHILL

PORTRAIT AND PAGEANT

KINGS, PRESIDENTS, AND PEOPLE

By

FRANK O. SALISBURY

C.V.O.   LL.D.   R.P.   R.I.

LONDON

JOHN MURRAY, ALBEMARLE STREET, W.

TO
ARTHUR MEE

WHOSE WIDE KNOWLEDGE AND STIMULATING GENIUS
HAVE WON THE ADMIRATION AND FIRED THE IMAGINATION
OF THE YOUTH OF ALL AGES OF THE ENGLISH–SPEAKING
WORLD, THIS VOLUME IS AFFECTIONATELY DEDICATED

First Edition . . *June 1944*
Reprinted . . . *June 1944*

Made and Printed in Great Britain by Butler & Tanner Ltd., Frome and London

PRELUDE

U.K. AND U.S.

THE hope of the world lies in the unity of the English-Speaking Nations. The attainment of that ideal does not appear a wild dream to a man who has divided many of his best years between the two sides of the Atlantic.

It has been the writer's good fortune to see much of the life of both countries, and to know at close quarters some of the chief personalities of the United Kingdom and the United States. He has found life a joyous thing in both countries and people very much the same.

We are all much alike to an artist ; is it not reasonable to think that we are really all much alike to one another ? Three kings, three presidents, many heroes, merchant princes, and not a few of the common folk whom God must like because He made so many, come into this book of memory. The painter with his palette sees many people, many sights, and many lands, and through it all he sees humanity, men and women with the cares of life weighing heavily on them ; the gay, the rich, the successful, the sorrowful ; the world in peace and the world at war. His is the radiant world of colour, of brilliant pageantry and impressive scenes, but there passes before him, amid all the pomp and circumstance, the dark, pathetic mystery of things which is the background of our human stage.

These memories are of people in every phase of life, and they show us that wherever we may be the world is very human. They come mostly from the years between two wars which brought about British and American unity in one great purpose, and it is hoped that they may satisfy the reader, as they have satisfied the writer, that the manifest goodwill of our two peoples is the foundation-stone upon which the peace of the world may be built up by the United Nations.

CONTENTS

LIST OF ILLUSTRATIONS

CHAPTER I

BEGINNINGS

TAKING the reins of the steed of memory back to the 'seventies, I remember the easterly winds of a winter's day rattling the Victorian windows of a room at Harpenden, with an Adam's overmantel and a mirror reflecting the scrolls and flowers of the papered walls. About the room were glass vases hung with prismatic dangles, in which glowed all the colours of the rainbow.

In that room I was a constant prisoner, often looking out with longing eyes at my brothers snowballing with their schoolmates. From this parlour window, my retreat when I was not kept in bed, the delicate boy of the family looked out on life in the lovely village of Harpenden. In those long and weary days I would stand at a small table with the paints brother James bought me from Winsor and Newton's, a beautiful water-colour box of moist colours. Somewhere even yet is a drawing of tulips and lilies of the valley with a technique so rough that it brings to mind the morning when, eager to get to work, I took a cup from the breakfast table, emptied the dregs of coffee, and filled it with water too hurriedly, for the sugar remained in the bottom and mixed with the colours so that after sixty years the grit of the sugar still tells its tale. This water colour is the first painting I remember, dated " 7 years of age " and signed Francis Owen Salisbury.

Looking back to that time I see nothing of exceptional ability in anything of mine ; my twin daughters Sylvia and Monica were much more promising with their first paints.

The handicap of ill-health kept me away from school, and until I was twelve the only schooling I can recollect is going to Miss Calcott's infant school for a month. I remember that Mr. Wix, the Inspector, visited the school, and when my map of Africa was shown to him Miss Calcott (I think possibly because of my frailty) put her head on one side as if imitating me, and gave me a smile of encouragement. How a little kindliness lives on through the years !

In my teens I was sent now and then to Mr. Henshaw's near by, and dreaded the return to school after being at home so long, finding myself so backward. When the time came to stand on a chalk-line in the centre of the room, waiting for my turn to read aloud, I would count the paragraphs to see which I should have to read; but one day I was caught, for the Master, evidently realizing what I was doing, asked me to read unexpectedly, and I could not find my place. I stumbled terribly, and in my humiliation the perspiration fell down my face and I was made an example to the school, caned, and kept behind to write a hundred lines—a bitter punishment, it still seems to me.

This ends my recollection of schooling, except that when spring came my parents sent me to Uncle Dyer's School at Dunstable, but the winds of that bleak place put an end to my schooldays in a week, and my sister Emmie, who was then starting her scholastic career as a student teacher, came to the rescue and took me in hand at home.

When I was about nine Mr. John Robertson, a dear farmer friend, prevailed upon my parents to let me go to his farm, promising to make a strong man of me with open-air life and milk straight from the cow. I went with him in his dog-cart, and drove to his farm at Cheverils Green, staying with him for three months, when he passed away. Each day we would ride in his pony trap round the fields, and my association with this fine old man is one of the first beautiful friendships I remember in a life which has been full of them since. After breakfast every morning the household would gather in the dining-room for prayers, and I sat on a hassock at his feet while he read the Bible, and on Sunday evenings I would sit at the foot of his bed while we sang hymns.

Those were remarkable days for men of character and sterling worth. Mr. Robertson was an eloquent local preacher, and so was Mr. Partridge, another neighbouring farmer. Well I recall their fine rugged heads, splendid subjects for a portrait painter. But, alas, I was no portrait painter; I meant to be a farmer, and went home very discouraged because my parents would not hear of it.

My father, to give me something to do, gave me one plot of land in the orchard and another in a field, and on these I grew wheat and mangel crops, making a drilling machine and a small dressing machine to separate the chaff from the corn. Evidently pleased with my progress, he allowed me to have a ewe and two lambs, which I looked after year by year until I had a delightful little flock which followed me whenever I changed their pen. At this time I kept pigeons, too, almond tumblers and carriers which gave me great delight, and for which I was awarded several prizes; but my brother, who now took me in hand, insisted on my giving all this up and getting to serious work.

Frederick Alpheus, my second brother, was a poet, gifted and artistic. As to-day the youth of our country is enthralled by the aeroplane, so in those days engineering was the magnet of our boys. Steam-engines were every boy's love, and we all had a craze for making models. My brother was working on an elaborate model of a horizontal engine in which I had a little side-show, and out of odds and ends I managed to make a vertical engine. I found a brass meat-jack, which I made into a boiler. The fly-wheel was the wheel from a screw tap, the cylinder was from a brass tube and some flat nails, and links from a mowing-machine chain formed the piston.

It took a long time to get it to go, for the methylated spirit lamp would not generate enough steam-power, so one night, before going to bed, I took it into the kitchen and put it on the gas-ring. Suddenly the piston rod shot up, and with one swinging touch away went the fly-wheel. The excitement was terrific. The whole family came and watched the fun, and that night I was allowed to stay up to celebrate my invention.

All this time, under careful treatment, I was growing stronger, and brother James thought it time he took my career in hand. It was arranged that I should be apprenticed to him in his stained glass works, so at fifteen I set out to St. Albans by the seven-thirty train every morning, and had three years of stern discipline. To it I owe everything. Brother James made it clear from the start that family relationship was not to come into business, and that I should be treated as an outsider and enjoy no favour. Every day I started work at eight and continued till six, and, curiously enough, I never recall being kept at home for illness. Force of circumstances were enabling me early to realize the vital truth that the most important part of education is what we give ourselves. By the misfortune of ill-health I was driven to be a student in the never-ending university of experience, with the motto over its ever-open door : " The doorstep of the temple of wisdom is the knowledge of our own ignorance."

As well as being odd boy in the studio I had to grind the colours for the painters, and then passed into the cutting shop and the glazing department, where I was able to watch the building up of a stained-glass window. After the first year I was promoted to making cut-lines and rough designs, but James felt that hard drudgery was the best discipline for me.

Once, when he was travelling for a week, there came a letter from an architect asking for a design for a window for a public-house called the " Eight Bells ", and, a little daringly, I made an octagonal design with a geometrical motif round a circle, showing the eight bells chiming and swinging in varying perspectives. The design was sent and secured the order, but in spite of this I was taken to task by my brother for going outside my range. Discipline was discipline ! For months I was kept tracing ornamental squares such as are often to be seen in villas, Victorian dreadfuls masquerading as art. The work, however, demanded concentration, a steady hand, a quick eye, and constant application, and it must therefore have been good experience.

For the first year of my apprenticeship I received a salary of five shillings a week, and seven the second year, but at the end of the second year I was already taking the place of a qualified painter and was working till nine at night without extra pay. I do not remember receiving my wages regularly ; being in the family apparently did count, after all ! The capital reserves of the business were not very substantial, and when pay-day came there was often not enough in the bank to meet the wages bill. It was then that I was sent home to my father with an S O S.

As my drawing was developing, James felt that I should attend a drawing academy in London, and took me to Heatherley's of Newman Street. Mr. Crompton generously offered to take me at an inclusive fee, allowing me to attend any classes I could manage, and this necessitated my season ticket being extended from Harpenden to London. The fees were paid by brother James, but were registered in a ledger against me, so that I could work it off against wages. I went to Heatherley's three days a week and worked the other three at St. Albans. The hour's train journey to London was useful to me, for I took the opportunity of reading such books as Plutarch's *Lives*, Boswell's *Johnson*, Carlyle's *Cromwell*, Macaulay, and Francis Bacon's *Essays*.

On entering such a famous studio as Heatherley's it was impossible for a young student not to feel bewildered by the classic antiques ranged round the room, the models in the Life Room, the easels with drawings and paintings in every stage of development, but it was a fine experience, suggesting the need for strenuous and concentrated endeavour. I felt that I had a long way to go. The hours were long and arduous, beginning at the school at ten with antique drawing, anatomy in the afternoon, and life classes at six, which meant a twelve-hour day for me.

One day I noticed a student, Alfred Lyddon, at work on some drawings from the antique and the life, and found that he was competing for a scholarship at the Royal Academy Schools. This fired me with an idea. I spoke to Mr. Crompton, and he was very disturbed and said I must have years of groundwork before I could dream of going to the Academy. I must have been about sixteen, but in the next six months I had my first try, and failed.

Many students in competing for the scholarships made their drawings from the Elgin Marbles at the British Museum, and I decided to work there in the day and do life drawings at Heatherley's in the evenings. My antique drawing was the Theseus from the Parthenon Frieze, and this time I was successful. I am still thrilled to think of the delight of the family when I won a Royal Academy scholarship for five years. I was just eighteen.

Years later, when Mr. Crompton retired from Heatherley's, the students honoured me by requesting that I should paint a portrait of his daughter Dorothea, for presentation to the principal to whom the whole world of art owed so much. I had to make a speech to voice the devotion of past and present students, and an illuminated address and an album of signatures was presented with the portrait. Nearly all the illustrious names of living artists were in the album, so famous was this school of art.

Work at the Royal Academy started in the Antique School, and after a course there one had to paint a still-life and copy an Old Master to pass into the Upper Life School. My copy was Owen's Boy with a Porringer. I had never handled a brush before, and it was the first piece of my work which seemed to show any satisfaction, ability, or promise. I now passed into the upper class and attended with fear and trembling ; we had three days a week painting from the head and shoulder, and three from the figure.

Mr. Seymour Lucas was my first Visitor, and I was terrified as my turn came. Mr. Lucas had a very enthusiastic and characteristic way of shouting his criticism, sometimes with caustic illustrations and merciless remarks which overawed the class. As he came nearer to me I wished the floor would open and swallow me up, but I managed to brace myself for the great ordeal. He stopped in front of my canvas, looked first at it and then at me, and asked how many heads I had painted. I said this was my first, and he said, " Well, you will make a great painter ; you have a fine sense of colour and an eye for beauty." I was lifted into the seventh heaven, and the humorist of the class came and gathered with a group of students round my easel in the interval and asked if I would sell my masterpiece now or let it go to Christie's.

The Seymour Lucas visit twelve months later was looked forward to by the whole class, and this time he taught me a great lesson. Looking at my nude study from life, he said, "Your man looks as if he had not washed for a hundred years : give me your palette." Taking a brush full of medium white and a slight flesh tone, he slashed it in a masterly manner across the high lights of the body, and it was astonishing how low in tone my colour now appeared. He then emphasized the importance of pitching a portrait in a light, brilliant key to stand the test of time. The Velasquez masterpiece must have been painted clear white in the high lights to be so luminous to-day.

Richmond, Sargent, Abbey, Crofts, Ouless, Marcus Stone, Storey, Cope, Alma-Tadema, Clausen, Solomon, Hacker, were all Visitors at the Academy School, and every month one of them gave us his best experience in the Arts. We were allowed to tap their brains, and these visits stand out as days of great inspiration. I remember how, one and all, they would emphasize the importance of composition and ideas. It was no use being able to paint brilliantly unless you had something to say, some idea to express. At the end of every month the Visitor would set a subject, and on the last day the sketches were put up in the lecture room and criticized before us all. The most painful day was Sargent's, whose subject was Jacob wrestling with the Angel. He was obviously nervous, and scarcely able to say a word except "This is good", or "I do not understand this". Solomon was very clever ; he went round and at a glance recognized the work of many students by their colour, style, or touch, only from having seen their work in the life class. I was surprised, but greatly encouraged, when he came to mine, to hear him say, "This is Salisbury's." Sir Lawrence Alma-Tadema was great. On his day most of the students were busy on the gold-medal work, and there were only six poor composition sketches to set up. The curator came up to me and said, "There will not be a criticism ; it is an insult to the Visitor," but to our astonishment we were summoned to the lecture-hall as usual. We were rightly ashamed of the sketches on exhibition, but the Visitor studied each one carefully, trying to see the best in the poorest effort, and made a memorable occasion out of hopeless material.

The next time Sir Lawrence visited the schools he set The Builders as the subject for composition, and was very pleased with my sketch, saying it would make a fine painting if carried out. After my visit to Italy I developed the idea, using the interior of San Marco at Venice —the gold mosaic arches with the olive-coloured flesh of the Italian workman on the scaffolding. The architect is seen in the shadow of an arch in perspective, instructing a workman busy on a mosaic. It was Longfellow's poem that gave me my first inspiration :

> All are architects of Fate,
> Working in these walls of Time . . .
> In the elder days of Art
> Builders wrought with greatest care
> Each minute and unseen part,
> For the Gods see everywhere.

The picture was eventually invited by the Worcester Corporation for exhibition at their gallery, and to my great delight they decided to keep it for the permanent collection. Some months later I received a letter informing me that the picture had buckled in the centre, and on going down to see it I found that my description of the picture had been glued on the back of the canvas. On this being soaked off all was well, to my very great relief, for it was the first picture of mine hung in a public gallery.

It was a great satisfaction to me that I was able to pay all the expenses during my five years of training, for I won the Landseer Scholarship (which was awarded by Lord Leighton), and was successful in winning a British Institution award.

My first visit to the Academy Spring Exhibition was an experience never to be forgotten. It was an awakening in an enchanted land with a mind fresh and receptive before the mysteries of the craft were known to me, or the critical faculty awakened. What a mistake it is to destroy the serenity of life's sincere creations by looking for failings when we should search out the beauties. Lord Leighton's masterpiece, " The Garden of the Hesperides ", was in this exhibition, and I still recall the exultation the picture stirred within me, unequalled by any I have seen since, even Michael Angelo's Sistine Chapel ceiling. It may seem strange that after all these years this sensitiveness to a beautiful scene should remain, but the artist is, of course, supremely sensitive to subtle influences, and to the changing faces of nature. Temperamental feeling may be his greatest asset or his greatest curse. Thanks to my disciplinary training I have conquered any natural reluctance to work and have not waited for inspiration. " Work for the inspiration : do not wait for it " has been my motto. Early in life I had a marvellous demonstration of the value of this. I regularly set myself to paint the sunset, and one day, sacrificing an exciting game of tennis, I climbed a mile to a vantage point, but the sky that had allured me to the spot was suddenly blackened and lost its beauty. Something whispered in my ear, " You can now go back to your game," but I was resolved not to be robbed of my prize and set to work on the black cloud scene.   Suddenly the sun burst through the horizon and sent its red and golden shafts of light transforming the clouds into magic splendour, and I was ready for it.   In a few minutes, with brushes full of the richest colours on my palette, I started on this glorious sunset.   I had my reward.   Yes, work for the inspiration ; never wait for it.   You may be too late.

CHAPTER II

DREAM DAYS

MY first studio was a small room over a workshop in Harpenden, in the yard of the old home. Here I painted my first gold-medal picture, " The Finding of Moses ", and a silver medal cartoon of a classic goddess. At my next studio, which had been a Congregational Hall, I painted my second gold-medal picture of Cleopatra clandestinely introduced into the presence of Caesar.

Towards the end of my course at the R.A. Schools I was impressed by the distinguished and rugged head of Sir Henry Gilbert, an outstanding personality in our village, and, being anxious to start portrait painting outside the family, I boldly asked him to sit, and he was glad to do so. My studio being too small for the sittings, I went to his house ; but the light was very poor. Before the time came for the sittings an attack of nervousness almost made me run away, but I mastered my fear and the portrait was finished. Some years afterwards Sir Charles Lawes-Wittewronge (who had succeeded his father Sir John Bennet Lawes at Rothamsted), took an interest in the portrait, and his sister, Mrs. Walter Creyke, asked to see my drawings. I walked with them to Rothamsted in fear and trembling, yet it was a glorious encouragement to me, for the family were charming, and have remained my treasured friends. More than half a century has passed since then, yet at this moment Mrs. Creyke is marvellously energetic half-way through the 'nineties.

To set out on an artist's career is for any youth no small adventure, fraught as it must be by struggle, failure, and disappointment. Living in a small village, with no influential backing, did not make life easy. Sir John Bennet Lawes had signed my papers for the R.A. Schools, and I remember that when I first met him he said, " I wish my son Charles Lawes were like you, having to make his own money ; then he might do something." It was a new experience for me to hear a rich man talk like this, and difficult to understand, conscious as I was of the years of hard work, disappointment, and uncertainty I must endure before I could succeed.

The problem of the future was being forced on me at this time because I had fallen in love, and the struggle going on in my mind was whether a student beginning a precarious career was justified in giving marriage a thought. Was it fair? However, these things were eventually taken out of our determining. Alice Maude Greenwood, daughter of one of the noblest women, decided that she would rather help me to make a reputation than wait until I had made one. She was the subject of my first Academy picture, which was sold on the opening day—a good omen. It was called " Reflections ".

In our Harpenden days we were an entirely happy, self-contained family ; indeed, we did not escape friendly criticism on the score of an excessive self-sufficiency which was held to amount almost to clannishness.

When I look back and the golden years pass before my mind I am conscious of a glow of wonder at the result of our parents' fostering care and mental and spiritual sustenance of us all. To safeguard us against the dangers of foreseeable failure, to nurture to healthy maturity, to educate and to inculcate the precious elements of character and reputable conduct in so big a family—we were five brothers and six sisters—was a notable achievement, even for a time blessed with a certain spacious leisure. In the incessant haste and ceaseless turmoil of our own days such a problem must be attended by difficulties increasingly acute.

I never remember my father formulating so rigid a formula as " Thou shalt not " or an insistent " You must ". His life and habits embodied the principle that example is better than precept. His presence combined simplicity with a natural quiet nobility of demeanour. He was our leader, our pattern, our exemplar. If we transgressed, a venial offence would usually involve no more punishment than the evidence of the pain we had occasioned, revealed in the sadness that showed in his eye, a mute rebuke that we found sufficiently poignant. If, however, our conduct quite transgressed the bounds of seemly behaviour we were sent into the orchard, there to select a stick from the filbert stems which each child thought fitting for the inflicting of chastisement compatible with the gravity of the offence. This mournful pilgrimage generally ended in true repentance, and brought us a happy reprieve.

Were I asked upon what code of ethics my father founded the principles that he set before us, my reply would sum up his creed in three phrases :

> Love of God,
> Love of King and Country,
> Love of work.

These ideals I embodied in the base of the design of the memorial window to my parents in Harpenden Church.

Our family, as I have said, comprised eleven, all of us married, with the exception of one sister. On the occasion of my parents' golden wedding anniversary the family gathering, including grand-children, numbered forty. Perhaps the happiest and most gratifying tribute paid to my father and mother was that of one of their grand-children, Flight-Lieutenant Gareth Salisbury, of the Royal Air Force, stationed as I write these lines, at Malta. This is what he wrote on Good Friday, 1943.

" I have received many letters from you all. . . . What a wonderful thing it is to have such a vast family so firmly bound together by love, in the greatest and widest sense. I think the Divine Architect of the Universe must have blessed every birth of our families. How other-wise could we have such complete harmony ? I fear we of this generation fall short of the high ideal set for us."

My brother Eustace, eighteen months younger than I, was very artistic, and we were like twins, so much alike that at the birth of our twins an old friend of the family came up and congratulated Eustace ! He used to say that as a boy he took all the whippings I should have had. He had a wonderful eye and a sound judgment, and never a picture left the easel without his approval. He, too, was studying art, and would have entered the R.A. Schools had not his drawings been stolen, which delayed his probation test until an attack of influenza spoilt his last chance. Curious how a life's career may be checked or determined by odd events !

We went to Italy together, starting with £60 between us, deter-mined to study as long as our money would last. It was a great time, and we stayed two months. On our way back I left him at Frankfurt-on-Main, where he worked for twelve months in a stained-glass studio, while I came back to London with a few shillings in my pocket.

Rome at Easter was filled with pilgrims, and the hotels were crowded. The proprietor of one hotel came to our rescue and introduced us to a lady who took in paying guests. With her we found shelter for a week, and as we were going on to Florence she begged us to be sure to stay with a friend of hers, Madame Garli. She was a relative of Sir Edward Poynter, we were told, and would make us very happy.

We arrived at Florence at ten o'clock on Saturday night, though we usually travelled on night trains to save hotels. Storing our baggage, we set out to discover Madame Garli, plunging deeper and deeper into a squalid neighbourhood. At last we came to what seemed to be the house. There was a dim light from an open door, where we found several Italians sitting on sacks, smoking and having their Saturday night talk. I asked if they could tell me where Madame Garli lived. They looked strangely at each other and laughed and then one man got up and asked us to follow him. We followed him through numerous alleys, half afraid, but, recalling the word of the Roman lady, who had warned us not to be disturbed by the outside appearance of the house, as it was beautiful inside. The man stopped in front of a dark archway and pointed up a flight of stone steps. We started to mount, and then a gaunt Italian with a candle leaned over the banister rail and demanded what we wanted. I said " Madame Garli ", and with a lean finger he beckoned us up.

Entering the room, there was before us a scene of squalor and dilapidation I shall never forget. In a chair in front of a table was a fat, untidy slut of dejected humanity, with empty bottles all round her, one used as a candlestick. Bewildered and a little horrified, I said we had come from Rome but would look in another time, and made for the door ; but our retreat was cut off by a man who came running up the stairs and stopped our exit, demanded what we wanted, and asked for our passports. Luckily he turned round to hang his coat up and we took our chance and fled down the steps and out into the night, eventually finding shelter in a *pension*. In the morning we related our experience to the proprietor, and he said it was a wonder we came out alive. To this day I have never been able to solve the mystery of Madame Garli.

At Pisa we had a curious experience. Going into a restaurant for a meal before catching our night train, we tried our Italian but failed to make ourselves understood. French and German interpreters came forward, but without result, and then a cripple from whom we had bought post cards at the Duomo came forward and we explained what we wanted. He turned to the waiter and told him in English, and all was well !

On my brother's return from Germany we took a studio flat for a year in Yeomans Row, opposite Brompton Oratory. For economy's sake the following year we moved to a cheaper one in Fulham Road, which turned out a terrible place. Some friends called upon us and I shall never forget their look of disgust when they saw the studio. It was a good lesson to me. For an artist to succeed he must appear to be successful, and we quickly moved. It was at Brompton Road that I painted my second Academy picture, " The Bouquet ", and Sir Lawrence Alma-Tadema wrote to congratulate me on it, inviting

me to his studio, the wonderful hall of classic beauty in Grove End
Road. Its marvellous interior, with column arcades, made the
setting for most of his famous pictures. What a privilege it was to
see this great artist in his studio, a setting of ordered and designed
perfection ! He spoke of my picture and I asked him to criticize it ;
as it was skied at the Academy I concluded there must be something
seriously wrong. When I showed him the photograph he said,
" Why, that is the picture I wrote to you about, and it was on the
line when I saw it." Although up, evidently it had come down in
the world in the curious hazards of hanging time !

This year (the first of our century) I bought a plot of land near
the old church at Harpenden, having saved enough money to pay for
it. It happened that my father and mother were the first to be
married in the church after its restoration in 1863, and my grandfather
lived in a house on the Church Green until he was 86, not having
had a day's illness. He was a keen amateur astronomer, but towards
the end of his days he took up astrology, and I remember that he
predicted his death. The fateful day came and he did not die, but
within a week of his date he died of disappointment. How fortunate
it is for our modern astrologers that they are not so sensitive about
their ridiculous predictions !

My parents both attained great ages, 86 and 89, mother outliving
father by three years ; but with his passing she became oblivious to
everything, so kind is tired nature. In her last years it was as if only
part of her seemed to exist. Her memory had almost gone, but
occasionally we would catch affectionate glances of recognition. For
any little help she would always say " Thank you through Service ",
broken mystic words that showed how the law of service had
dominated her actions and illuminated her life. Also rather remarkable was the fact that although her natural speech failed to be articulate
she could always recite the Lord's Prayer, which somehow seemed
to be engraved on the tablets of her memory and to come clearly
forth from her subconsciousness.

To enable us to marry, my father arranged a mortgage and I built
my first house, Elmkirk, making a studio of the first and second floors,
with a sky-light which was convertible. Maude and I were married
from Dorincourt, St. Albans, and had great delight in furnishing the
house and making the garden.

We spent our honeymoon in romantic Cornwall and at Oswestry
in Shropshire, where, curious enough, our hostess, Mrs. Parry-Jones,
was one night reading a book in which Frank and Maude were the

characters and they were on their honeymoon ! But at Tintagel a truly remarkable coincidence occurred, for there I received a letter from Sir Edward Poynter saying that he was impressed by a stained-glass design of mine exhibited at the Royal Academy and asking if I would design a window for a church on a very exposed position on the coast. How strange it would be, we thought, if it were for Tintagel, and immediately we went up to the old church on the romantic headland to check the size of the windows there. None fitted the size Sir Edward had given, however, but some weeks later I received a letter requesting me to proceed with the window, which was to be a memorial to the Earl of Wharncliffe in Tintagel church !

Another Tintagel coincidence comes to mind, for when the time came to make studies of the rough seas for a subject picture I wanted to paint ," The Last Drive of Hippolytus ", I could not find suitable rocks for the composition except in one of these Cornish caves. So I made careful studies of them. Imagine my surprise when, at the Royal Academy, under my picture in Gallery Three, was Sir Edward Poynter's " Sea Nymphs ", in which the President *had used the same rocks at Tintagel* !

We shall not soon forget those days in Cornwall, for it looked at one time as if our first married days might be our last. In a driving sea-mist and rain we drove in an open waggonette twelve miles over the moors from Helston, and later in the afternoon approached the headland, descending the steep zigzag down to Coverack. The church of St. Keverne, grim and remote, with victims of the Manacles in its churchyard and crocodiles on its west doorway, stood high above us, while crowning the opposite cliff stood the only hotel, *a blackened ruin*, keeping sentinel over the small hamlet below. At the foot of the hill was the stream and the millhouse, and a small number of cottages.

Now we were in a dilemma, for we had no rooms, but near by was a neat white-washed cottage, with a garden full of flowers. A woman was sweeping the steps, and I asked her if she knew where we could stay. She said she could take us. Her husband was a fisherman in summer and a carpenter in winter, and with them we spent some delightful days.

My wife was anxious to go to Falmouth, and as the only way was by sea the fisherman said that if the wind and tides were favourable he would take us in his fishing-boat. Day after day we waited, and at last he informed us that the prospects were favourable, and if we started at six the next morning we could catch the tide. We sailed like a swan across the Bay of Coverack, but were very soon out by the terrible Manacle Rocks, tossing in their choppy swirl for an hour, while the boatman entertained us with gruesome tales of shipwreck ! There, on the shore, were the skeleton ribs of a troopship wrecked during the South African War. Just beneath us at low tide you could see in the deep green waters the masts of a wrecked liner, the rigging looking like a forest of seaweed.

Then he told us how that ship, with a blaze of light, drifted out of her course by the strong current, struck the Manacles and sank in a few minutes. Suddenly, in a state of great excitement, he exclaimed, " We are drifting on to the Manacles ; we shall be wrecked." He decided that we must put out to sea, and our little boat tossed angrily as we sped over the ugly currents. For two hours we put out seawards until the Cornish coast was a thin line in the distance. " Here, " he said, " is where the great men-of-war plough up and down, 500 fathoms of water beneath us ! " He asked if I could row, and I said, " Yes, on a river, but never on the sea, though if you give me instructions I will." Taking up the oars, I started rowing manfully to be greatly discouraged when he shouted, " For God's sake, man, do not catch a crab or we shall sink to the bottom." This was enough for me, and I gave him back the oars and took the helm. There was no wind anywhere, but he kept exclaiming, excitedly, " For God's sake, man, keep wind in the sail."

Ahead over Falmouth was a dark cloud, and in a few minutes there was plenty of wind in the sail, and rain as well ! Suddenly he jumped up, snatched the helm from my hand, and shouted, " Man, let loose the starboard rope ! No ! no ! not that, the starboard one ! " At last I got the right rope, and the arm of the sail swept across the boat and nearly carried us overboard. Now we sailed towards the coast but, alas, we over-shot the mouth of the harbour by a mile, and had to tack back, finally arriving exhausted. A rest and a meal having revived us, and our shopping being done, we decided to return, the fisherman assuring us that he could get back to Coverack in an hour and a half. He asked me to steer the boat out of the harbour, and went on heedlessly, giving me no instructions. Racing on the seaward side was a fine yacht and in front were a number of tugs. I steered well in front of these and away from the yacht by my side, and suddenly he rushed up and pushed me from the helm, shouting, " Never go the windward side of anything." He turned the boat abruptly round, narrowly missing the yacht and remarking that " that was a near go ". Wind and tide were now in our favour and we rode to the top and dropped into the trough of the waves, reaching port without further mishap.

So ended our honeymoon adventure, and we breathed a prayer of thankfulness to the Providence which saved us then and has guided our lives through all these happy years.

In the following March we held our first private view at Elmkirk, before sending to the Royal Academy. My picture of " Hyppolytus " was finished, and also a portrait of my wife entitled " Memories ". The afternoon reception was a great success if numbers were anything to go by, and the interesting event of the afternoon was the appearance of a coach with four magnificent prancing horses, Baroness Eckardstein [now Lady Weigall] driving. She was the charming daughter of Sir Blundell Maple, and a great company of friends came with her.

The arrival of the twins Sylvia and Monica aroused great interest in the family about this time. My mother announced the news to me by saying, " Not more than others we deserve, yet God has given us more." I said, " What do you mean, Mother ? " And she replied, " You have two lovely little girls." I said, " What ! Is there not a boy among all that lot ? "

Though my pictures were well received at the Academy and the provincial exhibition, I made no advance financially ; things seemed to stagnate, and the situation was not helped by the fact that we had almost come to our last penny in the bank. Just then an old friend of the family gave me a commission to paint his wife and daughter. I heard afterwards that he could ill afford it, but he declared that the picture had always been a comfort to him. After this things seemed to turn, and a number of commissions came along, one on the twin's first birthday to paint another set of twins, Winnie and Dorothy Treasure.

It was a great joy to see our children growing more beautiful every day. Here were subjects indeed for an artist's brush. It happened that an art critic who came down to Luton to open an exhibition saw there my portrait of my father, and on his way back to London called to see me, saw the twins, and declared that I must give up the next twelve months to painting them ; it was a chance of a lifetime and a rare opportunity, he said. He secured my election to the Royal Society of British Artists.

We now systematically set to work to paint the twins. I say we, because it involved as much work for my wife as for me. Every morning they sat for an hour or more. What is more elusive, or more beautiful, than a child from one to two years old ? Never for a moment were they still ; never were their expressions long the same. How we all worked ! But in twelve months I could paint a head in an hour, and it is true that I learned more from the twins in that twelve months than in five years at the Academy School. To these studies of them I owe my quickness in painting portraits, for an artist, to secure a breathing likeness, must be able to catch a fleeting expression in a fleeting moment. I painted about thirty pictures from my perfect little models, and in the process of time they became constructive and helpful sitters. I exhibited the whole series at the Doré Gallery in Bond Street under the title, " Messages from Life's Morning ".

Many children's groups followed at this time. The Player children, the Curtis children, the Harvey girls, and the Ryder family, were all delightful subjects, and easy for a painter. An artist's work is rather like an adventurous journey, a road over which you never pass again, whose lost opportunities never return. If he is progressive and receptive, his style and technique will change as day by day the pano-rama of life unfolds before his gaze, and he interprets and perpetuates the living reality about him. The artist may be said to write his biography in his canvases.

At the outset of our home life we resolved to continue a custom which had been practised for generations in our family, by starting the day with morning prayers. I like to think of it as in some sense a memorial to the dear and noble lives of kindred gone before us. Difficulties attending this simple, time-honoured, and beautiful ritual multiply daily, and unfortunately its observance is dying out in our homes, but the B.B.C. every morning in " Lift up your hearts " before the eight o'clock news carries on the great tradition. It is a marvel to me that my father could keep it up so long with five boys always longing to get to their games ; for almost before the Amen of the Lord's Prayer there would be a regular stampede to the door. When Father was away Mother would conduct, and it is still remem-bered in the family that one morning, as she was praying most eloquently, she saw a mouse run under her chair, and after a little squeal finished the prayer standing *on* the chair.

One other morning we remember. We lost a dear little child Elaine, and soon after my wife, who read the Bible at our prayers, started the Twenty-third Psalm and came to " Yea, though I walk through the valley of the shadow of death ", when her voice faltered and she could read no more. Very quickly and very beautifully a young maid of seventeen stepped forward, took the Bible, and read on : " I will fear no evil . . ."

It is a good start for any day's work to open the greatest book in the world with its marvellous literature, comprising the whole range of human experience, sounding its depths and scaling its heights. It is like going on to the Captain's Bridge, meeting the Pilot, taking from him your chartered bearings, and setting your compass to the Guiding Star.

In these later days, when our small grandson Richard, aged 4, was staying with us, he had been up early one morning and was playing when he heard the bell ring, and said to his nurse, "Is that the bell for that jolly old game of prayers?"

The time came when the need of a bigger studio made me consider a fine site of land which came to be for sale on the west side of Harpenden Common, known from a group of cottages as Chapel Row. The old Wesleyan Chapel stood there, and tradition has it that John Wesley preached in it, an ancient of the village having given my father the poker with which Wesley poked the fire. I had just enough money in the bank to buy the land, and brother Eustace, who was studying architecture, planned a house which we called the Red Gables.

Eustace made a model of the house, the frontage facing the common, famous for its racecourse and the cricket ground in the distance, a noble clump of stately elm-trees at the end of the lawn sheltering the Lawes Rothamsted Laboratories. We had much fun in seeing our ideas develop, in turning old beams from a barn into overhanging gables; and at Red Gables we lived in great happiness for years. Here I painted "The Passing of War", and for Lord Wakefield the Royal Exchange panel of Alfred Rebuilding the Walls of the City of London. It had always been my ambition to paint a panel for the Royal Exchange. I was greatly interested in Abbey's panel, and had seen "William the Conqueror" by Seymour Lucas grow in his studio, hearing him tell the story of how the donor, a Billingsgate fish merchant, asked him if he would take the payment out in fish! Little did I dream that I would eventually paint three of these panels.

My next ambitious subject was "The Passing of Queen Eleanor", sixteen feet long. When I was painting this my dear artist friend, Fred Marriott, came into the studio and said, "Why, Salisbury, are you wasting your time painting that huge picture? No one will ever buy it." I had never thought of that.

In painting a historical scene there are many problems to consider which make absolute accuracy difficult. Here I had the funeral procession with the bier, on which rested the wax effigy of Queen

Eleanor, Edward the First following as chief mourner. The abbot and the monks from the Monastery of St. Albans were meeting the funeral procession as it approached the city, and the abbot was aspurging the bier. To be correct the king should have been at the foot of the coffin, but that would have ruined the rhythmic beauty of the procession, so I had the effigy carried with the feet first. The critics condemned the picture on the ground that I was wrong in having a wax effigy there at all, but my authority for this was the fact that in Westminster Abbey are remains of wax effigies as far back as 1300. Many years afterwards, at an exhibition of thirteenth-century art at the Burlington Club, the introduction in the catalogue, referring to the monument of Queen Eleanor in Westminster Abbey, said, " This is undoubtedly modelled from the wax effigy carried in the funeral procession ".

Exhibited at the Academy, the picture had apparently been of no help to me, and I thought of what Marriott said ; no one wanted it and no one was interested. Then I had to go to Liverpool to paint Sir William Hartley, and my delight may be imagined when my wife sent me on a letter from Lord Stanmore saying that a committee of the House of Lords was presenting six panels to the Palace of Westminster, and they wished the artist who painted " The Passing of Queen Eleanor " to paint the trial of Queen Katharine before the Consistory Court of Blackfriars. In a flash I had my reward. Somebody *was* interested.

But it was not until ten years after that the Eleanor picture found a resting-place. It hung in my studio all that time after a tour of provincial exhibitions. At last, at a private view in 1918, the Mayor of St. Albans, Alderman Arthur Faulkner, was among the guests, and as he was leaving he called me aside and said, looking at the picture, " Edward the First was the last Crusader, and our Army has just completed his work in the deliverance of Jerusalem. I want to present this picture to St. Alban's Abbey to commemorate the triumph of British arms so that it may be placed near the spot where the queen's body rested six hundred years ago." I feared the Ecclesiastical Commission would not give a faculty for it to be placed there, as it was not exactly a religious picture, but Mr. Faulkner achieved his purpose, and in that glorious abbey it hangs to-day, fitting as if it had been painted for its position.

CHAPTER III

A GREAT CHANCE

IN 1910 six artists were selected to paint six panels for the corridor between the House of Lords and the House of Commons leading from the Central Lobby. Edwin Abbey undertook to supervise and unify the work, the colour scheme was to be restricted to red, black, and gold, and the chief figures were to be five feet six inches. These were splendid unifying principles to start on, and we all met in high hope at Abbey's studio in Chelsea, and made our sketches. While the work was in progress Mr. and Mrs. Abbey motored down from London to Harpenden and paid us a delightful visit.

The research work for the panels was very exciting, for it was a wonderful and picturesque period of history, giving a fine chance to an artist. Holbein's portrait of Henry the Eighth and his drawings of court ladies provided a wealth of material to start with.

Sir Alfred Scott-Gatty, Garter King-of-Arms, undertook to supply us with all the heraldic information and was a great help. When I had roughly worked out my composition I went down to the College of Heralds and he showed me the historic Tournament Roll prepared for the celebration at Westminster in honour of the young prince, short-lived son of Queen Katherine. I studied the drawing of this ancient parchment, on which, preceding the State procession, were mounted heralds in cloth-of-gold tabards, each bearing a gold mace. I made sketches of these and of the long robe of the king. The roll was so long, illustrating the procession of horsemen in full armour ready for the lists, that it took me half an hour to get to the end of it.

Because Shakespeare says the king was preceded by mace-bearers, and Cardinal Wolsey by a mace-bearer holding silver columns, and because I had seen them in the Tournament Roll preceding the royal procession, I introduced mace-bearers supporting the king; but when the Garter-King saw my sketch he criticized these figures and said they were wrong. Unfortunately he questioned whether the roll supported me, and I could not show it to him as it would have taken half an hour to unroll it. But his argument was very interesting. He related how he had just organized the coronation ceremony of Edward the Seventh at Westminster Abbey, where the mace-bearer

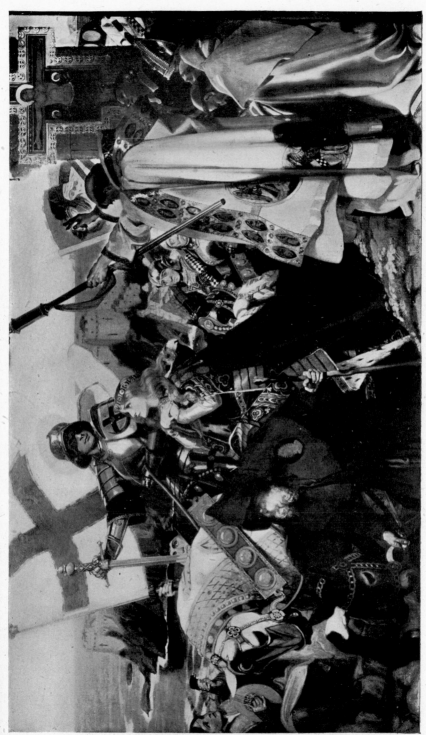

THE QUEST OF ST. GEORGE, IN THE NATIONAL MUSEUM OF WALES.
An early picture

The Sen Sisters.

stood at the High Altar holding the mace while the officials and foreign princes arrived, but immediately the King entered the west door the mace was covered. Also at King George's Jubilee service at St. Paul's the maces of the Houses of Parliament were placed on tables, but as soon as the king arrived were immediately covered. There is no doubt at that famous crisis in Parliament when Cromwell said " Remove that bauble ", the mace really represented the king. I remember that Sir Alfred used another interesting illustration to support his point—that the chalice, the sacramental cup, was used as a symbol of the presence of Christ in Our Lord's absence.

In spite of all these arguments, interesting as they were, Shakespeare and the painter of the Tournament Roll decided for me, and I stood by their historical recordings. I had an excellent model in my father-in-law, Charles Colmer Greenwood, who was in stature and bearing very like the king ; Lady Leveson-Gower sat for the queen ; and I was fortunate to find an architect friend who resembled Cardinal Wolsey. The idea that he would do for the cardinal came to me in a dream.

The cardinal's robe was Sir Henry Irving's, lent to me by Miss Edith Craig ; how many thousands have been thrilled by its appearance on the stage of our lost Lyceum ! The robe was, of course, a very valuable possession, and I well remember my anxiety when my model dropped a spot of coffee on the cape. Being of watered silk, it spread like a nightmare. Fortunately for his peace of mind, the architect had not noticed the accident, and as soon as he had gone we set to work with wadding and petrol and were delighted to be able to remove all trace of it.

By a curious coincidence Sir Herbert Beerbohm Tree's " Henry the Eighth " came on just when the pictures were finished, and I went to the first night. Bourchier was the king, and during the supplication of the queen, when she was kneeling at his feet, the actor sat. I felt that this was wrong, as after careful study of Henry's character I had decided that this was the crisis of his life, and he, in spite of his sovereignty, would have been standing. I wrote to the actor and expressed my criticism, and ever afterwards Bourchier stood at that moment in the play.

My wife sat for me as the first maid-of-honour, and assumed an anxious and serious expression in keeping with so tragic a moment ; and it happened that a friend, looking at the picture, remarked that the first maid-of-honour looked a tartar, and he would not like to live with her ! I did not enlighten his blissful innocence, but it is the only moment in our serenely happy lives when my wife has been anything like a tartar.

When the panels were all finished, the artists wanted them to be exhibited at the Royal Academy, but Mr. Lewis Harcourt, Commissioner of Works, was obstinate about it. He maintained that if they were exhibited before they were hung they would never reach the Houses of Parliament. He said critics would condemn them because of this and that, or because so and so was not asked to paint one. How wise he was, and how true a criticism of the critics !

One day I was down at Westminster early, touching up my picture, when John Burns came up, looked at the panels, and congratulated me on them all ! I said I had only painted one, and he said they hung together so well that they seemed to be all by one man. I thought it a tribute to the unity of the scheme, and especially to Mr. Abbey for his masterly supervision.

While we were at Red Gables Sir Charles Lawes-Wittewronge greatly delighted me by asking me to paint his portrait. Sir Charles became notorious through the famous libel case of Lawes versus Belt. In the Arts Club Lawes had said that Belt did not do his own sculpture. Lawes lost the case and had to pay a farthing damages with very heavy expenses, and as his father would not pay he went bankrupt. Sir Charles was a gifted sculptor, and President of the Royal Society of Sculptors to the time of his death. He sat for me in the vestibule at Rothamsted, where there was a splendid fanlight which I took as a guide for my glass dome when I came to build on Hampstead Heath. He made a wonderful subject with his velvet coat and a tapestry background, but at the Academy the portrait was skied three stories up, much to Sir Charles's disgust and my disappointment, for no one saw it. He told me that the R.A.'s said that if he wanted his portrait painted he should have asked a member of the Royal Academy to do it, but he himself was very pleased with it, and said to me, " Why should I go to an R.A. who could not paint a better potrait but would want double the fees because he was an R.A. ? "

I owe much to Sir Charles, a good and logical critic, the right help for a young painter, as colour and brushwork did not concern him. Composition, form, and sound elements of logical construction were the things he put first. Every Saturday morning he would cycle up to Red Gables and spend an hour in the studio. He was very outspoken, a little cruel, rarely encouraging, but I always listened and considered his point of view. He condemned the Queen Eleanor picture as all wrong because it was a panorama, the lines of the composition always passing through the picture, with no angles of 45 degrees running through to hold it in its frame. It seemed to be a logical idea, and to test it I painted " The Burghers of Calais " to work out his theory. It cost me a lot of trouble, but for a decorative picture fifteen feet long it was too restless and disturbing, and I am convinced, by the way the Eleanor composition stood the test, that Sir Charles was not right.

One day after a long visit he said that the test of the merit of a picture is whether you want to run away with it, and he never wanted to run away with any of mine ! (Certainly he could hardly have run away with Queen Eleanor.) Perhaps, as he already had four of my pictures in his collection, it did not matter, but my wife always knew when Sir Charles had been, because, in spite of his helpfulness, he generally left me depressed.

Nevertheless, I greatly valued his outspokenness. A friend is no good if he says only what you like to hear. Sir Charles told me he had never had a commission in his life, his theory being that an artist could only produce one masterpiece. That is why he remodelled his great group, Europa, so many times. He always started work at six in the mornings and, although very wealthy, lived a spartan life at his studio by Chelsea Bridge. When I asked him why he did not have a studio at Rothamsted he replied that the temptation to enjoy the country and the home would be too much for him and would distract him from his work. He spent only one night a week there (Friday), returning on Saturday afternoon to London. It was a great loss to me, and to the art world, when he died.

He was very interested in my house, as he wanted to preserve the beauties of Harpenden Common, and I had made a special feature of ornamental gates and the lay-out of the garden. One night in a dream I came out of my front door and found the woodmen felling a group of beautiful elms on the common, and the next time I saw Sir Charles I asked him if he would sell me the piece of land on which these trees stood, between my ground and his laboratory. He said, " Yes, I should like those trees preserved," but when the lawyers got to work it was found that the land was under the Lawes Trust and he had no power to sell for ninety-nine years. Alas, my dream came true, and the trees were cut down, ruining the beauty of that part of the Common and the vista from my garden. It was the beginning of the end at Harpenden for us. How strange it is, the guidance of our lives by such events.

While we were still at Harpenden Lord Brownlow commissioned

me to paint the portrait of Adelaide, Countess Brownlow, and still I love to look on this portrait when I would think of the days of our England that will never return,

> But the tender grace of a day that is dead
> Will never come back to me.

The magnificence of Ashridge House and the stately park with its herds of deer, the flag flying from the central tower, the carriages with the prancing horses taking and bringing guests, were a majestic scene in the great Victorian days. Lady Brownlow was a beautiful subject ; Watts and Leighton both painted her. She sat for me in her boudoir at Ashridge in a dress of rare red velvet and silk brocade, and luckily all went well. With so good a subject there is no struggling to get a decorative scheme ; the only anxiety is to do justice to all this elusive splendour.

A companion picture of Lord Brownlow did not go so well. He came to Red Gables, always with his beautiful countess ; it was like entertaining royalty to lunch. Lady Brownlow was very artistic, and anxious to watch the progress of the picture, and she would say to my sitter, " He is painting your head now, dear ; look pleasant," or " Stand up, throw your chest out ; do not stoop " ; or to me, " My husband's hands are not green," and so on, which disturbed me terribly. I saw the portrait not long ago at Belton House, and had to adjust the throwing forward of the chest as it spoiled the picture.

A charming letter from Lord Brownlow said they were happy to be thus handed down to posterity. They were fortunate portraits for me in more ways than one. When Lady Brownlow's portrait was exhibited at the Royal Academy an artist from Nottingham came up as I was touching it up on varnishing day and said, " You are not the painter of this ; you are too young," and on my pleading guilty he said, " There are a number of my friends at Nottingham who want their portraits painted ; you must paint them."

This opened up a delightful field of opportunity, and out of it came the Birkin Group and the Flensheim-Hersheim Group, the Player Family, the Hammond Group, Mr. and Mrs. Homberger, Miss Forman, Mrs. Perry, Mr. Knowles, Sir Edward and Lady Le Marchant, Miss Jackson of Bottesford, and Bishop Brindle.

Bishop Brindle was a glorious opportunity for any artist. He had a rare spiritual expression, a head very much like John Wesley's. He was to give me sittings at Red Gables and stay there with us, and the day was fixed. I prepared my palette and studio and met his

SIR CHARLES LAWES-WITTEWRONGE.

Bishop Brindle.

train, but there was no sign of the bishop, and no message. The next day I had to be in London, and when I came home my wife said, " Who do you think I have had here all day ?   Bishop Brindle." He came again the next day, and with his episcopal robes and in the fine light of the studio he looked magnificent.   Never had an artist of the great Middle Ages a nobler subject.

We started work at half-past ten, and after lunch I wanted him to have a rest, as he was eighty-two, but he said he never rested and would go on.   No sooner was he in his robes, however, than he went off to sleep.   I did everything I could to keep him awake, even dropping books, but I had to draw my easel nearer to the throne to prevent his falling off.

He was not disturbed when I apologized for his fruitless journey ; he said it was perfectly all right ; but I said, " You had an hour to wait at the station on your way back to London, owing to the fog."— " I had more time for meditation," he said ; " I recited my prayers." The portrait of this calm and serene spirit was hung on the line at the Royal Academy.

CHAPTER IV

LONDON

BISHOP BRINDLE'S lost day had taught me a lesson. The beauty of the Harpenden country, with its friendships and its lovely family circle ; the house we had built ourselves, with its choice setting, the garden with the clipped yews and smooth lawns stretching on to the rolling Common, the masses of gorse through the windows in spring, the lofty studio with all its amenities for work, had a fascination for me ; yet the thought of such disappointment for sitters, and the trouble of coming and going, set my mind on London.

My beautiful group of trees had gone from the Common, and we were reconciled to the change, but for months we made fruitless journeys to town in search of a new home. On one of these I met Sir Alfred East, President of the Royal Society of British Artists. He was recovering from an illness and was being wheeled in a bath-chair, but he had seen my Alfred Panel at the Royal Exchange, and told me that, ill as he was, he made it his duty to go to the Royal Academy to put my name down for membership, for on that work alone he felt I should be elected. I told him I was looking for a studio, and he said : " You can have mine and I will take yours : the change will suit us both." Sad to say, the dear man, the great artist, passed away within a few weeks.

Hampton's wrote saying they had just the house for me—Alma-Tadema's, for sale at £35,000. We laughed heartily at this, but they also sent particulars of Frederick Goodall's house at 62 Avenue Road, Regent's Park, which we thought might be possible. I found there was a wonderful studio and gallery, and the next day (June 17, 1913) we decided on the great adventure of uprooting after seven years at Red Gables. Before we took possession I had a letter asking if I would accept a thousand pounds profit and all expenses for my deal, as a friend of the seller (Sir Hall Caine) had set her heart on the house, but we could not change our minds. On November 18 I had my last sitting at Harpenden, and Miss Margaret Judkins was my first sitter at Avenue Road. Miss Crompton, that accomplished singer, arranged a musical programme for our first reception in the music room, the walls of which were lined with zinc. In this room Sir Augustus Harris had held many rehearsals for Covent Garden Opera, but for me the room will always echo with the voice of my wife as she played and sang with inspiring beauty. Here Gounod himself had been a guest : in this house he was ill with disappointment over the apparent failure of his Faust when it was first brought to London. After an evening reception in the house in those days the gas was left on by mistake and a maid striking a light in the morning caused a terrible explosion, and was killed. Pictures were blown sky-high, and parts of a famous canvas were picked up in the neighbouring gardens. The Alma-Tademas were there, and were both severely shaken.

Happily, our reception was attended by no such dire results. This move opened up for us a new and romantic chapter in our lives, but little did we dream that before our first year was out we should be plunged into the Great War.

One of the things to which I looked forward was the opportunity of making friends with many artists. I had little time for clubs, but as often as I could I would dine at the Arts Club in Dover Street on Saturday nights, and join in a game of snooker, when we had ten each side and played a shot every twenty minutes. So as not to interfere with work, I set out on my bicycle and called early after breakfast on the artists in the neighbourhood, and nowhere was I more welcomed than by Seymour Lucas, John Crompton, and Edgar Bundy. On one of my early visits to the Cromptons they produced a page from Pepys's Diary in which it was stated that " Mr. Salisbury the artist called early at breakfast time and had an interesting talk ". Mr. Pepys took Mr. Salisbury to an alehouse, but perhaps I may add for my namesake's good repute that it was " to see a picture which was being offered for twenty shillings ".

I found Seymour Lucas engaged on his panel of the Escape of the Five Members of Parliament, for St. Stephen's Hall, and as he was not accustomed to such a big-scale canvas he asked and welcomed my criticism. On his first visit to the new studio he was delighted with everything, and I remember well that he stood at the front door, raised his hat dramatically, and said, in response to my fears that it was a little too much for me. "No, this is just the place for you. It is not extravagant ; in four years you will have paid for it." He was right to the day.

After breakfast at his house he was talking of some recent election at the Academy which had surprised him and, turning to me, said, " You have plenty of time yet," to which I replied, " Do you realize that you had been an R.A. fifteen years at my age ? " He was greatly surprised.

During these days I called to see Sargent at Chelsea. I had been brought into touch with him as one of the judges who awarded me the honour of painting the panel of the Great Artists of Chelsea in Chelsea Town Hall. I found him busy on his decoration for the Boston Library, as he worked he made a wonderful picture, on returning home I painted my impression of him from memory. In conversation I spoke of the pleasure of being among artists, and able to exchange ideas, and to my astonishment he told me that I was the only artist who had taken the trouble to call on him for twelve months. This was a grievous eye-opener to me, for I instinctly felt that the good old days of art, the glorious brotherhood of the decade of Leighton, Millais, Watts, Poynter and Burne-Jones, had passed.

About that time Sir George Frampton, Master of the Art Workers' Guild, asked if I would paint a portrait of Sir William Richmond and present it to the guild. This I felt it an honour to do. So it came about that Sir William was the first distinguished man who sat for me at Avenue Road ; he was working at the time on the decoration of the roof of St. Paul's and was also Professor of Painting at the Royal Academy. Both he and his father before him were great portrait painters, and I naturally approached this task with some trepidation.

I called on him at his studio at Beaver Lodge, Hammersmith, where I made studies of various poses and secured a good one. He agreed to come to my studio for the painting, but was very busy and said the only time he could give me was Sunday. I was intensely disappointed to hear this, as I had made a rule never to work on Sunday, and on coming to London had decided not to start to do so. Was I to stick to my rule or not ? I remember that I dared to say to this great man, " I am sorry, but I do not work on Sundays," and he said, " Well, that ends it, because I have no other free time." My heart sank within me and I felt bitterly disappointed, but after a rather long pause he turned to me, put his hand on my shoulder, and said, " Why, that reminds me of my old Dad ; I will give you any time you want." So I asked for two whole days, and they were fixed.

I prepared my canvas by drawing in the composition from my studies and painted in the background so as to concentrate on the head when Sir William came. He arrived at ten in the morning, sat in his Oxford D.C.L. robe over a black velvet coat, and looked magnificent. I ventured one request at the outset—that he should not look at the portrait until I asked him to do so, and at half-past four, when I felt I had made a good start and the likeness was secure,

I asked him with fear and trembling to have a look. Imagine my relief when he said, " I shall not let you touch it again. That is the only way to paint a portrait—red hot. Nothing will hold back a man who can paint a portrait like that in a sitting." There was little more to do ; he, of all men, knew how to sit and to help a painter, and my own part was easy.

Sir William's conversation was very interesting. He was, of course, a great Greek scholar and had been giving lectures at the Royal Society. He told me how, after his lecture, Konody of the *Daily Mail* came up to him and started to criticize his remarks, with many people listening, whereupon Sir William turned to him and said, " Before you could eat without dribbling I was master of Greek." Looking round the studio, he recalled his many visits to this house in Goodall's time, when the artist was at the height of his fame and receiving £5,000 for a picture.

Sir George Frampton had told me how on his election as A.R.A. he had paid his duty call on Frederick Goodall, and before being shown into the presence of the R.A. had been passed on by three flunkeys in scarlet uniform and silk stockings. Our neighbour, Mrs. Berry, had described how, when the Goodalls dined with her, they drove up from next door in a carriage and pair.

A most tragic sequel to all this, Sir William told me, was that he had just received a letter from Goodall's widow begging for help, as she was destitute. This staggered me, and I made up my mind that if ever success came my way I would first of all provide for the future of my family.

Before the portrait was delivered I painted a replica for myself, and to my surprise the portrait I had painted in a day took me a week to copy, and was not the same personality. In talking over this with Sir William he said he believed that in a concentrated sitting something psychic happened which defied reproduction.

The portrait was exhibited on the line at the Academy and I received a delightful message from Sir Luke Fildes saying that it was the finest portrait he had seen in the Academy for years. After it was hung at the Art Workers' Guild the committee passed a rule that all portraits of past-masters should not exceed a canvas 30″ × 25″ in size, and I received a letter from the Master asking if I would give permission for my portrait of Sir William to be cut down to that size, as mine was 50″ × 40″. I replied that the portrait was theirs and I had no objection, but I felt it would ruin the picture. I added that evidently they were going in for chicken culture and required the spare canvas for roofing, for I had heard that week that the frame-makers of Chelsea were busy, not making frames for artists, but cutting down full-length portraits from big houses that were closed, the peers' robes on the canvases making marvellous roofing for chicken houses ! The portrait was not cut down and is still in the original state.

CHAPTER V

THE GREAT WAR

THAT summer the war clouds were gathering over Europe, and on the Fourth of August we were at war with Germany. In those days we thought of the Great War as the biggest in history, and the last; now, alas, in the middle of one far greater, we have to think of it as the old war, or as General Smuts says, the beginning of the 30 years' war.

It was probably the experience of every artist that all his work was stopped and all commissions cancelled. My rates and expenses almost doubled, and we were faced with a grave domestic situation. We economized to avoid disaster and came to the conclusion that the next thing to go was the telephone. But every tide turns. One afternoon the telephone rang and a lady asked if I could paint her with her children. It was settled in two minutes and solved our problem for six months. The telephone was not cut off.

It turned out that the artists were soon wanted again, for war was leaving gaps in many homes. Lord Bethell's eldest son was among the fallen, and from small snapshots, and with the help of his sister, I was able to paint a full-length portrait. In the first August also I painted the poet Colwyn Philipps, Lord St. Davids' son. The dear fellow had a premonition that he would not return, and he never did. He fell in 1915, waving his cap and shouting "Come on, boys" as they attacked the German trenches, and one of his fellow-officers said he was the bravest man he had ever met. In his note-book they found some wonderful lines about the magic healing of the night, which the fever of the day forgot:

> Be still, and feel the night that hides away earth's stain,
> Be still and loose the sense of God in you,
> Be still and send your soul into the All,
> The vasty distance where the stars shine blue,
> No longer antlike on the earth to crawl.

The tragic toll of the war was something our generation had not experienced before. Three of Mr. Gandar Dower's sons were called up and all sat for me. The eldest gave me a whole day when he was on leave and I was able to get a vivid likeness. Within a week of his return to France he was killed, and his body disappeared in space.

My nephew Ewart Stafford, a radiant youth of twenty in the R.A.F.,
sat for me from five till ten at night, and he, too, within a week
had taken his last flight. His sister Dorothy wrote a beautiful little
poem to his memory, beginning :

> Last year he flew with wingéd squadron high
> To fight earth's battles in the lowering sky,
> And nobly gave his youthful strength for right
> With all life's glorious possibilities in sight.
>
> And shall we mourn that his pure soul has fled,
> His glorious life for Right and Honour given ?
> No longer will we weep for him as dead,
> For he has joined the Flying Corps of Heaven.

The long war went on. The Zeppelins bombed London, followed
by aeroplane attacks. Air-raid alarms in those days were given by
policemen cycling down the road shouting " Take Cover ", a very
ominous sound which always reminded me of the carter's call in the
Plague, " Bring out your dead ".

In my spare time I started two pictures suggested by the war. The
first, " The Passing of War ", was inspired by Macaulay's *Lays of
Ancient Rome*, the great twin brethren Truth and Justice seeming to
symbolize the triumph of right over might. The picture suggests
these twin brethren, in spite of the massed powers of brute force
majestically sweeping forward, Justice with sword and balances, Truth
with the radiant flame on his helmet, ride forth to conquer while
the disordered combatants flee in confusion. The warrior hero of
battles lowers his standard and bows to the indomitable champions
of his cause ; Death with his coal-black charger halts and dismounts,
for in the blaze of the great light march the victors of freedom.

In the midst of the war a member of the British Red Cross Society
saw this picture and asked me if I would present it to the Red Cross
to be sold at Christies, which I was glad to do. It was sold and
presented to the London Museum. Exhibited at the Royal Academy
in the early days of the war, it failed to rouse any interest, the critics
appearing chiefly interested in their curious fancy that the figures of
the warriors in shining armour on white steeds resembled Mr. Asquith
and Sir Edward Grey, our dauntless leaders of those days of battle.

During the war the picture was hung in the banqueting hall at
Hertford House, where the Government entertained foreign visitors,
and, curiously enough, Mr. Asquith and Sir Edward Grey always sat
under the picture. I heard no more of the resemblances, but Sir Guy

Laking, Keeper of the Museum, told me that on the occasion when the Government entertained members of the Russian Duma the Russian Prime Minister in his speech referred to the prophetic significance of the picture and, noticing the signature, said he had not known that the great Lord Salisbury was a painter as well as a statesman !

An artist would seem to be of little value to his generation unless he interprets the spirit of his times. During the terrible and anxious days of the last Great War we never as a people lost confidence in the faith that brute force would be overcome by the ideals of justice and freedom, so I painted a picture illustrating this truth, calling it " God and St. George ". The picture shows the dragon of brute force coiling its tail and grinding its claws. The President of The Royal Society of S. George, that stalwart champion Lord Queenborough, took great interest in the picture as he felt it symbolized their ideals which once again are being so ruthlessly challenged.

On the day I was at work on the figure of Nurse Cavell in this picture (a victim of the dragon), I counted from my window twenty German bombing 'planes, and, turning almost overhead, they made for the City, doing great damage to St. Bartholomew's Hospital and the Bank area. One of the things they did was not so deplorable, for they brought the plaster off the gatehouse of St. Bartholomew's Church and revealed for the first time to this generation a charming little timbered front from Tudor days.

To enable me to paint this heroic warhorse of St. George, I had to model the horse in cement and paint from the model. The group came out so well that I finished it with plaster, gilded it, and coloured it, and it remains an interesting table-piece. A friend brought the headmaster of Felsted School to see the group, and he said, " That is what we want for our war memorial," so this led me to undertake the memorial screen in the school chapel, with St. George in the centre and the figures of Alfred and Galahad carved in oak.

Recently below a canvas on which I had started another subject, I discovered a large picture, an earlier rendering of St. George, which had evidently been inspired by my sculptured group. Realizing its possibilities, I restored it to the easel after a lapse of 25 years, and, midway through the Second World War, brought it, historically, up to date by blazoning on the warrior's standard the arms of the British Empire, and those of our Allies, the United States, the Soviet Union of Russia, France, Belgium, Greece, the Netherlands, and China. I added the swastika to the picture, and the dates, 1870,

1914, and 1939, the years in which Germany assailed the peace of the world.

The picture being finished, with the title—" Eternal Victory ", I sent it, in January 1943, to the Royal Academy Red Cross Exhibition where it was bought by Lady Maude Robinson and presented to Lord Somers (successor to Lord Baden-Powell as Chief Scout) for the central building of the Boy Scout Movement.

As the picture was dedicated to this great movement it was felt that it should have a universal timeless appeal, uncircumscribed by the historical events of our day. Complying, therefore, with the desire that the swastika should be removed from the dragon's head, I painted out the detested symbol, and with it the tale of the years of infamy. I had later a proof of the picture's appeal to youth in a letter from a boy telling me of the thrill, which he said he had felt at seeing St. George for the first time without his helmet, evidence, he thought, that the saint was not dependent upon earthly armour.

The whole nation was stirred by the story of a boy in the Battle of Jutland, where a lad from our slums leapt into immortality by a courage that has never been surpassed. He was Jack Cornwell. Lord Balfour, who was then First Lord of the Admiralty, felt that the incident should be painted as a tribute to the spirit of the youth of the Navy, and Sir John Bethell, M.P., whose portrait I had painted for East Ham (the home of the Cornwells), sent a friend to ask me if I would paint a picture of the scene. I was asked to call on the Financial Secretary to the Admiralty, Dr. Macnamara, and he told me what had happened, read me the official dispatch, and said, " There you are ; now go and paint it." I said I must get all the facts right first, must see the Captain, go to the ship, and take sketches, all of which he said was utterly impossible, as the ship was always at sea ready for action. There was, however, a chance when the ship came into port for refuelling.

I asked him if he would arrange it as early as he could, not too late in the winter, but I did not hear another word for months, and then a telegram came asking me to go to Rosyth. I arrived early one morning and found a gale blowing with heavy rain. H.M.S. *Chester* was anchored in the Forth, and as it was too rough for them to lower a boat I stayed at the hotel and could do nothing but watch the ship from the cliff. On the third morning a boat came ashore for me. It was quite an adventure getting aboard the man-of-war, as the current was so strong. I had a long talk with Captain Lawson, who described the whole action to me, explaining how he stood on the bridge and watched the boy. After the third round had been fired the gun was put out of action by a direct hit three feet from the gun, killing or disabling the gun's crew. Although the boy was mortally wounded, and the dead and dying lay all around him, he stuck to his post. The Captain called several of the sailors who witnessed the action, and the man who last spoke to the boy, but few of them could agree on the details of what actually happened.

The Captain told me that it was absolutely miraculous that they came through, as the *Chester* was the scout ship, discovering the enemy and drawing the whole gunfire of the German Fleet. Shells were bursting all round, and would raise columns of water fifty or sixty feet high. The Captain then took me on deck to the foremost gun, and on the actual spot we reconstructed the whole incident.

It was Jack Cornwell's duty to take directions from the bridge, and ear-'phones were fixed over his ears, the boy recording the directions on a dial in front of him, giving the gun's range. In setting to work on my sketch I found it impossible to erect an easel, so had my canvas stretched with cords to four boxes and my palette fixed to the seat, as it was impossible to hold it in the wind, which actually blew the paint off my brush. I held a corner of the canvas steady with one hand and worked with the other, and two sailors came to hold the canvas for me, another standing over me with a tarpaulin. It was exceedingly cold, although I had an overcoat on and painted (for the first time in my life) with gloves.

Before I left the ship I asked the Captain if he would suggest a title for the picture and he suggested a quotation from the Psalms, " Thou has set my feet in a large place ", which fitted the picture well. Physically the boy was confined in a very cramped position, yet he stood there representing the incomparable spirit and the matchless boyhood of the Navy. In the actual painting of the picture Jack Cornwell's brother sat for me.

The picture was exhibited in the place of honour at the Academy in May 1917. On varnishing day I thanked Sir Edward Poynter for the wonderful position they had given it, and he was good enough to say that the picture was placed on its merits. The end wall of Gallery Three, where it was hung, is traditionally held to be the place of honour.

The picture was formally presented to the Admiralty at the Mansion House. The Lord Mayor presided and the First Lord of the Admiralty (Sir Edward Carson) was present. I had to make a speech, which was to me a great ordeal ; but I managed to deliver the idea that as a

Chancellor of the Exchequer once said the last million pounds would win the war, as a Minister of War said the last hundred thousand men would win it, as a Minister of Munitions said the last hundred tons of munitions would win it, so a Minister of Fine Arts would say, not that Art would win the war, but that Art in its highest sense, if properly developed, would make all wars impossible.

The picture was placed on the deck of the Training Ship *Impregnable*, at Devonport, but since then it has been hung in a very good position in the Cadets' Training College at Gosport. A generous donor gave reproductions to every school in the country.

While the picture was on exhibition a sad little incident happened one day, when an official asked me to speak to somebody who had lost a boy on the *Chester*. He felt that his son had been not less courageous than Jack Cornwell, but his name had never been mentioned in the newspapers or the dispatches, and the poor man was heartbroken. What he believed was in all probability true, but it was hard to console him. I was able to give him a little comfort by emphasizing the title of the picture and by assuring him that Cornwell had been taken as typical of the spirit of all the boys on the ship and in the Navy, having been chosen for his dramatic position at the gun.

It seems fair that a word should be said about a matter which aroused much comment at the time. There was a controversy in the newspapers making much ado about what was called the abuse of the Cornwell Fund, which it was said was being withheld from the family in its great need. The papers did not know the facts, and the truth is that there was no abuse of the fund; there was only a desire to prevent the money being spent unwisely, and all that happened was that the allowance was reduced for reasons which were perfectly proper. It is one of the sad stories of the lives of the poor.

The Boy Cornwell, V.C., in the Battle of Jutland, on board
H.M.S. *Chester*, 1916.

GENERAL SIR HUBERT GOUGH.

CHAPTER VI

THE BATTLEFIELDS

SOON after the completion of the Cornwell picture, on our return from three glorious weeks on the rugged cliffs at Tintagel, watching the mighty tides of the Atlantic, the Lord Mayor asked me to meet him at the Mansion House.

Sir William Treloar was there and asked if I would paint a panel for the Royal Exchange. " I have selected my own subject," he said, " none of your musty old history for me." I pointed out that all the panels in the Exchange run in dramatic sequence, settled by a Royal Commission, and that the Gresham Committee would not accept a picture that did not conform to the order. The Lord Mayor said, " Nonsense ! I will not hear a word of objection. I am chairman ex-officio and I have a subject of worldwide interest and national importance, and, furthermore, here is a letter from the King promising all the help necessary to the painter. I want you to paint a panel to commemorate the visit of the King and Queen to the battlefields."

I must admit I was overwhelmed, and before I had time to think the Lord Mayor said, " We want it completed by the first week in November." That gave me just eight weeks. Sir William Dunn's term of office would expire on November 9, and he wished to present the panel while he was still Lord Mayor.

To me it was a staggering proposal, a panel 18 feet high by 11 wide, a visit to the Battle Front, and sittings from all the leading figures, in such vital days. But no artist could hesitate over such a proposal, and the next day I had an appointment with Sir William Robertson, Chief of the General Staff, who mapped out the King's route, which I had to follow. I crossed from Folkestone, having been given the rank of colonel, although I went in mufti. It was a very rough crossing and as submarines were busy the ship was escorted by three destroyers. Everything was made easy for me and I was taken through the customs without delay.

There was a car waiting for me and at my disposal as long as I was in France. It had no speed limit, and the tremendous pace and the risks it was apparently felt necessary to take in war-time did not add to my serenity.

We went straight from the boat to the British G.H.Q., which was near the Field of Agincourt and about an hour's run, as far as I remember. We arrived about dinner-time, and in the dining-room there was quite a distinguished company of visitors. Interviewing the General in Command, I explained the nature of my visit and he gave instructions for an officer to make all arrangements for me. The Ordnance department showed me the maps of the route the King took, and the next day we drove to Kemmel Hill overlooking Messines Ridge, in the sector commanded by General Plumer, of the Second Army. The officer took me up the hill through the wood by what was called the King's Way, and, entering the dug-outs, we made our way to where stood a red-bricked tower that had an iron cage for bears, for the hill was in peace-time famous as a pleasure resort. Smoke and thunder were continually rising from the guns, and an exceedingly courteous young officer in charge of a battalion explained the whole situation to me and pointed out the difficult position of the enemy. Aeroplanes were continually passing, but the enemy had been driven back considerably, and there was no danger.

A group of soldiers stood for me on the spot where the King, Lord Haig, and the Prince of Wales viewed the battlefields, a wonderful point of vantage, as we could see for miles and trace the battle front, while beneath us lay the ruined village of Wytschaete and the devastated country round it. I worked hard all day sketching, having lunch in the dug-out with the young officer and finishing work about four o'clock. Having an hour to spare the officer volunteered to take me into the front-line trenches, so we motored down the hill to the plain and away out along the white stretching road. He told me the histories of the ruined villages, where nothing now remained but red brick dust. We left the car, explored the mine craters, and walked along the trenches up to the front line, where I could see the Germans in the opposite trench. I was the first civilian, I was told, who had been so far forward, and I was not sorry when we were back. The devastation was appalling. Trees were burnt into blackened stumps strewn on battered earth.

We had rather an exciting experience returning. Climbing over a ridge, we were astonished by a sudden charge of field-guns, our own guns firing from beneath the ridge ! The shells passed only a little above our heads. The officer was furious, and took the man at the gun to task for not having given the signal when he saw us approaching.

Headquarters was to leave a message for me when the sittings had been arranged for the Commanding-Generals, but to my great disappointment I found on my return that no arrangements had been made. I thereupon saw the General of the Staff, who told me General Plumer would sit the next day. I had all the morning at my disposal so I asked the chauffeur about Ypres, and he said, " Oh, yes ; I have taken Muirhead Bone."

We started early and I shall never forget that ride. It was a beautiful autumn morning and for the first few miles there was little sign of war. Then we went through ruined villages where our troops were stationed, and at the Ypres salient, at the back of the lines, the congestion on the roads was terrific.

As we approached Ypres all the troops coming out were wearing helmets and gas-masks. My chauffeur was supplied with one of each, but I had neither. I thought we would go on, however, and finally we came to the precincts of the town, and had not advanced very far before a sentinel demanded our passports and wanted to know what I was doing there. My passport gave me permission to go where I liked, but he said no civilian had ever passed that spot and the enemy were dropping gas-shells. Directing the chauffeur to a place of safety, he said he must take me to the Town Major.

The Town Major was Lord French's son, and after wandering through long passages we came to his inner room. He wanted to know what I was doing there, and when I explained to him he said, " Well, the best thing you can do is to get out as quickly as you can." Then he told one of his staff to get down a book and, running down a list of names, he came to mine. " Oh, yes," he said, " you are all right." It seemed to me a wonderful proof of organization, for although I was not expected to be in Ypres I had been reported and tabulated right down the line. I told the Major that while I was there I should like to see the Cloth Hall and the cathedral, so he lent me his gas-mask and helmet, and the officer who had brought me in a prisoner offered to take me round the town.

It was an awe-inspiring sight to see the great cathedral and the Cloth Hall pounded into ruins, but I was glad to get out of the town, and back to keep my appointment with General Plumer. I remember the simplicity of his room ; by his bedside was a photograph of his wife and a well-worn Bible.

Punctually at two o'clock General Plumer came in. He was to give me two hours and there could be no second sitting, but (as always in these portraits) I had to keep in mind the composition of the big picture and decide rapidly on the most suitable position and

direction of the head.   He was very quiet, and from our conversation
no one could have dreamed that war was surging all round us.   At
four o'clock we went to tea, and at five I set out for Tramecourt,
when the chauffeur pointed to a château, the headquarters of General
Haig.   He seemed very nervous when I told him to stop, and as
we approached there were two sentinels with fixed bayonets demanding what I wanted, saying that no cars were allowed at that entrance,
and directing us to another.   Here we were stopped by a sentry, who
passed us to another sentry, who sent us to another officer, and finally
I was taken to Sir Philip Sassoon, the Private Secretary.   He was
resting in a camp chair at the back of the house and seemed very
surprised to see me, saying Sir Douglas was reviewing troops and
could not be disturbed, but he would give him my note and let me
know when he could give me a sitting.   Back at Tramecourt, I found
a message that I was to be at the General Clearing Hospital at ten
the next morning, when General Sir Arthur Sloggett would sit for
me, and other appointments would be made.   Breakfast was provided
for me, and after a long and tedious ride over the Field of Agincourt
we arrived at the Headquarters of the General Staff.   General Sloggett
was ready punctually and gave his time gladly, sitting all the morning.
General Sir Anthony Bowlby and Nurse MacCarthy also sat for me.
It was interesting to find the officers so full of optimism in the midst
of so much horror.

During the afternoon I had a message from Headquarters to ask
me to report to Tramecourt, so about dusk we set off on a hazardous
and nerve-racking drive, landing me at Tramecourt dead tired.   I
found that a liaison officer from Headquarters had been sent to look
after me and make my arrangements, this doubtless arising from my
surprise attack on the Headquarters of the Commander-in-Chief.
After this I had to follow strict military procedure, but it was certainly a great convenience to have a courier to make all my arrangements.   It was interesting to hear afterwards, at the clubs in London,
of the amusement created among the officers by my unconventional
procedure.

After early breakfast on Monday morning we set off for Dunkirk,
where General Rawlinson had the Headquarters of the Fourth Army,
but we found the General out, reviewing troops and not expected in
for an hour.   I met one of his aides-de-camp, Lord Methuen's son,
an artist and one of the handsomest men I have ever seen, a perfect
model for St. George.   He had a young son of a peer on his staff
and these two worked very much together.   Both seemed very per-

turbed over a mistake which had been made in failing to notify Lord Rawlinson of the appointment.

During the hours of waiting we walked about the long stretch of sands at Dunkirk, little dreaming that these beaches in the fateful years to come would be the scene of such a miraculous event in our history. The shore-line was uninteresting and forbidding with barbed wire and general desolation. Occasionally a mounted officer came galloping along the sands and we could hear the guns booming from the battlefield behind. As this was the first breathing-time I had had since my arrival, I sat down and took out my notebook to make notes, but my officer said that would not do at all, lest the notes might get into the enemy's hands. We went back to Headquarters to see if Lord Rawlinson had returned, for I was perturbed because my next appointment was thirty miles away with General Birdwood. It was not until one o'clock that I saw the General's car drive up, so I followed him to the hotel and was going to speak to him, but my officer held me back and said we must first see the aide-de-camp. What I could have achieved by myself at once took about ten minutes, until I was formally ushered into the presence of the General. I shall not forget the way he elevated his eyebrows and looked at his aide-de-camp for the explanation of an oversight which he evidently thought unpardonable.

He was apologetic for having kept me waiting, and I asked what could be done to work the sitting in without breaking my appointment with General Birdwood. He said he would sit for me after lunch and telephone General Birdwood that I should be much later. I lunched with his staff, and he sat for me in his private room, filled with maps and benches. The General was very interested, being very artistic himself, and after I had decided on my pose he very cleverly manipulated two mirrors so that he could see me at work. This was rather disconcerting, but he was very patient, sitting for hours, and it was singular that the conversation never once referred to the war ; these men all seemed to forget it.

After a hurried tea we set off to the headquarters of General Birdwood, commanding the Anzacs. I have not the remotest recollection where I went, but when we were getting near the camp most of the roads were made of sleepers brought from England, and we could not have been far from the battle-line. That was the 19th of September, and at dawn the next morning they began a great attack.

I found General Birdwood in a small army hut, the only light coming from a small window by the door. The General, quiet and impressive, sat until seven when the light began to fail, but as he was willing to sit until eight we arranged an electric lamp, and I completed my study. He asked me to join them at dinner and I sat with him surrounded by the finest group of men it was possible to meet, the pick of manhood and accomplishment. The room was covered with khaki canvas to make it a little more habitable, and this was quite an effective background to the smart soldierly uniforms and red tabs.

It was inspiring to hear General Birdwood talking to the men about their day's work. Even the youngest subaltern at the bottom of the table was not left out ; in fact, I thought he seemed to take extra pains to notice these. They were all very interested to hear about home, and on my telling them one or two things about conscientious objectors they seemed to sympathize with the genuine ones but had no sympathy with the shirkers.

Only two things throughout the evening disclosed the fact that there was to be an early morning attack. The General asked them if they had all had their watches synchronized, and said, " You must all go to bed early and get a good night's rest ". About half-past nine my chauffeur was waiting, and we set off to Tramecourt again. We rode all the way without lights amid gun-flashes, and once found our car within a few inches of a terrible precipice.

Soon afterwards I was delighted to receive this letter from General Birdwood (now Field-Marshal Lord Birdwood) :

DEAR MR. SALISBURY,

This is just a line to thank you so much for all the trouble you took in doing my picture. I think it is marvellous that you should have been able to complete it as you did, when you must have felt really exhausted after your long day, and in the bad light which was then left you.

I should like to congratulate you not only on your skill, for the picture certainly struck me as quite the best representation I have ever seen of myself in any form, but also upon your patience and good nature in carrying out your work.

You may be sure that my wife will visit your studio to see the picture when she is next in London, but this may not perhaps be for some little time.

I trust that the whole panel on which you are engaged will be a complete success, and will lead to further distinction for you.

You will since have realized from the papers that we were on the eve of a big fight when you were here. My corps was attacking the Germans at dawn the following morning.

Yours sincerely,

W. R. BIRDWOOD.

September 23, 1917.

The next morning General Gough was going to sit for me at the Headquarters of the Fifth Army, at a stately château in a park. He was delightful, and took a personal interest in doing all he could to get the room right for work. His portrait was one of the most successful I painted out there. Lady Gough was anxious that I should paint another portrait of him, which I afterwards did in the autumn of 1918, after the General's recall. I have never met a man who bore so nobly the greatest bitterness of his life, the catastrophe of the Fifth Army after he had borne the brunt of war for four years. He felt that in taking over thirty miles of front from the French he was placed in an impossible position.

He gave me the last sitting for the portrait on the day when all the successful Generals were being received in state at the Guildhall and Buckingham Palace. It was a cruel thing that he should not have been among them, but I remember well the cheerful front he put on that day. We talked continually so as not to think about it, but I could not help being impressed by the nobility of his character and the fine spirit he manifested at such a time. There was no bitterness, and his hearty laugh and joyous spirit rang through the studio and seemed to rise above it all.

From General Gough's Headquarters I was due to go to the Headquarters of the 14th Corps, where the Prince of Wales was going to sit for me at three o'clock. I was introduced to the Commander, Lord Cavan, who suggested that I should use as a studio the hut that had been a temporary hospital, but was now disused. I got my things together and the Prince was told that I was ready. He sat very well and was very quiet, smoking either a cigarette, pipe, or cigar the whole time. We were quite near the fighting line, and the guns were going incessantly. At four o'clock an officer asked if we would go to tea. The room was full of officers. I sat next to Lord Cavan, and the Prince came in a little late and sat according to his rank lower down the table. Lord Cavan remembered that he had known my father and had seen him at Wheathampstead. We went back to work and the Prince gave me another hour.

When the King and the Queen saw the portrait they liked it very much and the Queen said she would like to give it to the King as a Christmas present. They thought there was something a little wrong with one of the eyes, and asked me if, when the Prince was back on leave, I would go down to the palace and do a little to it, as the King and the Queen would like to see him with the portrait. The King told me that Lord Stamfordham and some of the Court thought I had made the Prince too youthful, and Lord Stamfordham, showing me a portrait of Lord Haig, remarked that was how I ought to make the Prince look. The King said he liked the way I had painted him ; he only looked 17 now ; why make him look older ? One day a telephone message came from Buckingham Palace saying the Prince was home for two days and would give me a sitting at noon. The Queen had arranged to give me a sitting at eleven so I worked on her study until twelve, and at noon the Prince came in, full of life and energy. He held his wrist up to the Queen and said, " Look at my new wrist-watch, Mother."—" It is very nice," said her Majesty, " would you like me to pay for it ? " and he said, " That is just what I wanted, Mother."

The Prince had not brought his khaki cap, so a messenger was sent for it, and when he put it on the Queen said, " That is exactly right ; you must not touch the portrait again. I had no idea that one eye drooped more than the other." There being so much I could do to it while the Prince was there, I pointed out several things to the Queen, who said, " Do you mind if I watch every stroke ? "— " Certainly not, Ma'am," I replied, " if your Majesty will excuse my back."

So, compelled to turn my back on the Queen, I was able to touch up the portrait and point out the improvements, whereupon the Queen said, " Don't touch it again. I should like the King to see it now." A messenger was sent to the King but came back saying that His Majesty was with the Italian Ambassador. We waited ten minutes, when Princess Mary came in and Her Majesty said, " I will go and find the King, and see if I can bring him." As she left the room she turned and said, " Do not touch the picture again ; we have been so unfortunate at times because artists have been over-anxious to improve their work." I promised her I would not touch it, and after fifteen minutes a messenger came running and said, " The King and Queen ! " With them came the Prince of Wales, the Duke of York, and Princess Mary. They looked at the picture, each making observations. I had at the same sitting my portrait of Queen Mary, and when they had all approved of the Prince's portrait they turned to the Queen's. One said the nose was very good but something was wrong with the lips and the mouth. Another would disagree and say something was wrong with the eye. King George said that reminded him of Sargent. When he had finished a portrait all the relatives and friends came to look at it. One said they thought it good but there was something wrong with the nose, and Sargent got his brush and altered the nose. Another said something was wrong with the ear, and Sargent altered the ear. So it went on, and in the morning they received a letter from Sargent saying that the touches he had made had spoilt the portrait and he had put his foot through it and it had ceased to exist. The King, after telling us this story, said, " You will have a letter in the morning from Mr. Salisbury to say that this picture does not exist."

During the sitting the Queen told me of their visit to Italy during their honeymoon. We spoke of Venice, and enjoyed talking of the marvellous equestrian statue of Bartolommeo Colleoni. The Queen asked me the name of the sculptor, but with my mind set on my work I could not for the life of me recall it, and next day I received a registered letter in the Queen's own handwriting saying, " The name we forgot the other day was Verrochio."

The next portrait I painted in France was of Lord Byng. The ride along the arterial road at the back of the lines from Arras was full of interest. We went over the Somme and through the country where the Germans had cut all the fruit trees down ; and from beginning to end it was one scene of desolation and despair. What had been the town of Arras was simply a road through the wilderness of rubbish and black heaps. As we approached Albert we saw the figure of the Madonna hanging at right angles to the tower, and super- stition had it that as long as she remained in that position the town was safe from the enemy, but as soon as she fell the town would fall.

We eventually came to the headquarters of General Byng, a house with an open verandah entering the garden, and under this we had tea. Lord Byng came in, looking very austere, and, greeting me rather brusquely, said, " Why have they sent you here in war-time to paint my portrait ? How long do you want ? " I said two hours. He said, " Impossible," and I said, " Well, two hours is not long to paint a head." He then informed me that his Generals were coming, and I said, " All right ; the Generals can come. I will be stone deaf and get on with my painting." He laughed at this, to my relief, and told me they were just going to plan their next attack, but he would give me ten minutes. That was hopeless enough, but, taking up my brush and palette, with a clean canvas in front of me, I thought I had better begin. He sat down and took the position I wanted, pulled out his pipe, and started to smoke, so I said if I was going to have only ten minutes I ought to have ten minutes without the pipe, and he said, " Quite right," and from that minute seemed to take an interest in the picture, saying, " I will give you as long as I can." I worked as hard as I could for about ten minutes, when his aide-de-camp came in and announced that Mr. Asquith was waiting to see him. The Government had just resigned, the Coalition Ministry had been formed, and Mr. Asquith was taking the opportunity of visiting the battle area. The General, saying he must see him, asked his aide-de-camp to give Mr. Asquith a cup of tea, and I said would he give Mr. Asquith two cups ? All the while I could hear the cars arriving with the Generals for the conference.

Mr. Asquith must have taken his tea very quickly, for the aide-de-camp soon returned to say that he was ready. General Byng said how sorry he was he had to leave, and I waited for three-quarters of an hour, when the light was beginning to go, and there was no sign of his returning, so in great disappointment I packed up. The curious thing was that when I had the sketch home it turned out to be the best study I had done, yet it was the work of twenty minutes under very trying circumstances.

This brought my battlefield studies to an end. I waited some days for the opportunity of a sitting from Sir Douglas Haig, but was informed from Headquarters that I might be there three weeks without having any chance, as they were planning a very important advance, which made it necessary for him to be moving up and down the lines all the time. He promised to sit for me in England, and I had to give up the idea of a sitting in France.

On deciding to return home I was informed that I must show my sketches to the censor, and there I met an officer who went through them all and put on the official mark ; he said he had seen all the studies that had been made through the war.

The next important thing was to get a sitting from the King, and this Lord Stamfordham arranged for me at noon one Saturday. I was to use as a studio the room over the central arch facing the Mall from Buckingham Palace, the room of the Balcony. Queen Victoria had sat in that room to Landseer, and Gilbert, and Sir Luke Fildes. From the window I could see down into the courtyard where the

King was holding an investiture, and was tremendously impressed by the wonderful way in which he received the men who had done such glorious deeds and risked their lives. He had a kindly word for every one, and each man, as he went away, seemed to feel that he really was the man the King was delighted to honour.

At noon the band played the National Anthem, and in ten minutes the King came into the studio, three minutes after Sir Derek Keppel had been to warn me that His Majesty would soon arrive. King George, in the uniform of a Field-Marshal, sat very well, talking occasionally.

This was my first sitting from him and I was naturally nervous, but was soon lost in my work. The messengers were continually coming in with State Papers, which the King glanced through. For a few seconds he closed his eyes and seemed very tired, and at the end of the sitting said that he was very sorry, as he felt he had not done me justice, but as a matter of fact he had been hard at work since seven o'clock. He looked at the picture and seemed surprised at the amount I had done, asking, " How many more sittings do you want ? " I said, " One more if it is long enough, Sir," and the King said, " If you will come to-morrow I will give you as long as you like." He gave me three hours, which I think must be a record sitting, and he was so pleased with it that he asked me to finish it up for him, and his valet came to my studio afterwards and put on the King's uniform so that I could paint in the ribbons and finish the tunic.

When the picture was nearing completion I received a telephone message to say that His Majesty had left the Palace and would be with me in twenty minutes, and punctually the King arrived. Looking round the studio, he said, " Where are the canvases—stacked round the walls and the paint on the floor ? That is what one usually sees in an artist's studio."

That week, going down to see my father and mother at Harpenden, I found them anxious to hear about these eventful visits, and I remember very well my father meeting me on the village green and saying, " Show me the man that is diligent in business : he shall stand before kings, he shall not stand before mean men."

General Smuts represented South Africa in the picture. He came to my studio and gave me two sittings. The first time was in an October afternoon when the moon was just rising, and as he looked at it he said, " Why don't you paint that instead of me ? " I have never met a man so noble yet so modest. He had promised to come again, but he was the General commanding the defence of London, and watched every air attack on London from the roof of the old Hotel Cecil, and it was only the day before he returned to South Africa that he was able to come back. " I promised to come and here I am," he said ; " one cannot keep much these days except one's word."

General Smuts has a fine head, very subtle, and when the time came for him to go my work was not a bit like him, and I was in despair. He said " I will give you another ten minutes," and in that time I was lucky, managing to secure a likeness which he said was the best portrait that had been painted of him.

Realizing what a great asset he was to our cause, I lamented the fact that he had to return home, and he said he had already been away so long that his wife would be forgetting him and his children were growing up and would not know him. I was thinking what a wonderful Empire Prime Minister he would make, but little did we realize that before his ship reached home he would be Prime Minister of South Africa, General Botha dying unexpectedly. The three great speeches of the First World War were by Mr. Asquith on our entering the war, President Wilson on America entering the war, and General Smuts reviewing the war from the world-wide and spiritual aspect. His first broadcast speech in this war (New Year, 1941), and his famous address to both Houses of Parliament, rank among the historic utterances of our time.

A God-given man to our age if ever there was one is General Smuts. The last time we saw him was at the Buckingham Palace Garden Party, when we had a little talk. He was returning to South Africa that week, and I said, " We need you here," to which he made a marvellous reply : " No, you do not want me ; what you want is God."

As this is being written a report has come of a speech General Smuts made to his church at Potchefstroom, and it seems remarkable enough to put on record in these days when Christianity and civilization itself are fighting for their existence :

Fundamentally the world has no need of a New Order or a New Plan, but only of an honest and courageous application of the historic Christian idea.

Our Christian civilization is based on an eternal order, an endless plan in the message of Christ. Let us follow the light which has once shone before us, and which can surely lead us to the better world for which we are all longing.

In the twilight of to-day I see on the horizon, not the man of Moscow, not the man of Munich, not the man of Rome, but the Man of Galilee. I see Him round the villages and districts, teaching, spreading the message of the New Kingdom, healing the sick and the suffering. And His message is :

Cherish in love your fellow-man, irrespective of race or language, cherish and keep the divine idea in your heart as the highest good.

The love for God and man is the final answer to all the insoluble questions of all ages. This is also the programme for the Church to-day, and for mankind, which is to-day milling round like frightened sheep without a shepherd.

The Man of Galilee is and remains our one and only Leader.

I was anxious to complete my studies of the General and make a portrait for St. Andrew's University to celebrate his Lord Rectorship. On his visit to England in 1942, on the eve of the turning of the tide of war, he was so busy that formal sittings were out of the question, but with the help of visits to his hotel and South Africa House, and the aid of the British Paramount Film Company who had taken a film of him speaking at Westminster, I was able to finish the portrait, which appears in this volume.

In those fateful days of war it was extremely difficult to complete a picture of this nature for a given date, as all the people concerned were engaged on vital war work and had no spare time. But finally all, with one exception, had given me sittings in time for me to complete my task. The exception was Lord Haig, who found it impossible, owing to his overwhelming duties as Commander-in-Chief. The War Office, however, kindly supplied me with photographs, enabling me to get a semblance of a likeness. The picture was temporarily placed in its panel at the Royal Exchange and the unveiling ceremony, on November 6, 1917, was performed by the Duke of Connaught's graciously accepting the gift from the Lord Mayor, who was supported by the City Aldermen, and by members of the Fighting Services.

As there was a general wish that this picture commemorating the visit of the King and Queen to the battlefields should be publicly exhibited, it was decided to send it to the Royal Academy in the spring. It was therefore returned to my studio, and during this time I had opportunities of making my studies of Lord Haig at his Kingston Hill home. There he showed me, among other interesting data, the map of the battlefields he had used in France, pointing out the place where the Armistice was signed.

I said to him, " As the armies had got so far, why did you not march to Berlin ? " He replied that they had calculated that to do so would cost the lives of a hundred thousand men. The hundred thousand lives were dear and precious, but the fact that the Germans never saw a conquering Allied army in their capital made it possible for Hitler to declare that the German military forces did not sustain ultimate defeat, that only civil defection brought the disasters of which their country became the victim and from that false assumption was born the mood that enabled him to nerve his misguided compatriots to an unprecedented re-arming, with all its calamitous consequences for mankind.   Truly as Lord Haig told me, we averted the loss of a hundred thousand lives at the time, but with what usurious compound interest in blood and anguish has destiny since made the world pay for that act of mercy !   I was surprised at the complete candour with which Lord Haig discussed the war-time conduct of politicians, notably that of Mr. Lloyd George, on whom his comments were severely critical.   The Field-Marshal's Diary, which is sealed until twenty years from the date of his death, may reveal highly interesting facts concerning his experiences as Commander-in-Chief.

The final touches to the portrait of Lord Haig had to be made on Sunday at Burlington House, where the picture was already hung.   I breakfasted there with Mr. Andrew Gow, the Keeper, who would not enter the galleries by the main entrance as there is an old tradition that this entrance was used on Sundays only by Royalty.   From the Academy the picture went to the Walker Art Gallery, Liverpool, before being finally hung in the Royal Exchange.

One of the moving spectacles of the war was the heroic stand of King Peter of Serbia and his tragic retreat across the mountains of Albania.   It was an event that will live in history with the gallant stand of the Serbs in the Yugoslavian mountains in the Second World War.   I was asked by the Serbian Legation to paint this scene, and the picture was shown at the Academy in 1917.   It shows the sorrowful figure of the King seated before an open fire with the remnant of his faithful followers in the wild and bleak passes of the snow-clad mountains of Albania.   A herald is carrying the national colours, and officers are studying maps over an old chest in which are the few treasures and documents the King had been able to save.

King Peter, as he set out on this sad journey, called the remnant of his scattered forces together, gave them all liberty to go home, and then said : " As for me and my sons, we fight on."   Not one man forsook him.

H.M. KING GEORGE V., 1917.

RANDALL DAVIDSON, ARCHBISHOP OF CANTERBURY, AT THE NATIONAL
THANKSGIVING SERVICE, 1919.

CHAPTER VII

THANKSGIVING

THRILLING as the battlefield had been, it was wonderful to be at peace again, and one day in the summer of 1919 the Sheriff of the City of London, Sir Banister Fletcher, called, and said he had the greatest possible subject for any artist. The Lord Mayor, Sir Horace Marshall, wished me to paint for the Royal Exchange a panel to commemorate the National Thanksgiving Service to be held at St. Paul's Cathedral two days hence.

The solemn pageantry of the subject offered to an artist fine decorative material, but the deep spiritual significance of such an event after a life-and-death struggle of four years seemed almost to defy expression in paint. The panels in the Exchange are only eleven feet wide but eighteen feet high, and the treatment of the subject must necessarily be governed by this restriction of space and shape, and the fact that the figures in the foreground must be life-size to correspond with the other panels. It was my first experience of an interior on so great a scale, and it did not occur to me to go to St. Paul's before the service, so that the choice of position was left to the chance of the moment. Happily an inspiration came at the end of the beautiful service, when the royal procession, the archbishops with the representatives of all the Churches, and the Lord Mayor and Sheriffs, moved in stately dignity to the great west door. The vast concourse of people outside joined in a grand old hymn and in the National Anthem, after which the Archbishop stepped forward with his crozier, supported by the Bishop of London with his pastoral staff, and pronounced the benediction.

In a moment I realized the immense possibilities of this scene, and took up a position at the foot of the steps, where I had a fine view of the impressive group, and a vista through the open doors as far as the great dome. A rich red and cream canopy gave a fine finish to the scene, and I felt that I had caught the right moment. Hurrying home, I quickly made my sketches, and in a few days the Lord Mayor secured the King's approval. With such a colossal scene it is impossible to work direct from models, so it was necessary to make separate studies, necessitating double work. The foremost ecclesiastical figures, with their splendid decorative copes, I decided to paint life-size, both making interesting portraits.

By the time all the other studies were completed I had not succeeded in getting a sitting from Queen Alexandra, and when Queen Mary came to see the picture I explained that it was almost impossible to introduce the Queen Mother unless I had a sitting. The next day I received a telephone message saying that Queen Alexandra would give me a sitting at Marlborough House if I did not keep her more than twenty minutes. The Queen was not well, and was seventy-five.

In her old age Queen Alexandra was very beautiful in looks as well as in nature. I found the best light at Marlborough House in the Queen's studio, and I was captivated by the beauty of her own water colours on the walls. As my time was so limited I had taken the precaution of painting in a figure to form a foundation, and it chanced that the Queen could see this figure through the back of my canvas, and said to her Lady-in-Waiting, " He is painting me over another woman ! "

After the sitting she invited me to sign the visitor's book, and a week later came to the studio to see the picture. I received a telephone message saying that Queen Alexandra had left Marlborough House and would be with me in twenty minutes, and Her Majesty arrived, unfortunately, when my wife was not at home. She was pleased with the development of the picture, and took a great interest in looking over the house, saying she was sorry to miss seeing my wife and would call again.

The study of Princess Mary in this picture came out quite successfully, and Queen Mary liked it so much that she accepted it for Buckingham Palace. The picture itself was completed before the Lord Mayor went out of office, and the panel was unveiled at the Royal Exchange by the Duke of York, our King George the Sixth.

CHAPTER VIII

THE UNKNOWN WARRIOR

THE eleventh hour of the eleventh month has become one of the noblest moments in the life of our generation.

In the Two-minute Silence of Remembrance the nation's soul has stood humbly before the throne of the Infinite, and those who have had the privilege of standing packed in that wonderful crowd in the heart of London, in the solid mass of humanity filling Whitehall from end to end, have felt in that surging tide of emotion a supreme unity, blending the hopes and fears and sorrows of a nation in the solemn silence that follows the chiming of Big Ben. What a significant fact it is that now, as we look back on those days, from this second devastating world war, we celebrate the Armistice but never the Victory !

The painting of this solemn event was an exhilarating experience. At this time the All-India Committee had come to London to arrange for twelve panels in the great hall of the Queen Victoria Memorial Building in Calcutta and it was when the King came to the studio to see these that he said, " You must paint the burial of the Unknown Warrior ; it is a wonderful subject which has caught the imagination of the public." How right he was in his clear vision of the significance of Remembrance Day !

I felt very nervous at the thought of it, realizing the solemnity of the event and the responsibility of the task, and I pointed out that I had still a great deal to do and that they were waiting for these India panels ; but King George said, " This is more important ; they can stand aside." Turning to Sir Bryan Godfrey-Faussett, he told him to see Sir Douglas Dawson and arrange that I should have every facility for making arrangements, and Sir Douglas sent me a police pass and asking me to go to the Colonial Office before the ceremony and ask for him. I took with me a number of plain post cards which would easily go into my pocket, so that I could make notes without being too conspicuous.

On the morning of the eleventh I went to the Cenotaph and met Sir Douglas Dawson for the first time. The Archbishop of Canterbury came up, and while we were talking Sir Douglas enquired how many seconds it took to recite the Lord's Prayer. The Archbishop said thirty seconds, and I then realized how the success of all ceremonies depends on a few moments of time.

Sir Douglas was an absolute genius in arranging ceremonies. Not one thing would be overlooked or forgotten ; the event from beginning to end was rehearsed in his mind, and all contingencies allowed for. I remember seeing him the next day, and finding him rather upset because he felt that the ceremony had not been the success it should have been. It seemed that the band had not paused long enough between the verses of the hymn, which therefore ended a few seconds before Big Ben chimed the hour for the Two-minute Silence. As the procession moved off from the Cenotaph, which the King had unveiled, I followed with the Cabinet Ministers, as they were in mufti, and went into the Abbey.

I shall never forget the overwhelming solemnity of the scene as we entered the sacred shrine of our race, or the spectacle of all those mothers, chosen from all over the country. These dear souls, who had been given the best seats available, were wearing the ribbons and the medals of their husbands and their sons.

The coffin was carried in at the north door, supported by the pall-bearers, followed immediately by the King and his sons, and then by the Cabinet Ministers. I had a marvellous position.

One of the conspicuous figures in that pathetic ceremony was Queen Mary at the column by the grave, obviously overcome by the sacredness of the occasion. No one could be in the presence of that vast congregation without being stirred. The ushers, as we walked down the nave towards the burial place, directed everybody to the north, but I instinctively turned to the south, so that I could have the light at the back of me. Had I gone to the other side I should have missed the impressiveness of the scene and had the backs of the admirals in the foreground of my picture, with the four queens behind me.

The service was so impressive that I felt half-afraid to take out my cards to make sketches, but during the singing of the hymn I was able not only to join in the singing but to make notes on the margin of my service paper. With these notes I was able to reconstruct the whole ceremony in the studio and went early down to the Abbey the next morning to make a colour sketch, though I was not able to work long after ten o'clock because the crowd began to file in. I found the ordeal of working there almost as great as the day before, the whole scene being so touching and stirring. There was a bunch of flowers, three faded daffodils, with a note from a mother who had

SKETCH-NOTES FROM MY SERVICE PAPER.

written "For my three boys—one of them may be here." The universal idea was so beautiful that it seemed as if every mother's son was there.

I made two sketches, one of the unveiling of the Cenotaph, the other of the service in the Abbey, and in a few days took them to the King, who called in the Queen to have a look at them. He said I must paint both pictures to hang in a public building, and in time for the Academy ; and he desired me also to paint a smaller picture of the unveiling of the Cenotaph for Buckingham Palace.

First I set to work on the unveiling of the Cenotaph, for which the horses and the gun-carriage were put at my disposal at the Royal Horse Artillery Barracks at St. John's Wood. It was well into the New Year before I was able to start on the burial picture. A room in the offices of the Ministry of Labour, which faced the Cenotaph, was put at my disposal, and I was therefore able to paint the Cenotaph at leisure.

The Duke of York was my first sitter, and the queens, the princesses, the clergy, the admirals, the generals, and the Cabinet Ministers all gave me sittings. Only one small difficulty arose during all these arrangements. Mr. Asquith gave me the first sitting at Bedford Square, and when I had been at work on the study for only five minutes Mrs. Asquith, who had just come in, looked at the drawing, and said, "That is more like Lloyd George than my husband." As my sketch proceeded, it resembled Gladstone, thus in a subtle way revealing the political type.

Lord French's sitting was delayed owing to his appointment as Viceroy of Ireland. During the intervening years Mr. Asquith had ceased to be Prime Minister and Lord French Commander-in-Chief in France. There had been fierce controversy in Parliament and the Press between these two men, and one day two telephone calls raised the tempo of the studio by several degrees. Lord French had to postpone his sitting, and rang to say he would come as soon as possible. Imagine my dilemma when, just an hour before Mr. Asquith was due, the telephone rang to say Lord French was on the way and would arrive at eleven o'clock, the moment Mr. Asquith was due ! I did not know what to do ; there seemed no way of preventing these bitter antagonists meeting on my doorstep, and as a last hope I telephoned to Mr. Asquith's house to see if it were possible for him to delay his sitting for an hour, from eleven to twelve. I thought I could complete a study of Lord French in an hour and this might save the difficult situation. Unfortunately Mr. Asquith could not come later owing to an early lunch engagement, but I was able to postpone the sitting to another day, and all was well.

The King came twice to see the picture of the Unknown Warrior. The size of the canvas was fourteen feet by eleven, and it contained forty life-size figures. In order to finish it according to the King's wish I had worked well into the night, setting my palette in the daylight and working by artificial light ; luckily I found that I could not perceive any difference in the work. The King was surprised at the progress I had made. I explained that I had worked more than eight hours a day and did not know what my union would say. " You don't belong to a union, do you ? " said he, and then laughed heartily on seeing that he had been caught.

As the King wished me to have the picture finished for the Academy towards the end of March, I informed the President that I should be sending it in. On the Saturday before sending it I received a message from Buckingham Palace that the King and Queen would like to call and see me the next afternoon, Sunday. They arrived unattended, the chauffeur and the footman putting the car under the trees by the front door and going on to the Zoo. I noticed that the King, when he came in, was rather quiet. He came down with me into the studio where the picture was, while the Queen remained with my wife in the music room.

In the studio, as we stood in front of the picture, the King said, " I am ashamed of the jealousy of you artists. I have actually been asked if it was my wish that your picture of the Burial of the Unknown Warrior should be exhibited. I replied that of course it was my wish ; it was a subject that had caught the public imagination and must be shown."

It was only a little later that Sir Frank Dicksee, who was President of the Royal Academy, told me of an unpleasant incident at the Council when three members threatened to resign if my picture occupied the place of honour again. Sir Frank courageously protested that it was a painful exhibition of professional jealousy and they could resign if they wished.

I did, however, receive many encouraging letters of appreciation, a beautiful one from Sir Luke Fildes, and one from Seymour Lucas in which he said, " I congratulate you on the great picture you have painted, or rather the great picture that God helped you to paint."

After this unhappy episode I felt that the King would give me no further work, but I was delighted soon afterwards to receive a letter from the State Chamberlain asking if I could paint a picture of Princess Mary's wedding.

The Editor of *The Times* very kindly gave me this simple description to be placed under the Burial Picture in the Houses of Parliament :

On November 11, Armistice Day 1920, the Unknown Warrior was buried in Westminster Abbey. Chosen by chance from the countless unnamed dead in France and Flanders, that the nation might honour in him without distinction of rank, birth, or service, all who fell in the Great War, his body was brought with full military honours to London.

In the Abbey simplicity dominated all that was done. The coffin, draped with the Union Jack, borne by non-commissioned Officers of the Guards, passed through the lines of a hundred wearers of the Victoria Cross.

The highest officials of the Forces were the pall-bearers. The King walked behind as chief mourner, followed by Princes, Peers, and Statesmen. As the Dean recited the Committal sentence the King scattered over the coffin soil brought from the battlefield. The service ended with the throbbing of drums and the clear call of bugles, sounding the Reveille.

The picture was painted by Royal Command.

At one of the first public dinners after the Armistice an American made a great speech in replying to the toasts of the guests. He had been in the crowd in Whitehall, he said, on Armistice day, and a bobby saw him, and, somehow guessing he was a visitor, beckoned to him to come forward and stand where he could see. In his speech the American said, " You English are remarkable people ; for a thousand bitter hours you console yourselves with one that is beautiful."

The original title of the picture was suggested by the Dean of Westminster, and it seemed to me that nothing could be more fitting than his choice, " And they buried him among the kings ". Alas, the title is not there to-day, for a reason which must surely seem extraordinary and beyond all understanding. When the picture was placed in St. Stephen's Hall, and the title was to be carved in the stone, the Commissioner of Works objected to the quotation, saying that the Socialists and the Labour Party would object ! So the painting was robbed of the dignity of these noble words, which I trust may be added one day. What a feeble and pitiful comment it seems to-day !

After the closing of the Academy the picture went round the provincial galleries, creating such interest at Wolverhampton that the Member of Parliament, Sir Alfred Bird, desired to ask the King to be allowed the privilege of presenting it to the nation. Unfortunately, before the idea was completed, Sir Alfred met with a fatal accident on attending a social function at the Duke of Wellington's

House at Hyde Park Corner, so his son, Sir Robert Bird, presented the picture to the Houses of Parliament as a memorial to his father. It was the first placed in St. Stephen's Hall. One day when I was fixing it there the Speaker, Mr. Whitley, discussed the question of filling the other panels. I pointed out that it was a mistake to fill the spaces with subjects without regard to historical sequence, saying that the panels should be treated as a whole, and he asked my advice. I said that the artists and historians should collaborate, and in requesting me to consider suitable subjects he said he felt that the Burial of the Unknown Warrior would fit in with the idea and should come last, remaining where it then was. In planning this out it was remarkable how right he was, the idea of the panels beginning with the foundation of all law, from Mount Sinai to Alfred, the founding of Parliament, the struggle for liberty and order through the generations, and moving on to the supreme sacrifice in obedience to Law. I submitted a series of sketches to Mr. Whitley, with a suggestion of the artist for each panel, but later the newspapers announced that the whole scheme was settled and the Burial of the Unknown Warrior was to be removed to a committee room. This raised questions in Parliament, and for a long time the picture was placed in the King's Robing Room, where all visitors could see it, but eventually it was hung in a committee room, out of sight for the public.

It is an easy matter to relate the outstanding facts of those momentous days now that they are remembered in tranquillity. I vividly recall, however, with what depression, with what acute anxiety I confronted the fact of sittings postponed, or of busy men unable to give me more than half an hour for my purpose. There comes back to me the recollection of sleepless nights, and of restless dreams in which I feverishly painted and repainted.

Whatever may be the judgment of time, seeing the picture in the Houses of Parliament again not long ago, and looking at it from a detached and critical standpoint after twenty years, I feel that it will remain my best contribution, historically and artistically, to our age.

CHAPTER IX

WESTMINSTER DAYS

AFTER all the anxious days of war through which we had passed it was a relief to be working on peaceful scenes again, and it happened that two or three ceremonies called me to Westminster Abbey, the wedding of the King's son and that of his daughter, and the installation of the Order of the Bath. The State Chamberlain having written to say the King would like me to make a small picture of Princess Mary's wedding, I went down to the Abbey for the rehearsal, the King and Queen being present. The question came up as to whether they should have floral decorations, and the King said, " Well, what does the artist say about it ? " I expressed the opinion that flowers would spoil the beauty of the Abbey, and, Their Majesties agreeing, the King said, " We won't have flowers."

I felt a little perturbed because the seats for the Royal Family were arranged with an unfortunate background, and suggested that they should sit on the side with the tapestry and the famous portrait of Richard the Second as a background. To my delight I heard the next day that this position had been decided on. A platform was erected for me at the back of a medieval monument so that I could work without being seen, fortified with a drawing-board and plenty of paper. The ceremony was of great beauty, and at times the sun shone on the stately uniforms of princes, ambassadors, and statesmen, and on the charming figures of queens and the princesses.

I remember that in my rough sketch of Queen Alexandra I drew the line of the sash of the Order of the Garter, then indicated the ribbons, and made a circle indicating that she wore some Order, and when the King saw that I had painted in the Order he said, " Oh, no, the Queen could not have been wearing that ; she would only have been wearing that in the evening " ; but the note on my sketch proved to me that something was there, and it turned out that she had worn it.

After the ceremony the bride and bridegroom, the King and Queen, and Queen Alexandra and the archbishops, went into the Confessor's Chapel to sign the register. It was remarkable that a shaft of sunlight fell right on the table at the moment, and as the Princess signed,

Burial of the Unknown Warrior, November, 1920.

"The King's Offering" at the Ceremony of the Most Honourable Order of the Bath, Westminster Abbey, 1928.

with the King standing by her side, the full blaze of light on the bride, and on the King's red uniform, made a striking effect.

Having finished my cartoon, I sent a message that I was ready for the King's criticism, and on the Sunday afternoon the King and the Queen came to the studio, and the King's first remark when he saw the picture was that I should not try to get in all the bridesmaids, and should leave the lamps out. I was much struck by the quickness of his judgment, and the wonderful way he seized on two points which had given me trouble, and were in a way spoiling the picture. So some of the bridesmaids had to go, and this meant, unhappily, that our present Queen Elizabeth was left out of the picture.

A serious miscalculation which caused me many hours of work was the portrait of the Duke of York. The Duke came to the studio and gave me a long sitting, and I was able to paint in a satisfactory portrait of him, but when the Queen was able to come, and I had advanced with her portrait, I found to my great disappointment that the Duke was about half an inch too near the Queen, which meant that I had to move his whole figure to the left. This was very tantalizing, because his portrait was at the time without exception the best in the picture.

At Chesterfield House the Princess Royal gave me a sitting with her wedding dress on, the first time the household had been able to see it, and the servants filed past with great delight. The Princess was anxious for me to finish the portrait from the study and not to take the dress away, but this I found impossible. My wife felt the dress to be a great responsibility, and we were very glad when it was safely back at Chesterfield House. When the picture was nearing completion Princess Mary came up and gave me a sitting, an immense help, for there is something that comes instantly and unhesitatingly from nature that is not to be secured without it. With some of these heads and figures I must have worked weeks from the study whereas from life a few minutes would have been enough.

The painting of the picture took a tremendous time, involving the grouping of thirty or forty figures, and the canvas was in the studio well on for two years. Just one portrait would hold it back for weeks. Queen Mary gave me a sitting at the Palace. It was fixed for ten-fifteen one morning and I liked to be there an hour before to arrange the light. Unfortunately that morning I was delayed a few minutes in leaving home, and as fate would have it I was held up by the traffic at Marble Arch. When I entered the park it was quite deserted and I could see a clear run in front of me, so I accelerated and was going at thirty miles an hour. At the next gate, to my astonishment, policemen stopped me and said I must wait until the inspector came up. I told them I had an appointment to keep with the Queen, but they insisted on taking all particulars, and I was late at the Palace, so that the Queen came in before we were ready. On explaining the reason why everything was not in order, the Queen hoped I should not be summoned, but in due course I received a summons, which cost me five guineas.

His Majesty was hoping it would not be necessary for him to put on Field-Marshal's uniform, but when Lord Stamfordham came to see the picture I pointed out what a great advantage it would be if the King could find time to let me see the uniform on, and it was arranged that I should go down to the Palace. I was taken up into the dressing-room and helped the King on with his uniform. Having just had a visit from the dentist, he said he did not feel very happy, but sat to me gladly. I was able to make one of my best drawings of him.

At this sitting the King, asking about the progress of the painting, said, " We will not allow this picture to be exhibited at the Academy," and, putting his hand on my shoulder in a comforting way, said, " I am not going to have you or my picture abused." Adverse criticism had made the King a good friend.

Sir George Frampton, who had just modelled portrait busts of the King and Queen, generously lent me his original plaster-casts and I found them very helpful. In returning the busts I rang Sir George's studio bell and impishly announced that the King and Queen had just driven up and were at the door !

As the sending-in day for the Academy came round the President, Sir Aston Webb, sent to Buckingham Palace and asked if they could exhibit the picture of Princess Mary's wedding. The reply was that they must apply to the artist, and the next morning I received a visit from the President, saying he had called to see the picture and to ask if I would send it to the Academy. Knowing nothing of the application to the Palace, I explained that I had nothing to do with it ; they must ask the King ! The picture was not exhibited.

Soon after this the marriage of the Duke of York was announced, and I attended a second royal wedding in the Abbey, at which I witnessed a touching and beautiful incident which should surely not be forgotten. The bridal procession had entered the great west door, and as the bride, leaning on her father's arm, approached the tomb of the Unknown Warrior, the procession paused, and the Duchess, looking up into her father's face as if asking him something, left his arm and placed her bouquet on the Unknown Warrior's grave. At the close of the service the King's orderly officers, in all the dignity and splendour of their Indian uniforms, marched, escorted by the officer-in-command of the gentlemen-at-arms and accompanied by the dean and chapter, to the Warrior's Grave, saluting and paying homage to the Fallen, an impressive subject which I painted for the India Office.

As the dark shadows of war receded and the effort to establish peace cleared the disturbed atmosphere, the ancient orders of chivalry gradually resumed their functions. The Most Noble Order of the Garter, the Most Honourable Order of the Bath, and the Most Distinguished Order of St. Michael and St. George, revived their time-honoured ceremonies in St. George's Chapel, Westminster Abbey, and St. Paul's Cathedral. Here illustrious citizens who had nobly served their country were installed, and plighted their knightly vows of chivalry.

The Installation of the Order of the Bath was held in Henry the Seventh's Chapel. The Chancellor and the Grand Master, in May 1924, authorized me to be present to make sketches, but the King's illness prevented him from being present, and it was not until 1928 that the chance to paint this great scene came. This time Queen Mary was present, a unique event in the history of the Order.

An artist will always desire not to be too conspicuous a figure in such a scene as this, and yet there are times when temptation is strong upon him, for he may see many little things that would be better otherwise. It was so at these rehearsals, when I noted that the canons stood too close to the King, cramping the scene. In talking this over the Dean gave me authority to group the canons more freely, but as the ceremony was to take place the next day I had no opportunity until the canons entered the chapel heading the long procession. I then dared to request them to stand back a little, but when the service began they gradually moved forward, so I quietly touched them on the shoulder to step back a pace. There was a rather interesting sequel to this the following week at a meeting of the Dean and Chapter, when one of the canons observed that it was remarkable to see the way the King was looked after during the ceremony, for he had noticed a man behind them in court dress, evidently from Scotland Yard, who twice during the service came forward and asked the canons to stand back so that he could keep his eye on the King. Sir Edward Knapp Fisher, Receiver General of the Abbey, said " Oh, that was not a detective, but Mr. Salisbury ! "

The Dean, who is the supreme authority of the Abbey (though he must act with the King), told me that the King had visited the Abbey that morning and emphasized that no one outside the Order was to be allowed in the chapel during the service. The Dean said, " But you have given Mr. Salisbury permission ? " and the King replied, " Oh yes, but Mr. Salisbury is a great friend of mine, and is painting a picture." The Dean turned to me and said, " You are a very honoured man."

It was a fine morning on the ninth of May, and, just as Canaletto had painted them so long ago, the knights walked through the precincts to the great west door, where the stately procession entered the Abbey, and the first part of the service took place in the presence of a large congregation. But the vital part of the ceremony was conducted in the chapel behind Torrigiano's closed doors.

There were two impressive incidents which appealed to me. The King, with pages holding his trailing robe, left his stall accompanied by the Grand Master (the Duke of Connaught) and the Officers of the Order (three of whom wore white silk robes instead of the rich ruby red, making a most artistic contrast), and came forward to the Altar steps to make the royal offering to the poor, which the Dean held aloft in dedication. Then followed the Installation of the new Knights. Standing in a double row facing the royal tomb, they dedicated their swords. The senior knight, Admiral of the Fleet Lord Jellicoe, proceeded to the Altar and surrendered his sword to the Dean, who consecrated it. Finally, holding the blades aloft, the knights sware to use them only in the service of God, Church, and King, the Oppressed and the Poor.

It was " The King's Offering " which gave me the best subject for my picture, which I made fourteen feet long by seven feet wide. In starting the work I adopted a new plan, painting the scene from models before beginning the portraits. The Dean was my first sitter, followed by the King, of whom I painted one of my best portraits. Then came the Queen, the Duke of Connaught, the Knights, and Lords Allenby, Byng, Jellicoe, Reading, Stamfordham, Bradbury, Hankey, and others. I felt that the great achievements of these men had indelibly left its impress upon their features. It was a privilege to paint them.

The picture was first exhibited in New York and Chicago. The portrait of the King was painted just before his serious illness, and was in fact on exhibition in New York during that critical time. After the exhibition at Grafton Galleries in London the Order presented it to the King to commemorate his recovery, and the picture now hangs in Buckingham Palace.

To be in Westminster Hall and look up at King Richard's great hammerbeam roof is a rather inspiring experience but to be up in the roof itself is something for a red-letter day.

At the time of these Abbey ceremonies I was naturally spending much time in the Palace of Westminster, and the scaffolding filled the Great Hall of William Rufus, as the death-watch beetle had attacked the oak timbers of the roof. The work of repairing this was started in 1913 but owing to the Great War it was stopped and the scaffolding remained up for years. In 1918 the work was taken in hand again. One day Mr. Tom Wilson, that excellent clerk of works for Parliament and most delightful man, whose death bereaved all his friends, told me that the roof was nearly finished, and that in three weeks the scaffolding would be taken down and cleared away. We climbed up together, and I was so impressed with the astonishing sight of these timbers that I wanted everybody to have a chance of seeing so great a triumph of the carpenter's art. I took out my note-book and there and then arranged to make sketches. I was only just in time, and I worked hard, often with the March wind sweeping round me bitterly, landing me in bed for three weeks. But I had obtained my material and was able to paint a picture reconstructing the scene of King Richard visiting the hall and inspecting the roof with his beloved carpenter Hugh Hurland, who worked on the roof when he was over eighty.

The original William Rufus roof had two rows of columns supporting the beams, and when it was found necessary to restore it King Richard called his carpenter and asked him to build a new roof, saying he must remove the columns supporting it and make a roof of one span. Hurland said it was impossible, as there were no oak trees long enough to give forty-feet timbers, but the king would listen to no excuse, and said, "I will have a roof of one span." The good Master Hurland set to work and devised this marvellous hammerbeam construction, which takes the weight by the thrust of a rising beam of over two tons. He designed a winged angel at the end of each beam, suggesting that the roof is being carried by a supernatural power, and as the King was the inspiration of the idea he gave each angel a shield bearing the royal coat-of-arms.

It was a most enjoyable piece of work to paint, and I was gratified to find Sir George Frampton enthusiastic over it; it was he who named my picture "The Great Roof."

CHAPTER X

AN INSPIRATION

THE idea of honouring the memory of the Fallen was growing throughout the country, and the Lord Mayor of Liverpool (Mr. Frank Wilson) asked me to visit the city to meet the Arts Committee and that great Liverpool citizen Alderman John Lea, whose portrait I had painted for the Walker Art Gallery. They were contemplating a series of frescoes for the Hall of Memory in the Town Hall.

The approach to the hall was not good, nor was the hall well lighted, but already in the oak panelling on the walls were thirteen thousand names. The twelve lunette spaces gave a great chance for fine treatment, and the Lord Mayor asked me to suggest subjects for twelve frescoes, preferably not khaki, and if possible a connected *Story*. For two or three days the only ideas that came to me were complicated and involved, and I became depressed. Almost in despair I went to bed, but the next morning came my inspiration, for among my letters was one from a lady unknown to me, enclosing this poem she had written in appreciation of my picture of the Burial of the Unknown Warrior, which she had " a curious and inexplainable desire to show me ". It was entitled, *A Story*. *My Prodigal*.

> Long years ago Love's consummated fire
> Fashioned within me by God's cunning hand
> My little son, the babe of my desire,
> My mite towards the manhood of the land.
>
> Mine only when within my breast he lay,
> And baby fingers seemed to touch my heart,
> Yet even then I heard a whisper say :
> Give me my substance, that I may depart.
>
> I gave him life, and in his golden youth
> He took his stand, a man among brave men,
> And vindicating honour, right, and truth,
> He gallantly gave back my gift again.
>
> He took his stand, a spendthrift in the fray,
> Impetuous, without a backward glance,
> And royally flung all my gifts away
> Upon the bitter blood-soaked fields of France.

Somewhere in that red shell-torn battle zone
They buried him in haste where he had died,
Flesh of my flesh and bone bred of my bone ·
An unknown soldier, unidentified.

Only God knows a mother's cheated pain,
And God has heard my pitiful requests :
" Though I may never see my babe again
Lord, let me know where my beloved rests."

For King and State with God-inspired accord,
Though knowing not his name nor his degree,
Went reverently, guided by the Lord,
And brought my heart's beloved back to me.

The motherhood of England at his side
Wept healing tears over his glorious place,
And, lo, I saw my comfort and my pride
Reflected in each sorrowing proud face.

O, God, I heard the comfort of Thy voice
As they laid him in Thy consecrated ground :
Be comforted, O mother, and rejoice
For this thy son, that once was lost, is found !

It is surely a remarkable poem, and coming just at that moment
seems something more than a coincidence, for it solved my problem.
From it I obtained the three leading ideas for the twelve subjects.
The start of a human *story*.

"*Infancy.*" Love's consummation, God's Almighty hand, our
mite towards the manhood of the land.

Duty's Call. A man among brave men vindicating Honour,
Truth and Right.

Sacrifice. He took his stand impetuous in the fray without a backward glance, loyally gave his gift of life away.

Then followed *Renown.* One generation to another shall show
honour and their names liveth for evermore.

Immortality. Be comforted, O mother ! for this, thy lost, has
passed into the fadeless light.

To the final subject—

Remembrance. Tranquil they lie, their knightly virtues proved, their
memory hallowed in the land they loved.

The Hall of Memory was dedicated in the summer of 1923 by the
Duke of York—now King George the Sixth—accompanied by the
Duchess of York, the Lord Mayor and all the representatives of the
Services of the Crown.

CHAPTER XI

AMERICA

FROM our small enchanted land America calls to every artist, for there Art has rich lovers and a boundless field of inspiration. We arrived for the first time in that great country in an ideal hour in 1925, sailing up the Hudson when the sun was setting, and the lights of the majestic sky-scrapers came out to meet the stars in the clear evening sky. For the Englishman who has not seen it before it is one of the astounding sights of his life, and there is awaiting him in America an experience he will never forget, for these people, our cousins, are as marvellous as their country.

A few weeks before sailing we were at a dinner party with Sir Charles and Lady Allom among the guests, and I happened to say I was going to New York to paint portraits. Sir Charles said, "I can lend you a studio, and will cable at once and get them to prepare it." This he did most nobly, for when I arrived in New York there was a fine studio above his beautiful offices.

It happened that I had just been the guest of my friend Dr. Stuart Holden at Glassburn, his lovely Scottish home, where I met Dr. Harris Kirk of Baltimore, the famous preacher. We had a wonderful time together, and Stuart Holden tried to initiate me into the art of salmon fishing. I had no success in casting the line, however excelling in hooking up weeds or entangling the line on the banks, so I abandoned fishing and took to the brush, and at the end of the day I had two sketches, but Stuart Holden had no salmon. Dr. Kirk sat for me and was my first American portrait, the forerunner of so many.

I had an astonishing proof of his memory. Sir John Tweedie, the great eye specialist, was also sitting to me, and in our conversation we discussed the work of old Dr. Martineau of Brighton. I found Sir John interested in the famous preacher, and he asked me if I had read his sermon on "The Tides of the Spirit". He lent me the volume containing this discourse, and it made a great impression on me. When Dr. Kirk was sitting the name of Dr. Martineau was mentioned, and I asked if he had ever come across this sermon. He immediately started to quote from it, reciting long passages word for word, though he had not read it for twenty years.

It is no small task disembarking in New York if you have luggage.

Mrs. Myron C. Taylor.

Myron C. Taylor, President of the United States Steel
Corporation.

THE REV. DR. S. PARKES CADMAN.

On my first 1925 visit I took a number of pictures for exhibition. There is no duty on original works of art but frames are dutiable, and if the value is more than five hundred dollars the Customs may send the pictures to the appraiser's office, which often takes three weeks. The case containing Queen Mary's portrait was held up for a long time, the delay being mainly because on the embarkation form it had not been stated how the case had been packed—whether in hay or straw, so that the Queen's portrait was actually delayed because they were afraid of foot-and-mouth disease ! It appeared to me that the dock authorities did not see the humour of this.

Mr. Clarence Bowen took us to our hotel, the Gotham in Fifth Avenue, saying he would call for us at eight-thirty, as he wanted us to go to a reception at the Central Art Galleries. It was a delightful evening, and we met many artists and architects, including Mrs. Dunlap Hopkins, President of the Women's School of Design, and Mr. and Mrs. Ernest Greene, who became devoted friends. Out of this gathering came a chance of meeting Mr. and Mrs. Myron Taylor in their beautiful home, adorned with the glory of Spanish, Italian, and Gothic arts of the finest periods.

Mr. Taylor, who followed Judge Gary as President of the Steel Corporation, has sat to me for four portraits, one for Cornell University, and Mrs. Taylor, whom I painted as a companion portrait to hang in the beautiful Gothic building they gave to the University, sat for me a second time in a picture of a very unusual character. At the celebration of their silver wedding they attended a fancy dress party, and Mrs. Taylor put on her wedding-dress, with wreath and veil, looking charming. It was hard to believe that so many years had passed, and Mr. Taylor insisted on my painting his wife as " The Bride ", twenty-five years after.

So began a lifelong friendship. With his friend Captain H. Hier-Davies to complete our company, a very happy trio we were, Three Musketeers of kindred tastes and sympathies. Great was our delight in exploring survivals of the beauties of medieval England, and one of our early adventures embraced a visit to St. Albans to see the grand old abbey, the ancient Roman city of Verulamium, and the ruins of Francis Bacon's house. This was the climax of the day, as we stood under an oak older than the United States Mr. Taylor said, " I would give anything to have this tree in my home at Long Island, for my ancestor, Sir Edward Underhill, was secretary to Francis Bacon, and may have sat in the shade of this noble oak." The Underhill branch that settled in America were Quakers, and I have seen their old meeting house on Long Island. Lady Jane Grey was godmother of one of the daughters of the family.

My first sitter in America was Judge Elbert Gary, famous as President of the United States Steel Corporation. Fortunately the portrait went well. His house was near the studio and he would come early before going down to Broadway. It was a privilege to talk to this remarkable man, who for twelve years fought the Government on the Trust Suppression laws, and won. Sir Joseph (afterwards Lord) Duveen came in several times while the portrait was in progress and I was gratified beyond measure when he said, " Raeburn could not have painted it better," though I may be forgiven for not accepting his compliment at its face value.

I painted the Judge three times. The first portrait was completed at Christmas and Mrs. Gary arranged a lunch at which their friends could see it. Among the guests were Sir Joseph and Lady Duveen. The dining-room was surrounded with Old Masters on the walls, and Sir Joseph, being invited to describe them, spoke eloquently of their artistic qualities.

When he had completed his survey, I reminded him that he had overlooked my favourite, a fine portrait of an Old Man by Raeburn. Turning to the picture he pronounced it an outstanding masterpiece— in the sale this fetched a record price.

The whole setting of the luncheon party, with the guests round the table, the features all illuminated and the vista looking into the hall from my point of view next to Mrs. Gary, made a fine subject for any artist's brush. On a later occasion I painted the scene, looking from the hall.

Their beautiful house, with an elaborate curving staircase of marble going up three or four flights, must have cost an immense sum of money. At the end of one of my visits I called to say good-bye to the judge and found him unwell and in bed. I was taken to his room and had a delightful talk, and this was the last time we met, for he never recovered. When I next visited New York and walked up Fifth Avenue the house was being pulled down to make way for an apartment building. I understood that the wonderful staircase was sold for five pounds.

Another early sitter in America was Mr. Herbert Fordham, who, as he had no children and intended to leave his Long Island home to the public, wanted his portrait to hang in the house. His sittings were very amusing. He sent me copious typed documents on the history of his ancestors, as he thought it was necessary that I should be sure of the right atmosphere ; and he also thought it necessary that my wife should become familiar with his salient characteristics, and those of his family. He kept me deeply interested by his flow of language regarding the qualities of his Quaker ancestors on the one side and the hard calculating ancestors on the other ; the cold steely glint in his eye, he said, came from the hard side ! When I was painting his hands he wished me to notice that his fingers were rather short and stubby, and assured me that it would be beyond my power to calculate the strength of his grip.

The great moment came when his wife was to see the picture. He himself was very pleased with it and was anxious for her to be pleased. On catching sight of it, however, she began to cry, and for a long time no one spoke. The silence was painful, and he came across and whispered to me that it was a compliment to the portrait if I did but know it. He could not get her to say anything, but gathered that she felt the portrait a little uncanny. I suggested that it would be a good idea if they came the next day and studied it quietly by themselves, and we made that arrangement with the house-keeper. The result was that in the end she was delighted with it, yet he thought there must be something wrong to have caused her such emotion, and he felt that perhaps it was too ethereal, and that I must get him " more a man of the earth, earthy ". I had many letters from him relating to the portrait, and had to write whole essays on the salient points of his character, often points that he did not himself grasp. I remember that he was disturbed because I had made his finger-nails too elegant, which was an excuse for a week-end visit to Long Island, where I added a few touches to please him.

When the Hitler War broke out in 1939 I received from Mr. Fordham a long discourse warning us of ultimate defeat and begging me to listen to the voice of a scholar of history, a letter he wished me to send on to influential sources of power. My reply, during the Battle of Britain, was not to his liking, as he wrote back requesting me to keep cool, saying that signs of cerebral excitement existed in no small degree. He had followed all world-wide broadcasts, he said, and studied more reliable information than Britain could obtain, and " Again I say unto you, make peace while you may, or, if you prefer the words of an earlier prophet, read the last seven verses of the fifth chapter of Daniel, ' Thou art weighed in the balances and found wanting.' " In reply I reproved him for giving the British Navy the trouble to bring such a quisling message to the Island which was fighting his battle, and begged him to ponder the words from the 92nd Psalm, " Thou, Lord, art most high for ever-more, for, lo, thine enemies shall perish ! All the workers of inquity shall be scattered ".

I had the pleasure of meeting Mr. William T. Dewart of *New York Evening Sun* fame. We had an exceptionally delightful time together, discussing the international situation. The second day of the sitting was Thanksgiving Day, November 20 (commemorating Independence), and at the end of the day he said, " I have rediscovered England, and we will call this the Thanksgiving Portrait."

On my first arrival in New York I was impressed by Cadman's Daily Counsel in the *New York Tribune*, and I heard also of Dr. Cadman's famous broadcasts every Sunday afternoon from Brooklyn. I wondered if this was the Dr. Parkes Cadman who, as a student from Richmond College, used to come to Harpenden to preach, staying at our old home. I went over to the men's service at Brooklyn and found it an inspiring meeting, with the singing lead by angel trumpeters in white. After the address questions were collected from the audience, the secretary taking them one by one and reading them out for the doctor to answer right off, without any warning. I have rarely seen such a brilliant working of a man's mind, and such evidence of a profound store of knowledge. I recall one or two of the questions. The problem of Home Rule had just been up at Westminster, and question number one was : " What will England do now that Ireland is free ? " The answer came promptly : " My man, you have made a mistake ; it is England that is free ! " I remember telling this to King George the Fifth and to the Prime Minister of Northern Ireland, and both thought the answer remarkable.

When the meeting was over I joined the long procession of those who wished to shake hands with Dr. Cadman, and my mentioning Harpenden and my father brought back to him a sudden flood of happy memories of forty years. From that moment was forged a link of friendship between us so deep and true that nothing could break it. It was while Dr. Cadman was sitting for me in New York that I received the information from St. Andrew's that the University had resolved to confer on me the honorary degree of Doctor of Laws, and I was much moved by his enthusiasm. He said it was a most coveted honour from one of the oldest and most honoured universities in the world.

A tower of strength to any man who had his friendship, Dr. Cadman, with a fine sense of humour, had always an interesting story up his sleeve, and his soul was on fire with the thought of the living and eternal powers of the universe. What a God-given privilege to have such a friend ! He twice became a victim of my brush. Once, when posing, he had his closed hand to his chin. " Could you tighten your fist just a little ? I asked, and he said, " You put a five-dollar bill in it and see ! " My daughters came in during the sitting and their criticisms always favoured the sitter. One of them, quietly touching her chin, asked if I could not make it less double. She had hoped she would not be observed, but Dr. Cadman caught the suggestion and laughingly told us of the man whose face was not all it should be, and who was at a Methodist class meeting, where all the others were testifying what the Lord had done for them, all this poor fellow could say was, " Look what a mess the Lord has made of me ! "

The passing of Dr. Cadman was a deep sorrow and a national and international loss. In his sermons and broadcasts he always spoke generously and brotherly of Protestant, Jew, and Roman Catholic alike. He preached his last sermon at Pittsburg. During the afternoon he was in great pain and had to see a doctor, who forbade him to preach in the evening ; but he said he could not disappoint fifteen hundred people, and preached. After the sermon he collapsed and was taken to the only hospital near the church—a Roman Catholic one, and the only available doctor was a Jew. These dear people wrestled with the angel of death for this great man's life, but the fateful hour had come. His work was ended. The Protestant minister kept watch at the door, praying that " neither life nor death nor principalities nor powers should separate them from the love of God " ; the Jewish doctor stood by the bed ; the Mother Superior held the Crucifix over him ; and his chariot of fire took his soul beyond the horizon and the sunsets.

Truly he left us enriched in memory but distressed in mind, a veritable Ambassador of God, filling one of the loftiest niches in the Pantheon of Civilization. As my good friend Judge Fawcett said, he is of the great immortals, St. Augustine, Thomas Aquinas, Martin Luther, John Wesley, and the rest of the glorious host that has laboured through the ages to advance God's Kingdom.

One of the most enjoyable adventures of personality that has come to me was in painting eight different portraits of Mr. George F. Baker, one of the last of the industrial giants. The first was for the Genealogical Society of New York, the next for his great friend Edward Loomis, and others for various universities and the Steel Corporation. Though of great age, he sat for each one, and with each portrait our affection grew. When the sittings were all finished he would come into the studio some afternoons and sit watching me work, but would soon fall asleep, though when he sat for me he did not even doze. Up to the last day he would never miss a board meeting, and I was told that, while he invariably went to sleep, if any new problem came up, or any important decision had to be taken, he was instantly awake to it.

He gave me an opportunity of painting an impressive portrait in the robe of Doctor of Laws, which I thought would be appreciated as it was for Yale University, which had honoured him with the degree. But to my disappointment his son objected to the robe, saying it made him shudder, as his father was a purely business man and not a scholar. Artistically the portrait came so well that I could not alter it, so I decided to start again and paint Mr. Baker without the robe in a business suit. It was finally decided that the two pictures should be sent to Yale for the University to decide, and they chose the robe.

After Mr. Baker had been seriously ill for twelve months he recovered enough to give sittings for another portrait, and to celebrate his return to health he wished us to dine with him at his house on Madison Avenue. Our daughters were with us, and he particularly wanted them to join the party. Everything was done in grand style, with full gold dinner service, and he himself had prepared the menu, which started with oysters followed by turtle soup, then a rare and exclusive dish of terrapin, then venison, then " hot Virginia ham ", and at last Stilton cheese—very high, as all the rest had been. The poor girls could touch nothing, but enjoyed the ice cream. Mr. Baker kept a watchful eye on all our plates and would urge the twins on, saying, " You are not getting on at all well," and to save the reputation of the family my wife went through the dinner like a hero.

When we last shook hands and said good-bye he said he would look forward to seeing me on my next visit if he were not in the seventh heaven, but within two weeks the dear man was in his seventh heaven. I remember that my wife, on taking her gloves to be cleaned in a shop on Madison Avenue, happened to mention Mr. Baker, and they said they knew him very well, as they turned all his suits for him—an odd fact, seeing that he was one of the richest men in America, and it was peace time.

The last of the eight portraits I painted of Mr. Baker was perhaps the best. The portrait was on the easel when Sir Charles Allom came

Joseph E. Davies, sometime American Ambassador in Russia.

George F. Baker.

Mrs. Edwards Harkness.

Edwards Harkness, Founder of the Pilgrim Trust.

[75]

into the studio with Sir Joseph Duveen, who said it was the finest portrait he had seen for twenty years, and it must be exhibited in London. I happened to say that if I sent it to the Academy it would be thrown out, and he stood in front of the canvas and shook both his fists, saying, " They dare not reject this." I said, " Well, I will test it," so I secured permission to bring it home, and it was rejected.

There is a quality in human nature that prospers on the challenge of difficulties and disappointments, which rightly accepted, so far from depressing, stimulate the will. Here my experience had an immediate and gratifying sequel. Contrary to common practice in such contingencies, the United States Steel Corporation, for whom the portrait was painted, were not, as is so often the case, prejudiced by the rejection. On the contrary, their President, on missing the portrait from the Royal Academy during a visit to London, came straight to my studio, commissioned me to paint four outstanding Americans, and said, quite simply, " Why exhibit at the Royal Academy ? "

Two artists, both Academicians, on seeing the portrait on my easel exclaimed, " Why did you not send this to the Academy ? " I was about to narrate the story of my experience when one of them exclaimed, " Do not tell us ; it is too painful."

Before he died Mr. Baker had asked me if I would go to Baltimore to paint a portrait of Dr. Wilmer, the renowned eye specialist, and I said he was the one man I would go anywhere to paint. However, he came to New York to sit for me and it was a marvellous privilege to meet such a man. He told me that early in his career, when the gates of success were opening for him, he had to decide whether he would serve humanity or seek fame and fortune in the fashionable world, and both he and his wife agreed that he should seek to serve humanity. Mr. Pierpont Morgan once wished Dr. Wilmer to come to New York to attend to his eyes and even offered him a house in New York as a reward, but Dr. Wilmer refused, and as Mohamet would not go to the mountain the mountain had to go to Mohamet. Chartering a special train, Mr. Morgan went to Baltimore and Dr. Wilmer saw him, in due course sending in his account for the small fee he charged to any hospital patient. When the portrait of Dr. Wilmer was finished, a lady looked at it and said, " That is the most Christlike face I have ever seen," and I felt that I had portrayed something of this dear man's life of service to humanity.

Perhaps the most difficult American sitter I have ever had was Mr. Andrew Mellon, the millionaire Secretary of the Treasury, and a great art collector. On the Thursday before I was sailing for home he called me on the telephone from Washington and asked if I could paint his portrait. I said I was sailing for London on Wednesday, and he said he was sailing for Bermuda on Tuesday. I asked if he could give me two days, and he said, " Come to Washington to-morrow, Friday." I replied that I would, and I arrived at the Treasury about three in the afternoon. I was shown straight into his room, and he said he was very busy and would not be free for an hour. I said that was perfectly all right, as I had to get the studio ready, and he explained that most artists used a room at his apartment, so I suggested that he should inform them at home that I was coming along, so that they could have the room ready.

On arriving I had a most difficult task, as all the windows were too low, with mosquito screens cutting off the light, and though it was six o'clock before I was ready my sitter had not come in. When he did at last arrive it was dark, and I started making studies in arti-ficial light. Mr. Mellon said he had never known an artist work by electric light and didn't seem over-pleased, but we went on. At eight o'clock a number of poses were settled and I enquired about the arrangements for the next day. To my dismay he found he was full up with engagements until four o'clock. I managed to prepare the canvas from my study, and had the background painted in and the drawing ready before the light faded. Then my sitter forgot he was sitting for me and had a bad habit of looking up, showing his profile instead of full face. Famous as an art collector, he had little understanding of how to help an artist. Now I knew why all his portraits were failures, and said to myself, " Poor Orpen," as Orpen had taken the line of least resistance and painted a profile looking up. At last, in desperation, I said, " It takes two to paint a portrait," and he replied, " Do you want me to take the palette ? " I said I wished he would, and then he realized he was not being helpful, and for ten minutes sat well, looking at me and more or less keeping the pose ; but he soon drifted again into oblivion.

I have never been in such despair as then, and with the light going I felt like giving up the portrait, but, instead, I said to my inward self, " Salisbury, take your coat off and go for it." I thought of some financial subject to enlist his interest. Mr. Churchill was then Chancellor of the Exchequer, and I asked Mr. Mellon if he had met him. He said he had not long before had breakfast with him in Downing Street, and this started a conversation which enabled me to catch his vital expression at last. He said, " Surely you cannot talk and paint at the same time ?" My reply was that I am so fortunate as to be able to do both simultaneously. To that, however, I must add a qualification. In the easy flow of normal conversation my share is perhaps subconsciously sustained, for I find that a direct question may find my mind a blank on the point involved. Thus a sitter once asked my views on the Creation, and I had to admit that the consideration of the subject necessitated my putting down my palette.

On another occasion I was asked if I could give an illustration of Immortality. "Yes, my canvas and palette can answer that," I jokingly ventured to reply.

And that leads me to a thought on which I frequently ponder with the deepest interest. We gaze with wondering eyes at a portrait by one of the Old Masters—mere canvas and paint—which yet recalls a vital personality as conceived by the artist's mind and by his brush bodied forth to endure through the ages. Artist and subject have long been one with the mortal dust from which they sprang, yet the portraits, limning form, features, and personality long since one with oblivion, lives on. It survives as the mutely eloquent product of the fervid spirit, the creative energy, the genius made manifest, of that master mind, silent still, and functionless through the centuries that have intervened between the painting of the portrait and the hour in which the enraptured observer beholds it. So such works attest the seeming miracle of the spirit that animated the hand and fancy of the artist whom, but for his creative work, the world would have forgotten long centuries ago. Through his work he lives immortal, and, through him, his work. Thus genius and inspiration outlive their physical tenement.

In spite of the many difficulties I encountered Mr. Mellon was very pleased with the result and on Monday I returned to New York with the portrait. Sir Joseph Duveen came to the studio the next morning and pronounced the picture a success, saying he would write Mr. Mellon and congratulate him.

Mr. Mellon took me round his collection of Old Masters, and as we looked at the Rembrandts, the Vandykes, the Raeburns, all with their glowing and flowing robes, he said, "Why have we no artists now who can paint pictures like these?" I said, "Do you realize the heavy handicap a modern artist has to struggle against, seeing that men and women arrayed like these are now seen only on the stage ? This desolate, inartistic age has stripped life of all its pageantry. What can an artist do with a small turn-down collar, a narrow strip of

material masquerading as a cravat, and a tight-fitting cloth suit?
Could a magician, let alone an artist, make a dazzling picture of such
poor stuff?" Mr. Mellon replied that the point had never occurred
to him.

Clearly that is why so many artists have made great names by
going back into the past and painting medieval and Tudor days,
illustrating Shakespeare or the vast range of life covered by the Bible.
A fine picture must have a decorative lay-out of material as well as a
play of light and shade. Out of his experience an artist can often
make a fine thing of poor material, but living portraits must be true,
and men to-day are not arrayed like Holbein's men.

One of the most noble and one of the most modest men it has
fallen to my lot to paint was Mr. Edwards Harkness. Many times his
friends, anxious to secure his portraits for Harvard and other places
to which he was so great a benefactor, tried to prevail on him to
sit, but he shrank from the ordeal, and at last I was asked to write to
him, emphasizing the fact that it would not be a long or painful
process. He replied that even if he sat he would be no good to
any one after an hour, but added a postscript saying that he would
call round to see me the next morning. This was his undoing. A
sitting was fixed, his robes as Doctor of Laws of St. Andrew's were
sent to the studio, and the work began. After he had been sitting
two hours I saw that he was getting tired, and liberated him on
condition that he came back in the afternoon. In the meantime I
had a model who donned the robe and sat for the figure, so that when
Mr. Harkness returned I was ready for the vital touches.

He came only once more, but rarely has a portrait gone so easily.
Many of his admirers, Harvard and Yale, and the Presbyterian Hospital in New York, begged for portraits, but Mrs. Harkness claimed
the first. It happened that Sir James Irvine, President of St. Andrew's
University, was visiting at the same time in New York, and said
that if the portrait was a success they must have one for St. Andrew's.
When Mr. Harkness told me this I felt that, remembering all that this
great and noble American had done for our country, the least I could
do was to present his portrait to The University of St. Andrew, where
it now hangs in an atmosphere which meant so much to him. It
hangs as a memorial to a rare and truly illustrious figure, whose
simplicity of life, generosity to all good causes, devotion to humanity,
and great love of England and the British people, was most exemplary.
It was between the old war and the new one that he founded the
Pilgrim Trust so quietly one day at lunch with three friends, to whom

he said he would like to do something to show his appreciation of what this country has done for the world and wished to set aside two millions sterling for good causes. It is to such men as he that the world, looks in these difficult days to promote the spirit of unity and peace. Such characters inspire our race and forge new links, binding the English-Speaking nations in deeper understanding. It was a sad day that took Mr. Harkness from us, but in our memories and in his works he lives on.

Mrs. Harkness also sat for me and I remember a very touching tribute while the picture was on the easel. Mr. Harkness came with his wife and a friend to see it, and the three stood a long time looking quietly at the portrait. Nothing was said, but the gentleman who had come with them walked silently up to Mrs. Harkness and kissed her.

One day in New York I was rung up by the private secretary of a man who wished to be unknown but asked if I would paint two portraits. He turned out to be Mr. Henry Clay Folger, President of the Standard Oil Company, but better known as the founder of the marvellous Shakespeare Library at Washington, which was then coming into being. He wanted portraits of himself and his wife which could be hung in the building. Mr. Folger had a Doctor of Laws robe of Cornell University, which was black and white, and a silver frame suited both the picture and the setting so well that they seemed to be part of the architect's design. As the library was not completed when they were finished, the portraits were put into a case and stored for years in a depository with Mr. Folger's Shakespeare collection.

At one sitting, when I said I should like him to be holding something in his hands, he brought with him, wrapped up in newspaper, a precious Shakespeare publication published before the First Folio, for which he had paid thousands of pounds and refused half as much again ; yet, coming to the studio that day, he carried it in a newspaper wrapping and came by the subway, alone.

What a noble memorial he and Mrs. Folger have left the world, a heritage for all generations ! Mrs. Folger's right hand was crippled with writer's cramp through cataloguing the collection, but what of that ? They would think nothing of crossing the Atlantic and returning by the next boat with a book from Christie's or Sotheby's.

Mr. Folger's library now stands by the Capitol at Washington, having cost £400,000. It contains 79 of the 200 known copies of the First Folio edition of the plays, published in 1623, nine plays issued in quarto size in 1619 and purchased for £20,000, volumes of the poet's works which belonged to Charles Lamb, Coleridge, George Washington, and Abraham Lincoln, and letters about Shakespeare by great authors. Altogether the collection has seventy thousand volumes by or about Shakespeare and his contemporaries. No wonder Mrs. Folger's hands were crippled in cataloguing them.

Lest it should clash in style with other buildings at Washington the exterior of the Shakespeare Library is designed in simple classical lines. Around it are reliefs of scenes from Shakespeare, Macbeth and the Witches, Lear in the Storm, and so on, happily ranged below the windows. One wing contains a reconstruction of an Elizabethan playhouse, the courtyard with overhanging galleries, the outer stage on which the gallants and their ladies used to sit, the inner stage, and above it the balcony stage. To give the illusion of open-air a canopy is stretched across the theatre below the ceiling, electric light giving a daylight effect. The whole building is an appeal made by one of America's hardest workers and most successful business men for the right use of leisure. He found time to read and to write books on Shakespeare, and planned a little room in this shrine to which he and his wife could come and continue their studies. Hardly less stimulating than the idea of the wonderful building they have given us is the example they set of zeal, industry, and love of fine things.

Mr. Edward Loomis had one of the best heads it ever fell to the lot of an artist to paint, and our happy times together established a deep friendship with his family. Often on his way up to town to his home on Fifth Avenue he would drop in at the studio and look at my work. As an influential man on Wall Street, and director of many business concerns, he knew most of my sitters, and was a good critic. He would look carefully at a new portrait, and if I heard him say " Don't touch it again ", I knew it was right. If he said " I don't quite get him ", I knew something was wrong. What a gift to any man is a friend with an opinion so wise and helpful ! I used to call him my Director and Overseer, and his enthusiasm was an inspiration. A quiet evening with his family was always a joy to us. In the library one could always see the *Weekly Times*, the *Illustrated London News*, and the *Manchester Guardian*, and constant visits of Mr. and Mrs. Loomis to this country were a precious link across the Atlantic.

One of the most vital personalities of any age was Mr. Charles Schwab, President of the Bethlehem Steel Corporation. While sitting for his portrait he told me the romantic story of the building of submarines for the British Government. Admiral Jellicoe had called urgently for submarines, and Schwab said he should have them. He was met in the Atlantic on a liner and taken on board a man-of-war to Scotland where he saw Admiral Jellicoe, whose wants he promised to supply in nine months. He was sent on to the Admiralty, and Lord Fisher said it was impossible, for no submarine had ever been produced in less than eighteen months. Schwab said that if he did not complete his contract he would pay a penalty of half a million dollars, and he returned to America and started work. He was offered twice the money by Germany not to build submarines, but scorned to break his word. The Germans then charged the American Government with breaking the Neutrality Act, and the result was that Schwab was ordered to stop production. He demanded that the Government should give him a month's notice, and in that time transplanted his factory over the border in Canada. He delivered his submarines to the very day.

The Genealogical Society of New York has naturally deep and lasting ties with this country, as so many of its members trace their descent from the voyage of the *Mayflower*, or to some famous town in our Island. Mr. Clarence Bowen was the society's president for many years, and in securing portraits of its members he greatly stimulated interest in portraiture generally. There is a fine portrait of him in the Genealogical Society's gallery by an American artist, but it fell to my lot to paint him for the family. I recall a very interesting evening at his house, when after dinner he informed his guests that he had a remarkable man, an Egyptian, waiting to entertain us in the library. We were introduced to this tall, thin, and very striking personality.

The company consisted of seven or eight representative New York business men with their wives, and as we were standing together the Egyptian came up and asked us to think of our telephone numbers. Then, one by one, he told them all correctly. It may seem easy, but not so the next experiment. Our host announced that the next test was going to be a very difficult one needing help, and requested us to be as quiet as possible. The man was blindfolded at the other end of the room with his back to us all. I was given a sheet of paper, and he asked me to draw a geometrical pattern. I drew a Greek key pattern. I was then asked to write the name of a famous man, dead or alive. I wrote Gary, *not* Judge Gary. Then I had to draw an animal and I drew a conventional rabbit. A number of other guests were asked to do similar tests, and finally the Egyptian's eyes were uncovered and he came to the table, took a pencil and paper, sat down, and, starting with me, asked me to think of the geometrical design I had drawn, while he reproduced my drawing almost exactly ! " Now," he said, " I will draw the portrait of your man ; he is Judge Gary." The result was astonishingly good, but not so astonishing as the fact that the Egyptian had fathomed our secrets.

His last request to us all was to think of a number, and after a time he said, " Gentlemen, you are all thinking of the number seven," and it was so. He was correct and astounding all through the evening, and I leave the matter there as one of the world's mysteries. However it may be, this demonstration of the psychic influence of mind-control gave me an assuring thought that the human mind, in constant relation with its Creator, could, in an attitude of receptivity, receive the impress of His thought and will.

There was a very interesting dinner at the Metropolitan Club in New York, when Mr. Coolidge, Senator Hughes, and many representative Americans were present. Mr. Clarence Bowen, who presided, made a speech of welcome to the guests, and cleverly asked another of the company to continue his speech when he sat down. He then carried on the link of speeches to other guests one by one, and at last said, " We have an Englishman here who will speak to us." In great expectation I looked round to see who the Englishman was, when to my horror he called upon me to take up the thread. This reminded me of my father, who in the early days at home would call upon each one of us to get up and speak on any subject he chose for us, a practice which has often stood me in good stead, and on this occasion helped me out of a difficult situation. Yet I failed to use my trump card, for I forgot that I had in my pocket a letter from King George the Fifth saying how deeply he was touched by the American messages that had reached him, and the evidences of American sympathy, in his recent illness.

The Women's School of Design wanted the portrait of its founder and President, Mrs. Hopkins and Raeburn himself can never have had a finer sitter or a more distinguished character. Her artist's soul made my work easy, for she was rhythm itself and knew how to help an artist—very unlike the headmistress of a college who was sitting for me, a lady methodical and precise, who said, " Let me know when you are painting my expression, so that I can fix my face," which is, of course, just what no artist wants. Mrs. Hopkins knew better. A pioneer with her ideas of training girls in all branches of arts and crafts, she was invited to England by Princess Christian to talk to an educational gathering at the Imperial Institute.   Up to the time the portrait was being painted she told me that twenty thousand students had started artistic careers, and been able to earn good livings, through the School of Design ; and the American nation has since acknowledged her service to art and education by presenting her with a much-coveted gold medal.

Mr. Daniel Willard, who was President of the Baltimore and Ohio Railway, came to New York to have his portrait painted for the company.   I had a most amusing experience while painting him, for every few minutes he would jump down to look at the easel.   I discovered that he had been painted so many times without success that he was over-anxious.   His life-story is remarkable, for he began life as a stoker's boy and an engine-driver, and rose to be president of the railway.   When the portrait was nearing completion he looked at it and said, " Yes, you have the head slightly leaning to the left shoulder ; that is because for years I leaned out of the cabin of the engine to watch the signals.   Also you have one eye closed more than the other ; that is because I had to close that eye owing to the wind and the dust when I was looking out."

The General Motor Company wanting to commemorate the work of their President, Mr. Alfred P. Sloan, he sat for me, and I made a companion portrait of his wife.   At that time his companies throughout the States were producing seven thousand motor-cars a day.   The corporation also wanting his portrait, I went for this to Detroit, where I met the manager, Mr. Knutson, since famous as Minister of Supply.   I was motored to their testing-ground, which covered hundreds of acres, and was told that any new car designed and manufactured in England was brought over, put on this track, and run until it fell to pieces.   Each run at the end of the day was tabulated, and all the fine points and weak parts of the car were discovered.   The tracks were divided into different speeds, the course being elaborately tabulated with conspicuous notices.

Mr. Walter Gifford, of the American Telephone and Telegraph Company, also sat for me for a portrait for the board room, he being then the youngest American controlling so vast an enterprise.

I had the pleasure of painting Mr. Stephen Baker, President of the Bank of Manhattan, and well do I remember the delight with which he planned the portrait as a surprise for his wife.   The picture was finished and the moment of delivery was staged, my subject playing the part like an actor   He arrived at the studio with his wife, enquiring the way as though he had never been before, looking at every picture, and at last casually enquiring, "What have you got on the easel behind?" The easel was turned and the surprise seemed overwhelming, but was a great success.

It is sometimes interesting to see the reaction of relatives to a portrait at first sight, and one story comes to mind of a subject I had painted in a rather unusual light—from the left, with a reflection from the right, so bringing out all the fine modelling of my subject's head. He was delighted with the result, and said, eagerly, "When can my wife see it?" The next morning was fixed, and his wife stood in front of the portrait for such a long time that he whispered to me, "I think it is all right." But after a long pause she sighed and said, "What a pity we have not a good photograph of you—nothing but those terrible passport photographs, and this is worse!" My sense of humour happily saved me, for I knew I had a good portrait. I advised my sitter to have the portrait home for a month, and promised that if they did not like it then I would paint it again. The test came in an unexpected way. I wanted to borrow the portrait for an exhibition and the wife said it could not possibly be spared, as she could not live without it!

I was soon to have another curious example of this reaction to a portrait. I had painted a distinguished American, and he asked me to paint his wife. She was a wise and excellent lady but not a good subject for an artist, and frankly said that she was the last woman in the world to be painted. I inwardly agreed, yet the husband was persistent, and at last I explained that I was so full up with work that I could not undertake it unless it could stand over for another year. He would take no excuse, however. I chanced to meet their two children, and they confided in me that they were very anxious for a portrait of mother, "but not an artist's ideal conception of her". I thought this very beautiful, and one day the husband brought her into the studio and persuaded her to sit. Her handicap was slight facial paralysis, but she was a truly noble character and I felt that there was a possibility of an exact likeness and a good picture. In the end it proved a great success, if we are to judge by its popularity with the family, and I remember a curious thing about it. I was painting at the same time a very beautiful young girl with a most striking and artistic dress, and I felt that the subject would attract everybody who came to the studio. As it happened, the two portraits were finished together, and I was very struck by the fact that every visitor went straight to the portrait of the lady who seemed so plain and never looked a second time at the beauty. "That is a fine portrait" they said of the mother who had wished to be painted as she was. How subtle a thing beauty is, springing from the inmost depths of the soul, and not from outward things !

One day at an exhibition where this portrait was exhibited I was in the gallery when a man came up to me and said, " I am a stranger to you, and to the subject of this portrait, but I have followed your work and have seen some of your portraits that I like and others that I dislike. I should like to give you my opinion that the portrait of this lady will one day be fought for by our galleries." An artist, it would seem, cannot choose his subject with any certainty of success. It is best to take the tasks that are set for us and depend upon the strength that is given us to fulfil it—the strength that God gives us to paint our pictures, as Seymour Lucas would say.

Sargent once said to me that he was giving up portrait painting because he always made an enemy of his sitters. He was at times rather cruel, such a realist, so dexterous a master with his brush, that he would register everything he saw before him at the moment, making no allowance for his sitter being tired, or for any other chance or mischance. In the days when I was a student at the Academy and Sargent was a Visitor, he would follow Seymour Lucas, who had impressed upon me the necessity of selectiveness, and who, with the model in front of the class, would demonstrate the importance of not bringing a dark edge against the outline of the head, but keeping the darkest towards the edge of the canvas to give scale and brilliancy. " Never ", he said, " have a dark shadow cutting hard against a light."

Sargent followed Lucas as a Visitor, and I was carefully observing the rule I had learned from Lucas, when Sargent looked at my painting and at the model and asked for my palette and brushes, and told me to look at the model. Just then, from where we stood, the dark fold of the curtain made a black shadow cutting out against the light of the face. By moving a foot or by moving the curtain it would have been as Seymour Lucas would have wished to paint it, but no, there it was, and by the gospel according to Sargent I was wrong. Sargent took a brush full of Vandyk brown and painted into my picture exactly what he saw. He was thinking, no doubt, that the student should paint what was in front of him without question, and not trouble about canons of art ; and I realized then that this great artist accepted nature exactly as it was before him, with no question of selectiveness, no thought of ideal moments.

This period of simple portraiture which I was now enjoying seemed child's play after the exhausting tasks of ceremonial pictures. One

canvas one subject ; no restraint of procedure or court etiquette ;
no getting into trouble through painting a profile or a back-view ;
only the joy of the individual before you, each portrait a discovery
of the scope and adventure of personality. It was all a great relief.
I painted Mr. Douglas of Quaker Oats fame, and at breakfast at his
Lake Forest home his wife enquired, " You don't know anything
about Quaker Oats in your country, do you ? " whereupon my wife
replied that her husband was brought up on Quaker Oats, which
much amused them. Then came Mr. Kellogg of Kellogg's Corn-
flakes, a strong, reserved, and austere man, always silent, in whose
presence you could remain quiet without being awkward or feeling
that you must entertain him. Very different was my next sitter,
Mr. Colin Crawford of iron and steel fame. We had no sooner
settled down to work than the romance of his life was unfolded before
me, interesting as a novel, illustrated with many strange pictures and
illuminated by extraordinary triumphs of integrity. I say integrity
because I mean it. I recall, for one thing, the story of his beginning
as a poor boy of nine in Ireland, doing odd jobs on a farm. Full
of a boy's spirit of daring and adventure, he conspired to steal his
aunt's savings which she had hidden in a stocking, to go to America,
but resisted the temptation and arrived eventually by a straight course
in New York. His career has been crowned with success, and is
a striking example of the triumph of right principles.

I have always thought that Mr. and Mrs. Siddley were two of my
most satisfactory portraits ; if the unity and bond of friendship means
anything they should be. Mr. Siddley was Chicago's Chief Attorney.
Mrs. Philip Swift and her sister Mrs. Dexter Cumings gave me a good
opportunity of getting something vivacious and charming. But one
of the most interesting Americans I have painted, is Mr. Joseph E.
Davies, the Ambassador to Russia. His fine head and impressive
personality made him an easy and pleasant subject. His book on his
Mission to Moscow reveals many truths that were then locked up in
the diplomatic compartment of his brilliant mind. I painted his
famous and beautiful wife, too. It is seldom that an artist has a sitter
who knows to perfection the gowns and jewels that suit her best,
or where in the house the portrait should be hung, and who with
tactful grace can pose without cramping the artist's work, but such
was Mrs. Davies. Her portrait made a decorative picture, with a
dress of ivory satin and a rich red velvet cloak. She had a remarkable
silver strand in her hair which was also inherited by her charming
little daughter Nedena, who, while I was painting her, had two

detectives guarding her night and day, as it was during the unhappy period of the kidnapping of the Lindbergh baby.

It was delightful to see so many great houses in American cities. They have the richness of museums with the atmosphere and comfort of a friendly home. Especially was this so in Chicago, where I have spent three months on each of my American visits. My first Chicago portrait was Mrs. Moses John Wentworth, whose house on Lake Shore Drive I can never forget for its collection of Old Masters. Soon afterwards came a commission to paint little Sarah King, the golden-haired grand-daughter of Mr. and Mrs. Thomas W. Hinde. This began an ideal friendship with them and their family circle in Lake Forest, the centre of ideal and beautiful homes where I found myself at home at once, for on the walls I continually came across fine portraits by such British artists as Oswald Birley, Harris Brown, Harrington Mann, and Sir William Orpen. The portrait of Mr. Philip Swift is one of the finest Birley has ever painted.

Here it was that Mr. Edward Ryerson, who had been impressed by the portrait of my grandfather, asked me to paint his family. Mr. Ryerson was a distinguished patron of the arts and I greatly enjoyed my work for him.

Mr. Cyrus McCormick made an interesting subject. He had more or less retired from the business of the Great Harvester Company, and had developed a peculiar physiological weakness, for as he was talking or writing he would suddenly fall asleep, fading away in the middle of a sentence. He was fully aware of this, and warned me, but all went well. After the portrait was finished, and as he was saying good-bye, he turned to my wife and said, " When your husband gets his coat-of-arms he must have a palette with brushes rampant and the motto, Every portrait a friend."

On one of my visits to Chicago I broke the journey at Cincinnati to paint a portrait of Mr. Ethan Beresford Stanley, and another of Mrs. Stanley with their little grandson Dicky. Whenever Dicky was sitting for me alone a watchful eye was kept on him every moment, with constant visits and interruptions. The nurse would come in with a comb and pass it through his glorious golden head of curls, and after one of these visits Dicky sat with his little head on his hands and said, " I cannot stand these hold-ups."

I had the pleasant opportunity of painting Mrs. Ward Seabury, a beautiful subject, and Mr. Seabury, both pictures a link with the Motherland, for that splendid family are direct descendants of Samuel Seabury the first American bishop, who crossed the Atlantic to be consecrated at Aberdeen. I painted a memorial portrait of the bishop from a woodcut which revealed the nobility and grandeur of his features, and the portrait now hangs in the Seminary of the North-Western University.

One of my Chicago sitters so astonished me by his intimate knowledge of the political and business situation in Europe, and of London in particular that I took it for granted that he was often in England. To my surprise, however, he said he had never crossed the Atlantic, and I asked how it was that he understood the situation so perfectly. He replied that he did business with London, and read every week the *Times Weekly* and the *Manchester Guardian*.

Mr. Edson White, President of the Armour Company, the great packers, told us that he had so often been urged by his wife to have his portrait painted that he would like to have it done as a surprise for her at Christmas. The portrait was nearly finished and was hidden away in my cupboard, when Mrs. White came and asked me to paint her as a Christmas surprise for her husband ! During the sittings she would tell me what a handsome man her husband was, adding, however, that he was very obstinate and could never be prevailed upon to sit to an artist. It took my wife all her time to keep the secret, for it happened that one day Mr. White called while Mrs. White was in the studio (the very next room). Happily, all went well, and when each received the other's portrait on Christmas Day the friendly deception was well justified by the pleasure it gave to both.

Chicago is a city of opportunity and enchantment, daily qualifying to become one of the greatest cities in the world—more than ever so, it is expected, in the days when we all travel by air, for the situation of Chicago in global geography is truly wonderful. I once had the opportunity of telling a director of the *Chicago Tribune* what many Englishmen have felt, that the headlines in their daily papers greatly misrepresented the city to the world. I had been there, I said, for three months each year for some years and seen nothing of gangster activities, except that a friend of one of my sitters, going home from the opera, was driven to the kerb by a red police car and commanded to stop, and a man in police uniform, with a revolver, demanded her jewels. All he got were imitation ones. The police car had been stolen. I also heard that when the English players were touring Chicago they each had telephone calls asking them to subscribe 100 dollars to some charity, and it was said that an official was calling round in the morning to collect it, which so scared the players that so..1e of them returned to New York by the next train.   Apart from these things I found Chicago a city of happy home circles, of most interesting society, and of churches and institutes like those of London or any other great city.

The last time I was there was on Armistice Sunday and I strolled into a church by Michigan Avenue and was thrilled to see the Stars and Stripes and the Union Jack being carried in procession to the altar while the organ played both national anthems, which were lustily sung by the congregation.   It was soon after the crisis on the eve of the war, when Mr. Chamberlain returned from Munich triumphant as a peacemaker, with Hitler's signed pledge of friendship, a compact never to go to war with us !

History will have to pronounce on the Government's action in those days.   I remember that my friend and neighbour Lord Inverforth, who was sitting for a presentation portrait which was destined for the Royal Glasgow Institute of the Fine Arts, in discussing the situation felt that when history is written Mr. Chamberlain would be remembered as among our greatest Prime Ministers.   But public opinion in America had been critical and antagonistic, and it was good to see that when I arrived it had changed more favourably ; in fact, at the Chicago Club a number of leading men were discussing the situation and declared that Mr. Chamberlain could not have done better or acted otherwise.   The oustanding remark of that discussion made a great impression on my mind—that England " always has the right man at the right time to lead her ".

Mr. Eden, who had resigned from the Government, was in New York and stayed at our hotel.   I attended the banquet at the Waldorf when he spoke to four thousand representatives of the Chamber of Commerce.   Notable men of all the vital industries had assembled from all over the States ; never have I seen a more representative gathering.   Everyone was expecting our late Foreign Secretary to make some startling disclosures and to criticize Mr. Chamberlain, but Mr. Eden was an English statesman first ; he did not make his visit a political platform.   He made a fine speech and had a wonderful reception.   His outstanding words were of prophetic significance, for before very long, he said, " Britain would have to fight, whether she liked it or not, the serious menace to the peace of the world, and we should fight alone in a terrible conflict ".

Dining one evening with Mr. William Dewart, a leader of New York opinion through his popular *Evening Sun*, I referred to the tremendous reception Mr. Eden had received, and asked if it was because he represented the element opposed to Mr. Chamberlain's policy. Mr. Dewart said, "No, certainly not; it was because he was an Englishman, and if he had been a blacksmith his reception would have been the same."

At times it seemed to me a little overwhelming to be painting portraits in a house hung with renowned masters. When I was painting Mrs. Herbert Satterley, Mr. Pierpont Morgan's sister, I was conscious that it was to hang on the walls which were ennobled by such immortal works as Gainsborough's "Duchess of Devonshire", and as I looked on this portrait I could not help recalling the story I had heard of it at a City dinner in London. One day it was in the news that Mr. Agnew had bought the Gainsborough for over ten thousand guineas, a world's record price, at Christie's. A friend told Agnew that he knew the history of the picture, and related this story, new to me and without any authority as far as I know, though the dates of the two duchesses seem to fit. The duke had commissioned Gainsborough to paint the portrait of his first duchess, and while it was in the artist's studio the duchess died and the duke married his mistress. Then the duke asked the artist to paint in the face of his new duchess, which Gainsborough would not do, with the result that the portrait was left on his hands. After the artist's death the duke bought it from Gainsborough's widow and got another artist to change the face to the likeness of the new duchess. Mr. Agnew was a little disconcerted to hear such a story, and when Mr. Barclay (who had related the story) told his wife of the conversation, he remarked "That picture will disappear." Soon after came its dramatic disappearance. It was missing for many years, but eventually turned up as the sensation of the whole art world, and was bought by Mr. Morgan.

CHAPTER XII

PRESIDENT COOLIDGE

I HAVE had the good fortune to paint three American Presidents, beginning with President Coolidge. It was my first visit to Washington, a romantic experience. I had come by the night train from New York on Christmas Eve and the crisp dawn lent enchantment to the beautiful city dominated by a dome which sets an Englishman thinking of St. Paul's. I was braced with expectancy and enthusiasm for the adventure of this visit to the White House.

The President's car came to meet me and I was taken to the suite of rooms for visitors, where, after breakfast, the secretary came to say that the President would be ready to receive me at ten o'clock. He asked if I had brought two canvasses and I said I always carried an extra one. It was customary, he told me, for the artist who painted the President to paint his wife also.

The usher came at the appointed time and took me down to the President. He was very kind, offering me a cigar. On my explaining that I did not smoke he said, " Well, there is very little in these days that we can offer you," for it was during Prohibition. There was a dish of fruit on the table from which he took an apple and pared it, cutting it in two, and offering me the top half. He took me round the White House, showing me the pictures. On the first landing were two bust portraits, one of Mrs. Coolidge and one of the President, which had just been painted. They were rather caricatures, and the President explained that the artist had insisted on his saying with a snarl every few minutes, " Tiger ! Tiger ! " It seemed to me a wild idea, and surely the last thing in the world to express the character of Calvin Coolidge, the silent man. He introduced me to Mrs. Coolidge, whose charming personality and gracious smile had won all hearts. After this I was driven round Washington to see the city.

I was tremendously impressed with the Lincoln Memorial, very beautiful and wonderful, and surely among the most impressive monuments ever erected in memory of a great man. England has set up this heroic man at Westminster, with his eyes fixed on the Abbey and with our own heroic Cromwell across the road ; America has set him in a noble shrine in line with the Capitol and the Washington Column, and it may be doubted if anywhere in the world is a monument that can compare with this for majesty and simplicity. Simply he stands in both the centres of the English-Speaking race, but, while in London the people throng past him, here he sits enthroned in lonely splendour in a stately hall of Ionic columns. It has often occurred to me in passing his statue at Westminster that the chair behind him is the only empty chair on the route of our great processions to the Abbey, and that surely it would be a lovely thing, and a pretty gesture of friendship, to offer it to the American Ambassador on our procession days, for the use of any countryman whom he would like to honour. Here in Washington is no such opportunity, for in this majestic hall a solemn silence reigns which only sacrilege would break. It stands in its glory like an ancient temple on the banks of the Potomac, approached by broad flights of steps, and with its noble columns reflected in the water, a shrine fit for the Acropolis of Athens, for a heroic figure worthy of the Parthenon.

Washington is, of course, marvellously designed and laid out ; I was told that the architect was sent to prison for squandering public money. Its streets run in Roman fashion to the points of the compass, some known by numbers and some by letters of the alphabet, and avenues are named after states. The Capitol, all white, is 750 feet long and nearly half as wide, and a statue of Liberty crowns the great dome. It was begun in 1793 and completed with wings and dome in 1865. The White House was begun about the same time, but greatly extended at the beginning of our own century.

The City's chief monument, of course, is the great Washington Column, which puts our Nelson Column in the shade, for it would need three Nelson Columns to match the height of the obelisk on the banks of the Potomac. The column is set on a white marble base and rises 555 feet high and it is said that the site was chosen by George Washington himself. But the obelisk was not begun until 1848 and was for years abandoned, being finished in 1884, and having cost a quarter of a million pounds—a high price, surely, for a plain stone column, shaped rather like Cleopatra's Needle. The Lincoln Memorial has been designed so as to give one of the best glimpses of the Washington Memorial through its mighty columns.

I returned to the White House for lunch round a big circular table, and sat by Mrs. Coolidge. The President scarcely spoke to anyone at the table, but took great interest in his white collie dog, directing most of his conversation and attention to it.

At three o'clock I was summoned to be ready to leave for Sapelo Island, the country home of Mr. and Mrs. Howard Coffin. The

President and Mrs. Coolidge took the first car, with four detectives on the running-board and several police on motor-cycles. I came next with Colonel Starling, the secretaries and officers following. At the Grand Station a special train was waiting, and on it were sixteen reporters and kinema men. I had an apartment to myself, and settled down to a quiet read. In the evening the President sent for me to sit with him in his parlour, and we had an interesting talk before going to bed.

The train went through Savannah on to Georgia, where we were met by Mr. and Mrs. Howard Coffin, whose yacht we boarded for Sapelo Island. We had left Washington in snow ; here we were in the beautiful semi-tropical climate of South Carolina. A lovely morning it truly was, and I very much enjoyed the cruise among the islands of the coast of Southern Georgia. The photographers were all busy when we embarked, taking every movement of the President, who was quite used to it, giving them every opportunity, facing each camera in turn.

Only a few minutes after our arrival at the beautiful villa the President said he was ready for me. I found him a splendid sitter. It was quite unnecessary for me to talk, as it was natural for him to be silent and quiet. The work proceeded well and rapidly, and on the third day I started on the portrait of Mrs. Coolidge. During her sittings the President would occasionally stroll in without saying a word to either of us and go out in the same way. When the portrait was developing he looked at it quietly and then at his wife, and said, " It is like—it is actually like you, dear ! " We both laughed at this, for he seemed truly surprised that a portrait should ever be like anyone.

Everyone took a great interest in the painting, and all were enthusiastic. I worked constantly, and had very little time to see the island, except after dinner. It was remarkable to go out into the woods at nine o'clock at night without a hat or coat on, remembering that it was Christmas. The huge oak trees with festoons of moss, and the blue sea in the distance, were very beautiful, and I chose this scene as a background for Mrs. Coolidge's portrait, as it fitted the colour scheme admirably.

I painted Mr. Coolidge in a light suit. We tried a robe and a black suit, but he looked like a parson. I remarked that he looked distinguished in the light suit, and he said in measured tones, " This is a very distinguished suit." He had a great sense of dry humour.

I was never able to fathom his silence, whether his mind was actively solving some abstruse problem or whether it was a mere blank.

There were five of us who sat down to meals every day, but he seldom joined in the conversation. Only once during the whole visit do I remember him talking at the table, when we were discussing a very important subject relating to the political situation, and he astonished us by joining in with a very terse sentence which summed up the situation. Beyond that we had our jokes and conversations, but he might have been deaf or absent during meal-times. After dinner he would sit in the drawing-room for coffee, and on one or two occasions entered into lengthy talks with Mr. Howard Coffin concerning conditions in the motor industry. Then he would get up quietly and go to the ballroom, where a kinema was being arranged for him, and later we would all go and sit in a row in front of the screen, just five chairs, the President sitting silently through the film. When the film was over he would get up and go to his own rooms which were next door. As I was near the door I would open it and say good night, but the silent man passed out silently.

The house was surrounded with sentinels, and wherever the President went a bevy of detectives went with him ; they followed him like Mary's lamb all over the island. What surprised me was that they were all dressed in soft hats and shabby mackintoshes, which gave no dignity to the Presidential party. The officers and the secretaries, however, were all smartly dressed. Mrs. Coolidge, whenever she went for a walk on the island, also had a detective with her. I could not think who this man was just ahead of us or just behind us, until she explained that she could not even go to the draper's to buy a reel of cotton without a detective.

On Sunday we went to the yacht early after breakfast, and sailed to Augusta. It was arranged that the President and his party should attend service in the church where Charles Wesley was rector on his first visit to America. The service was carried on exactly as in Wesley's time, and was a most interesting experience for me. We sang some of the fine old Wesley hymns that have echoed through our churches at home for generations.

We lunched at St. Simon's Isle, and in the afternoon explored the old Spanish monasteries, now in ruin. In the evening a fire was lit in the grounds and the Negro students from the college of Savannah gathered in the firelight and sang their marvellous spirituals. I shall never forget the impressive and moving beauty of it all. For supper oysters were roasted by the fire, and wild turkeys that had been shot were hanging up in the trees. One of the old keepers imitated the turkey call, which they practise when they are out shooting these birds. They have to be very careful, he explained, because if they make the call too persistent the cock bird will take no notice ; they must be shy and diffident—a human lesson, he said to me.

One morning we got up at half-past three and went into the deep forests to shoot wild turkeys. We rode about seven miles by car and then walked through the thicket until we divided into three parties, keeping very quiet until dawn broke. It was a delightful experience for me to attend the Awakening of Nature. The first to greet the morning was the croaking frog, and then the dove, and one by one the whole aviary of the forest joined in the chorus.

Our keeper gave the turkey call, supposed to be the call of the hen bird, but we had only one response and waited without any success. On our way back I had a talk with the keeper, a very old Negro born on the island and living on it all his life, and I was able to get an idea from him of the conditions before the suppression of the slave trade. He said conditions for them on the island had been much worse since slavery was abolished. I asked if this was a primeval forest, and he astonished me by saying, " Oh, no, sixty years ago this was one of the most wonderful cotton and tobacco plantations in America." I was surprised to see how Nature could go back to the wilderness in two generations ; it showed me what a tremendous amount of work the early settlers must have had to do in clearing the ground for their plantations.

On our rejoining the others it appeared that no one in the party had fired a shot except the President, who, it was said, had got three turkeys. We returned home and the secretary came in to tell the President that the New York papers had been ringing up saying they must have photographs of the President shooting. Would he go out and be photographed with the turkeys he had shot ? Although he was sitting for me, he left at once, changed into shooting rig, and was photographed, and in about three-quarters of an hour came back, seeming unusually quiet and very cross. When the secretary came in soon after he said, " Of course I am not going through the whole thing again," but the secretary explained that they had the Movietone, and that the gun had failed to synchronize, or something of the sort. I was astonished and greatly amused at the trouble the President took to satisfy the clamour of the Press. It is inconceivable that anything of the sort could happen in our own country.

At the end of the week the President was anxious that I should stay and paint the portraits of our host and hostess (Mr. and Mrs. Howard Coffin), and this I did, having very much enjoyed my stay with these delightful people on this romantic island. The visit ended pleasantly with this letter from the White House :

My dear Mr. Salisbury,

The portraits of Mrs. Coolidge and myself have come and we are much pleased with them. You have all the permission I can give to exhibit them anywhere. Please accept my thanks for all your service and care.

Yours,

Calvin Coolidge.

The Broadcasting Company of America asked me at this time to broadcast a talk on ceremonial painting, and I appealed to the American people to give their artists a fair chance. Why not let their judges wear gowns and wigs, robe the President, and precede him with a mace of office and uniformed supporters ? The next morning some of the papers displayed on the front page a reproduction of the King and Queen's coronation photograph with the heads of President and Mrs. Coolidge inserted in such an impish way that the crown was slightly rakish, and the headlines were : " Artist Crowns King Cal and his Queen ".

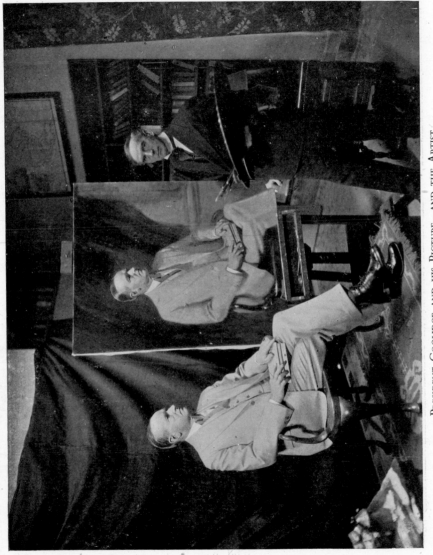

President Coolidge and his Picture—and the Artist.

JOHN WESLEY.

CHAPTER XIII

JOHN WESLEY

WE have lived to see William Blake's "Jerusalem" win its way to rank almost with the National Anthem, but could anything be more utterly unlike his green and pleasant land than the place where he lies in Bunhill Fields, the Campo Santo of the Nonconformists, as I think Dean Inge has called it. Certainly it is a sacred place, for here we may stand and almost touch without moving the graves of William Blake, Daniel Defoe, Isaac Watts, and John Bunyan, while a stone's throw away are the home and pulpit and grave of John Wesley. The sacred Bunhill Fields should surely be made into a worthy place of pilgrimage, with all its squalor swept away. What a glorious opportunity when we are rebuilding London.

While I was showing this place to Dr. Harris Kirk of Baltimore, during the Blake Centenary celebrations, the minister of Wesley's Chapel, John MacNeal, came across and asked us if we had ever seen Wesley's house. As we had not he showed us over this historic place. I was very disappointed at the state of it, Victorian linoleum in the hall, horse-hair furniture in the front room, photographs of the Presidents of the Conference on the walls, and not one good portrait of John Wesley. I said the place was a disgrace to Methodism, and promised Mr. MacNeal that if he would restore the house to what it was in Wesley's time I would paint a portrait of Wesley to hang on the wall. He was enthusiastic and replied that it should be done. We fixed the whole thing up. Mr. Taverner, my builder, carried out the work and wrought a wonderful restoration.

But now I had let myself in for a formidable task. I had painted posthumous portraits from snapshots of soldiers, and sometimes finding a relative with a strong family likeness had helped ; but I had nothing to help me with John Wesley, although I had been brought up in the Wesley tradition. Sir William Richmond had, however, told me of a new life of Wesley, which I read with great pleasure, and I saturated myself in the literature of this great man's life. It would seem that anybody could write a book on Wesley and find a sale for it, so great is the exalted position he holds in the temple of fame. What an amazing life ! There appear to have been two

Wesleys, the scholar and the missionary, sacrificing everything, giving his goods to feed the poor, going to America to preach. Returning home at thirty-five, feeling that he was a failure and could never preach again, he must have felt the truth of the immortal passage of St. Paul in Corinthians, " Though I speak with the tongues of men and of angels ", that mysterious something which seems to link up the eternal purposes of God. After a prayer-meeting with the Moravians in the iron foundry in City Road a transformation came over him such as befell Paul on the road to Damascus, and the result was that in a few weeks five thousand people waited at five in the morning to hear him, and fifty thousand on Blackheath. The live coal from the altar of God had touched his lips, and, behold, the Prophet of God ! I remember reading in Arthur Mee's book on Kent that Wesley would preach at five in the morning in a village churchyard while William Blake was fast asleep next door.

How was I to paint so wonderful a character as this ? The museum authorities and the Methodist Bookroom helped me all they could, trusting me with precious relics, his preaching robe, his preaching-bands, and his study chair, which was an old cock-baiting chair ; he used the back as a desk and sat straddle-like as on a horse. The number of Wesley pottery mugs, vases, and ornaments, outnumbered even the Queen Victoria collection of such things.

The original model of one of the china busts by Enoch Wood, which they have at the museum, struck me as being an exact piece of modelling ; it is referred to in Wesley's Journal as being the best portrait ; perhaps because his secretary begged him not to read while sitting for it, but to give the artist a chance ! Although the size of the head was only three inches, the bust was a tremendous help to me. I got my friend Horace Sequeira, the well-known actor, to sit, wearing a wig like the wig of this bust, and made a number of studies in black and white. Then a piece of great good fortune came my way. One day at the Methodist Bookroom, studying the collection of relics there, I saw in a glass case a parcel marked " Wesley's Surplice ", and exclaimed with delight that this was just what I wanted.

Dr. Barton, who was showing me round, looked surprised, raised his eyebrows questioningly, and said, " I fear it is not John Wesley's : we have had it a long time and I am six feet, and when I put it on it hangs a foot on the ground." This was very disappointing, but the doctor said that if I wished he would put it on, unless it fell to pieces. He did put it on, and, sure enough, it dragged a foot on the ground ! Much bewildered, I studied it carefully, and discovered a button on the collar which suggested that it was not put on properly. I found that if it were wrapped round the body and buttoned up at the back, behold, it was then one foot off the ground ! The Rev. F. Barton was so surprised and delighted that he gave me permission to borrow it, for I had proved to his satisfaction that it was Wesley's surplice. It was a full double one, which he needed for warmth as he preached so much out of doors. It may have gone round England with him, the robe in which he preached to the people on the village greens.

Another episode occurred while I was searching for data in the Victoria and Albert Museum. My wife stopped me and said, " You have just passed a bust of John Wesley," and there was a marvellous bust with an excellent profile. I asked the director if I could have a cast of it and he said it would take three weeks to make one. As I wanted it at once he replied that he would see what could be done, and the next morning I received a letter from the Museum saying that they had decided to let me have the bust, and would have it cleaned and sent up to me at once.

So, having collected my material and visualized my subject, it only remained for me to materialize it ; but I needed a living personality who bore a likeness to Wesley and was of Wesley's age, about 75. It came suddenly to me that there was only one man who would do, and that was Charles Voysey, the famous architect, so, going down to the Arts Club where I knew I should find him, I told him my idea. He looked at me in astonishment and said that nothing would give him greater pleasure, for he was a descendant of John Wesley. This was a great surprise to me.

He came to the studio, put on the wig, the robes, and the preaching-band, and might have been Wesley himself. I said I felt that all he lacked was the fullness of the lower lip of an orator, and begged him to push his lower lip forward, which he did, thoroughly enjoying doing it. After the first sitting in daylight from my model, I went on with the painting by artificial light well into midnight and went to bed very happy feeling that I had got John Wesley. I painted also a portrait in profile and called it " The Ecclesiastical Statesman ".

The portrait was completed in time for the Union of the Methodist and Wesleyan Churches, and the great meeting at the Albert Hall at which the deed of union was signed. King George and Queen Mary were there, and the inspiring message of the King to the Methodist Church said, " In this act I see a prophetic significance foreshadowing the unity of all the Christian Churches." The painting was exhibited at the Academy. At the completion of the restoration of Wesley House my wife opened the door with a golden key and the portrait was unveiled by Dr. Parkes Cadman, as President of the Churches in Christ throughout America and the world.

It was this portrait which gave Dr. Cadman an idea that I should collaborate with him in his book of the Prophets of Israel, asking if I would paint these great characters. As I had painted our modern prophet, why should I not try to portray the historic figures of the Bible ? It is wonderful to think of the revelation that opens up when we read with intensity the words of these inspired men. I could not help taking myself to task for allowing so much of my life to slip away without coming more intimately in touch with the Prophets. What a loss ! A great scholar who came into my studio looked at the paintings and spoke of Isaiah and Jeremiah and Elijah with an intimacy as of personal friends.

I have painted three windows for Wesley's Chapel since then. The Methodist Freemasons throughout the Empire, wishing to have a memorial in the heart of the Empire, decided that Wesley's Chapel was the right place and asked me to paint a window for them, their subject being " Sacrifice—Greater love hath no man ". I painted Christ supporting a wounded soldier, and soon after its completion an Australian freemason, Mr. Cato, commissioned another window to commemorate the sending of the first missionary to Australia, the idea of this being Spiritual Power.

A memorial to the founder of the Wesley Guild was the third of these windows, and as Sir Galahad is the Guild's patron saint this heroic figure made a fine theme ; I showed him fighting the seven deadly sins with his uplifted sword, the sword of the Spirit. The light radiated from the sword, and I was wanting some words to express the secret power when the telephone bell rang and Dr. Douglas Adam spoke, his first words being : " I took for my subject last Sunday *the immediate availability of the divine resources.*" I begged him to repeat these words, and said, " They are just what I want at this moment ; I will put them in letters of gold into my picture."

Self-portrait of the Artist making Studies for the Coronation Picture in
Westminster Abbey, 1937.

Mrs. Frank O. Salisbury.

CHAPTER XIV

SARUM CHASE

THE mystery of open and closed doors is a problem for the imagination of a philosopher. Somebody has said, talking of the disappointments of life, that whenever a door had been closed against him he had had good reason afterwards to be thankful for it. The slamming of the door of 62 Avenue Road in our faces seemed to us a catastrophe.

The great change threatening came in the winter of 1931 while we were in America, letters from home bringing reports of the cutting down of trees and the building of a house sixty feet high which had a ruinous effect on the garden and the studio. I cabled to the ground landlords asking them to protect my interests, and they replied that the new building was a great acquisition to my property. The housekeeper in charge, however, who had been with us twenty-five years and could be trusted, wrote that it was ruinous, and assuring us that she had found a site on Hampstead Heath where a house could be built. My reaction to this, however, was that it was out of the question. Her reports proved not to be exaggerated, and the hopelessness of the situation on our return home was depressing beyond measure.

For ordinary purposes such a thing would not have greatly mattered, but for an artist light is vital, and as the new building was a south wall the result was that when the sun shone the reflections of the great red house turned the light of my studio red, so that all my sitters were blushing! It was terribly disheartening. I was advised that it was an obvious case for damages, in view of the fact that my ideal studio was utterly ruined, but my solicitors thought it would involve litigation ending in the House of Lords, and there was nothing to be done but to look round for a new home. Luckily, the site Susan had found for us, though hilly and very difficult, was ideal for situation if it could be managed.

Telegraph Hill rises from the junction of Platt's Lane and West Heath Road to one of the highest points in Hampstead overlooking London, with a wonderful view across country to the Chilterns. It was the place where the beacon was lit to carry the tidings of the Spanish Armada. What a place for a garden! What a situation for a house ! The land was as bare as the heath itself except for a group of giant oaks in front, and it was the glory of these trees which ultimately decided the matter. I took an option on the site for a month.

This was the last primeval site on Hampstead Heath, the very summit of London, and I resolved to have a house worthy of the situation. I rang up Sir Giles Scott asking him if he would build the house, but he could not undertake another commission owing to his responsibility for Liverpool Cathedral and the Cambridge Library. It happened that Vyvyan, the son of my brother Eustace, the architect whose passing was such a bitter grief to me, was following in his father's steps, and he designed for me such an impressive erection that I decided that he should be the architect. He very soon set up a scale-model of the land with the correct gradient and elevations, from which we found that the main level of the house must be twenty feet above the road, which created no small problem in getting to the front door.

Having worked out the possibilities, I bought the land and it turned out that the owners were also builders and would sell only if they could build the house. This seemed a snag, but they studied my interests as if they were paying the bills themselves, and made a wonderful job of the work.

Many of my friends urged me not to build on such a costly site, but Uncle James Price, the only link with the older generation of the family, came to see it, and to my delight declared that it was the finest site in London and that I was not to spare either art or money in making the house worthy of its dramatic situation.

This wonderful little hill at the very top of London was a wilderness of stinging nettles and wild plants, and it was thrilling to look forward to what might be made of it. As we surveyed the landscape in the solemn stillness of the sunset my wife suggested that we should dedicate this lovely place to the creation of beauty and the service of the highest. We have done our best together.

My wife cut the first sod and the clearing of the site began on the 4th of September, 1932. I gave instructions that the work was to be carried out in American style, and every morning at nine o'clock I was there to watch progress. I resolved that all materials should be on the spot at least a week before they were needed. We searched England for a beautiful two-inch facing brick, and I shall never forget the story of how we found it at a kiln in Sussex which was closing down for want of orders. I arrived there and found the owner of the kiln ill in bed, greatly disturbed about the future of his business. I asked his wife if he could make me some bricks, and the answer came that he could, if he had a good order in time to make them before the frost came. How many did I want? I said a hundred thousand, and I think the good news brought the brickmaker leaping out of bed and gave a new lease of life to him and to his business. So the bricks came to the last building site on Hampstead Heath, and I remember that when Sarum Chase was finished the architect of the fifty-storey Woolworth Building in New York, Mr. Cass Gilbert, was so delighted with the colour and quality of my bricks that he ordered some to be shipped to America.

The work went on splendidly during the winter months. The weather favoured us, and the first three months of the year were so dry that, although the roof was not on until the end of March, by the end of June the frescoes were fixed on the walls and have never since shown any signs of damp.

All through the progress of the house I took a series of moving pictures, so that we have a complete record of its growth, even to the robins nesting in the rooms. During the week-end, and even while the men were working seven robins built their nests on the site, and one successfully raised its brood and actually held up work in the studio for three weeks. Rarely have I seen such an example of devotion in the animal world. All the time the windows were being put in, and the planing-machines and the carpenters were making a terrible noise, the mother remained with her young. She flew in and out of an open window to feed them, and one morning the foreman told me that she had very proudly escorted the young robins on their first flight. That was the first picture in my studio, the living picture of the flight of seven little robins.

The skylark soared overhead, the hawk haunted the neighbourhood, and the heron came to steal the goldfish already in the pools. So much had we of the country within a twelve-minute car ride of Trafalgar Square.

My experience of studios gave me the opportunity of a lifetime in getting the lighting as perfect as possible. Lighting is half the artist's battle, for no picture can be properly painted unless it is right. A concentrated effect of light makes painting easy, yet many artists handicap themselves by giving no consideration to this vital problem.

It was not until I began working at Sarum Chase that I realized what I had lost in lighting values at Avenue Road. The heavy shadows of the gallery and the dark panelling there were too insistent.

How necessary it was, after all, for me to be turned out ! The closed door which seemed a disaster had once more been a blessing. True indeed it is that half our troubles never arrive.

We moved in on July 4, 1933, and on the 27th and 28th held our first reception. The walls of the hall afforded fine spaces for frescoes, and, an American friend suggesting the idea, I decided to fill these spaces with a series of frescoes of the Saga of Life, an impression of life's experiences. The walls facing the front door comprise three motives, " The Divine Overture ", " The Human Awakening ", and " The Historic Struggle ", and on the main walls of the staircase are two other scenes, " The Supreme Challenge " and " The Eternal Victory ".

In " The Divine Overture " a balance design of entwining and climbing roses makes, as it were, a grille through which we peer into the inscrutable mystery of the origin of human life. Dimly seen are the fleet-winged cherubim bringing in protecting arms the embryo of humanity to the kneeling mother, the background seeming to enshrine the group with a glow of divinity. Above are Carlyle's words, " Heaven and earth are but the time vestures of the Eternal, and the universe a vast symbol of God ".

" The Human Awakening " shows youth, grown to manhood, crossing the threshold of Home, a Gothic doorway forming the background. With radiant expression Youth puts his foot on the step of high endeavour, clad in armour and holding aloft the Sword of the Spirit, with a double edge affirming good and denying the reality of evil. The Angel of Duty points to the path of the steep ascent, holding in her hands a helmet symbolical of God's watching spirit, the all-powerful protection against evil, signifying that Providence never sets us a task without strengthening us to carry it out. On the scroll round the nimbus of the Angel are the words, " The immediate availability of the Divine resources ".

" The Historic Struggle " shows life's conflict, with its disappointments and sorrows, a figure bowed and almost overcome in the shadows of death, a skeleton holding the hourglass of time and the scythe of death. The problem of suffering, being a profound mystery, is also seen through a grille of entwined roses, with the mystic vesica behind suggesting the underlying thought that sorrow has its purpose and that death is not an ugly thing to be feared but a step onward in the Universe. At the top of this scene are the words of Isaiah in letters of gold, " The crooked shall be made straight and the rough places plain ".

Mounting the staircase on the south wall is the next subject in the scale of progress, " The Supreme Challenge ", a young man standing with his foot on the head of the dragon, holding with a firm grip the lance ready for combat to conquer or die. In the background are the arms of Britain, representing King and Country ; Church and State are represented by schools and colleges ; and a curved line running through the design suggests the golden circle of accomplishments, representing music, art, and science, engineering, agriculture, and navigation—our heritage. " What are we going to do with it ? " is the supreme challenge for every one.

" The Eternal Victory ", the final subject in Life's Saga, on the west wall, shows Youth exhausted and almost prostrate at the summit of the hill, his sword broken, his strength failing. Lions and wolves strive to tear the mantle off his back, and it hangs tattered and torn from his shoulders. The evil forces he has conquered pass defeated into the dark abyss at his feet, and in his extremity he looks up, stretches out his hands to Heaven, and, lo, the heavens open, and out of the gold comes the triumphant chariot with the mighty steeds and the angel of power reaching down, grasping the hand of the young crusader. It is William Blake's aspiration come true, " Bring me my chariot of fire ", the consummation of human and divine co-operation, Eternal Victory.

In the background of these last two frescoes is a rising shape holding the composition together from the base to the top, a mystic radiation of stars and rays of golden light, suggestive of a carrier-wave of the spirit linking man with his Maker. Two heraldic panels representing Fortitude and Courage, Beauty and Strength, were painted by my daughters, who are very gifted, Sylvia in miniatures and Monica in water colour : they were anxious to have some share in the work. The colour of all the frescoes is restricted to a simple palette, and the harmonious range of tone adds greatly to the effectiveness of the scheme.

All through my life the words of Sir Joshua Reynolds have been before me as an inspiration. " Nothing is denied to well-directed labour ", said our great immortal, and as this thought has played a great part in my work I set the motto in the decorative design of my studio ceiling, balancing it with another which seems to grow out of it and to crown it, " God meets man on the pathway of his highest endeavour ". In the central scroll of the ceiling, surrounding a compass which is set and truly polarized, are the arms of my native village of Harpenden, the arms of the Glaziers Company of which

I was master, the arms of America because so many Americans have sat for me, and the royal arms in token of the royal sitters in the studio.

Outside the house an experiment I ventured to make with cement for modelling was a great success, and resulted in my making several such models for my work, as they stood up splendidly. Coloured with bronze, they are very effective and durable.

It was the need of two figures for the doorway that moved me to this experiment. Having failed to find satisfactory antique figures, I decided to model St. George and the Princess in cement, a thing which I believe had never been done before. Experts declared that the cement would never tone with the stone of the house, but I was content to risk that, and the figures proved just right. Now, after a few years, the tone and colouring are perfect ; a little treatment with animal and vegetable matter soon killed the harshness of the cement, which I had prepared in the warm tone of Weldon stone, and few experts would guess that these figures are anything but stone. It is of remarkable interest that they have come unscathed through the Battle of London, standing the shock of high explosive bombs which would have cracked and crumbled stone.

A garden is as important as a house, and few sites ever gave such scope as Sarum Chase. Vast quantities of earth were removed to make the terraces, which are formed in a crescent radiating from the drawing-room doors, the centre of the building. The sloping lawns, the rising steps, the sculptured group by the French sculptor Corrat, gave scope to an interesting design, and the making of the garden developed simultaneously with the building of the house.

The test of a garden is that it should look well in winter as in summer, and therefore we used yews, rhododendrons, laurels, box, heather, and hollies with much advantage. The borders under the terrace walls are facing north, and, as the sun rarely touches the earth except early and late in the day, nothing would flower there success-fully. In the third year I tried lilies. Wallace's, the lily experts in Kent, said that I could create a sensation with lilies, and for two years they were right. Starting with madonna, candidium, and crocium, the orange flowers, followed by the regali and then by the prince of all lilies, the auratum, we had a dazzling display of natural glory, yet, although the bulbs were carefully replaced each season, we could never repeat our first success. But what majestic flowers they are ! Not even Solomon was arrayed like one of these.

An expert lily grower walking round one day pointed out a most

SARUM CHASE.

SIBYL CHASE. THE DRAWING-ROOM

wonderful thing to me. In a broken stem a small bulb was being formed ; the dying plant, as if knowing it was doomed, was putting forth its last energies to carry on its life ! The Eternal Mind of the Universe works on unceasingly.

To shelter the stems and roots after the lilies have flowered is no small task in a formal garden. We finally succeeded with a variegated holly, which has a beautiful effect all the year round. A flower garden must have a constant supply of bedding plants, and plenty of glass and space. The light sandy soil and the sloping hillside heights caught all the winds that blow at Sarum Chase, and to counter this we had three-inch net stretched on iron standards to support the stems of the lilies as they grew into it. There was no tying-up or damaging the bulb roots by driving in canes or stakes, and the net, painted green or tarred, is also lost to sight.

To overcome the difficulty of irrigation I had a watering-system installed with sprays rotating in the shrubs and jets on the lawns, the water worked by an electric pump from the pool round the beautiful fountain Sir William Reynolds-Stephen designed for me. Touching a button will bring a shower of water all over the garden, and the plan has been a great success. Sir William was one of our great friends, and his death has been a sad loss to us, as it is to the nation. The Brains Trust may deride our sculpture, but his work will stand when all the words lightly spoken are forgotten in oblivion.

Two of our first visitors to Sarum Chase were Americans, the Bishop of Long Island and Mrs. Stires, who were greatly interested in what had been done on this great site I remarked that I was now anxious to do my best work, as such a studio was a challenge, and the bishop made this wise observation : " You must possess beauty before you can give it out. It is a mistake to be over-anxious to do good work ; over-anxiety might defeat the very desire. Christ said, Let your light shine, not struggle to make it shine, or to be over-anxious for it to shine ; just let it shine, like the sun, and all will be well."

It seemed to me a beautiful thought, and the words have remained in my mind. One other remark has remained with me, the words of a Cabinet Minister who said, " Well, this is a beautiful house ; enjoy it till you are taxed out of it."

CHAPTER XV

INDIA

THOUGH I have never been to India, I have done some interesting work for that great country. The architect and committee of the All-India Victoria Memorial in Calcutta, visiting my studio while I was at work on the National Thanksgiving panel, wished me to paint twelve lunette panels in the great hall of the memorial building, the selection of the subjects being left to me. I began with The Call to the Throne, the First Council, the Coronation in Westminster Abbey, the Prorogation of the Queen's first Parliament, and the First Visit to the City of London. For the panel facing the central entrance I painted a symbolical subject entitled "Empire", and then came the Queen's Wedding at the Chapel Royal, the Durbar Proclamation as Empress of India, a central panel called "The Apotheosis", the Jubilee Service in Westminster Abbey, the Diamond Jubilee Service at St. Paul's, and finally the Lying-in-State.

King George the Fifth approved the ideas and gave me the use of the royal pictures, and with the help of the officials at the British Museum and the Guildhall I was able to obtain all the historical facts. A series of subjects of this nature naturally caused many difficulties. In the Jubilee scene the group of royalties threatened to overwhelm the central figures of the Queen and Archbishop Benson, and King George advised me to leave them out, as I wanted to do. So I painted them all out and the composition was immensely improved. The King said to me that in his opinion all ceremonial subjects should be painted twenty years after the event, so that the artist could leave whoever he liked out without getting into trouble.

When the great canvases were rolled up for sending to India it was necessary to protect them from ants, for the architects informed me that out there these creatures will run a covered way of sand up a wall in a short time, attacking and soon destroying any fabric. Fixing the canvas to the wall with white lead ultimately overcame this trouble, and the scheme was completed ready for the Prince of Wales to dedicate when he opened the Memorial Hall in Calcutta.

This work brought me in touch with the India Office and with many distinguished Indians. One day Sir Rajendra Mookerjee brought with him to the studio three Indian princesses, so beautiful that I could not resist asking them to sit for me. With their black and gold and rich green saris they made an enchanting group, and rarely have I found a picture go so well and straightforwardly. The calm serenity of the Indian spirit is well seen in these three Sen Sisters ; it seemed to me as they sat there that out of their dark eyes flashed the light of the East. The picture created much interest at the Royal Academy, and later in America.

In New York, at an afternoon reception at Mr. Myron Taylor's house, somebody asked Mr. Taylor if he had visited the Royal Academy in London that year ? He replied that he had, saying he was not an artist but he thought he knew a good picture, and the one that impressed him most was a circular picture of three Indian princesses, the Sen Sisters. Thereupon Mrs. Hopkins said, " How singular ; here is the artist ! " Mr. Taylor laughed and said that it was lucky his remark had been complimentary. A lady joining in the conversation then said she had been to the Royal Academy that summer, too, and the picture she remembered was a painting from the seat of a car with the headlights on, called " The Enchanted Road " (painted for Lord Kenilworth), whereupon Mrs. Hopkins said, " Here is the artist of that also." Twice lucky was luck indeed. It was at that reception that we first met the Myron Taylors, who have ever since been sincere friends.

The following spring the picture of the Sen Sisters was included in the Duveen Exhibition in New York, and there it strongly appealed to a patron of the Arts who desired to present it to the Metropolitan Museum. This, however, was not disclosed to me before it had been shipped to Liverpool for the Walker Art Gallery. The authorities informed the patron that the picture would be acceptable, and that they would pay all expenses for it to be returned, so I cabled to Liverpool, who replied that they wished to purchase it for their permanent collection. I had to tell them it was too late and it was duly returned to New York. It had been at the Metropolitan Museum for six weeks when the generous donor who wished to give it reluctantly informed me that in the meantime a rule had been passed making it impossible for a living artist's work to be accepted.

This incident does not conclude the story, for Lord Duveen informed me that he wished to present the picture to the Tate Gallery. I was, of course, delighted, but his secretary rang me up one day to say that the committee had voted against its acceptance. My wife, who is my best critic, ranks it as one of my finest pictures, if not my best, and is anxious that the Metropolitan Museum should have it when I have conformed to the rules by dying. In the meantime the Three Sisters, having been so nearly hung in three great galleries, remain at Sarum Chase.

In the middle of India at Medak, in the Dominions of the Nizam of Hyderabad, is a noble Gothic cathedral which grew under the inspiration of Rev. Charles Posnett. The stonework was carved in England, transported, and built at Medak under the architectural supervision of John B. Gass. Several years ago I received a drawing of one of the most beautiful five-light tracery windows imaginable, heroic in size, each light over four feet wide and twenty-five feet to the top of the tracery. A letter with the drawing asked that I should design and paint glass for it, the suggested subject being the Ascension. The design worked splendidly, but when I came to work out the cost I was staggered, and I felt that no mission station could possibly afford it, though they had four thousand members. But I sent the drawing, in colour, and to my surprise received a cable that they would have the window at any cost. The Indian Christians all took a great interest in it, and the window was fully subscribed for before it was unveiled. It has fifteen thousand pieces of glass, one-fifth of them painted.

A few years ago I received another request from Mr. Posnett to complete a companion window for Medak, this time in honour of Woman, as the women of the church sat facing this window. So I painted the Nativity, the Shepherds and the Wise Men, with the Father Everlasting encircled in the rainbow splendour of the Throne, and a circle of angels proclaiming " His name shall be called Wonderful ".

Surely no vehicle of human expression (unless it is the sublime music of Handel and the great Masters) can express or suggest splendour as richly painted glass can do, with its glorious range of colour. Nature seems in the changing light to claim it for itself, and to give it supernatural enchantment.

This window was completed and fixed up in the studio on September 2, 1939, and on the next day, Sunday, the B.B.C. early announced that at eleven o'clock the Prime Minister had an important statement to make, and would speak to the whole country and Empire. We knew that a serious crisis had arisen.

The blow came ; we were at war with Germany. Hardly had Mr. Chamberlain finished speaking when the sirens sounded for our first air-raid. The All-Clear went in a little while and then we had a second warning.   The war had begun, and it was clearly not to be a soldier's war on distant frontiers, but a people's war, with our own doorsteps as the battle-front.

It was impossible to think of sending out the window to India, so we packed it in the car, although it weighed nearly a ton, and took it into the country, where as I write it still remains.

CHAPTER XVI

PRESIDENT HOOVER

ON my second visit to America in the autumn of 1926 it was suggested that I should paint the portrait of Mr. Hoover, but though we were both in Chicago he could not spare a moment for sitting, and invited me to go to California. This I could not do, and he said that the next time he was in New York he would sit for me.

Soon afterwards, when I was painting Mr. and Mrs. Elbert and Patricia at Green Pond, on their plantation in South Carolina, I had a telephone call saying that Mr. Hoover was in New York and could I attend the Lincoln Banquet, over which he would preside, on the following Tuesday ? Having just time to finish the portraits, I left for New York, arriving at seven in the morning at the Waldorf Hotel, where my studio was and where Mr. Hoover happened to be staying.

As I was going to the President's apartments, whom should I meet but Dr. Parkes Cadman. I told him I was going to see Mr. Hoover and he said, " He is a good friend of mine ; I will come with you." We went in and greeted the President, who never once looked at either of us. Dr. Cadman said to him that he had been a great public servant, and it was his duty to leave a fine portrait, and now was the time. He mumbled that he did not like sitting, and that his time was all booked up, but if I would come down to his apartment he would give me five minutes in his bedroom ! This I thought was the limit, and I had no further interest in Mr. Hoover, but as we walked away Dr. Cadman said, " You just stick to this and once you have had your sitting you will conquer."

I wrote to the secretary telling him that I had been faced with many hard problems and had painted Generals at the Front under very trying circumstances, but I had never been faced with the proposal of a five-minute sitting in a bedroom. I added that it always takes two to make a good portrait, and if Mr. Hoover would come to my studio and give me half-hour sittings I could do something. The secretary telephoned to say that the President would sit for me at half-past seven the next morning, and give me an hour.

Exactly on the stroke he came in, accompanied by two men, a secretary and a detective, I thought. I had determined that I would make a life-size oil study of the head, and decided in about five minutes which way he should sit. He asked if his visitor could stand behind me. I said I was sorry, but it was impossible to have anyone standing behind me while I worked, but he could sit down in a chair in front of me so that I could see over his head. Then they carried on a conference. They began to talk and look through newspaper cuttings, which provoked me to appeal for consideration, as it compelled Mr. Hoover to keep looking down. He appeared surprised that I should object, but they were quiet for a little time, and finally my sitter gave his attention to me.

I started to talk about the Lincoln Banquet, which I had attended the night before in order to study him. I mentioned the fine speech of Dr. Frank. Mr. Hoover listened, but addressed the man, and not me, in reply—much as in Queen Victoria's days a princess out shopping would address the shop people through the lady-in-waiting, or a prince would tell his officer what to say to the barber who was cutting the royal hair ! I went on with my painting, and presently the man lit a cigarette, puffing the smoke between my eyes and my sitter. Again I had to plead for consideration, and the cigarette was put out. The next interruption was a message that a senator wanted to see Mr. Hoover, who, however, said he had no appointment and did not realize that anyone knew he was there. I went to the door and found a delightful man, who said he had an appointment with Mr. Hoover at eight o'clock. I invited him in, and he took the seat at Mr. Hoover's feet. I was surprised to see how difficult the situation was. The senator was charming, but Mr. Hoover gave him no lead, though he had evidently been a man of great power in Mr. Hoover's Cabinet. They spoke of the air disaster to the giant Zeppelin, to which Mr. Hoover said he had been opposed. The senator stood up and looked at my study, and said, "You are going to have a jolly fine portrait here ; you ought to give the artist time," but at half-past-eight, exactly on the tick, Mr. Hoover said he must be going, and the senator, evidently understanding his friend very well, said, "Oh, there is no need for you to go ; you had better stay." Mr. Hoover left, however, with the promise that he would come back later in the day and give me more time. There was nothing to be done but to wait, and in the afternoon I had a ring from the secretary to say that Mr. Hoover was going back to California in half an hour, and what was to be done about the portrait ! I said that would be the end of it, and it would have to be left as a portrait study. So it remains.

I have never known anyone so silent as Mr. Hoover—not even Mr. Coolidge ; a journalist on one of New York's greatest papers told me he was with him a whole week and in all that time he had had no single greeting from him, no nod of recognition. Certainly I have never had a more difficult sitter, or one who seemed more aloof from his surroundings ; he was apparently in the wilderness· and not in office. It was as if the whole burden of the world was on his shoulders and he could spare no minute for mere humans.

CHAPTER XVII

MUSSOLINI

IN the Spring of 1934 we went to Italy, where I was to paint the portrait of Mr. Myron Taylor for the Steel Corporation of the United States, of which he was Chairman. Mr. Taylor had three villas on an estate in Florence, and we were to live in one of them while a smaller one was to serve as a studio. The prospect was delightful enough in any case, but was especially pleasing to me because arrangements were being made for me to paint the portrait of Mussolini, then in the zenith of his power. The terrace above the studio overlooked the marvellous country towards the monastery of Fiesole, the little town which crowns the hill, the cradle of Florence, and to be here in such companionship was a never-to-be-forgotten experience. Mr. Taylor sat for me till the sun poured into the studio and made it impossible to go on working, when we went out and strained our muscles on the hard courts. The portrait was finished in time for a reception and I am glad to say it was enthusiastically received. The Queen of Roumania and her two sisters came, with the Ladies-in-Waiting to the Queen of Italy and a large number of American friends.

Mr. Taylor received a despatch from the Italian Foreign Office for me, which I found to be a letter from Mussolini, saying he would be pleased to give me all the time necessary to paint a fine portrait, and asking me to report at the Foreign Office. First of all, however, Mr. Taylor arranged for us to have a day in the galleries of Florence, and we also went by car to Perugia. As we entered the magnificent church there, with its artistic atmosphere and its tradition of the ages, the beautiful organ was playing Handel's "Largo" and we had a magnificent recital for our special benefit. I could not help remarking how wonderful it was that this should happen, and I found that our host had arranged it all, having telephoned for the organist to be there when we arrived ! In Perugia Myrom showed me the great masterpieces of Pietro della Francesca, and after this we said good-bye to our friends and to this old town and motored on to Assisi and then to Rome, where we arrived late at night. A countess we met at the Sunday afternoon reception told us to be sure and mention her name, and we were grateful for it, for it was magic at the Grand Hotel.

At ten the next morning I went to the Foreign Office and interviewed the secretary, who said that Thursday was a general holiday, but Mussolini would be ready to sit for me on Friday morning at the Palazzo Venezia. I tried to impress on the secretary that to be prepared was everything and that it was necessary for me to go to the palace either on the Thursday evening or very early on Friday morning so as not to waste any of the Duce's time ; but he did not seem to understand this at all. I tried to assure him that painting was like soldiering and the stage must be set for action, feeling that this might appeal to a Fascist, but it was all in vain. Not till the British Ambassador, Sir Eric Drummond, rang up the Foreign Office for me was I able to arrange for admission to the palace in time to make my preparations. It was settled that I should go down at six o'clock on Thursday, which I did, though without any success. They said they could not admit me until half-past eight the next morning, and informed me that there was an easel and everything necessary for me at the palace.

At half-past eight in the morning I arrived, and had to pass two sentinels, who made a careful examination of my credentials. I found that the magic pass was not the letter from the Foreign Office, but the blue initials of Mussolini ; the magic signature made them all anxious to help. In the guard room I had to go through another examination and give my card, and after much formality and delay the guard came back to escort me. We went through the entrance hall, where two sentinels stood at an iron grille door. This was opened and we passed up the stone staircase, the iron gate being immediately locked behind us. At every door two guards were at attention. I was taken to a room, where I was allowed to open my canvas, which I had brought in a roll with a stretcher, and five guardsmen watched the process of unpacking. In spite of their friendliness it was hopeless for me to appeal to them to let me into the room where Mussolini was to sit ; but at nine o'clock Mr. Brenton, of the American Academy, appeared on the spot with an easel, which seemed to me perfectly miraculous, and saved the situation. He was able to assure the guard that all was well, and they took me into the Duce's room, a palatial apartment, with three great windows, a table, Mussolini's chair, one chair for a visitor, and a map on an easel ; there was nothing else. It was all very simple and dignified.

I continued setting my palette, and at a quarter to ten bells were ringing in all the rooms and the guards sprang to attention. All round I heard them saying " He has arrived ". In about five minutes

an usher came to call me. Two men carried my easel, another my
canvas, and I followed the stately procession with my palette. The
door was flung open and the guard made way for us ; we were in
the august chamber of the great ruler.

The walk up the room to the Duce's chair was quite an event,
but as I arrived Mussolini rose, came round the end of the table, and
shook my hand warmly. He said he was very busy and overwhelmed
with work that morning, but that he would pose for me whenever
he had a chance. This did not seem very encouraging, for the
table was some distance from the window, and the light was not
good, half the face being in shadow as he sat at his desk. However,
I determined to go ahead and decided not to paint or use a canvas
then, but to make a study in chalk while he was looking at his papers.
The secretaries were standing on either side, and in a few minutes
one of his ministers came in with much ceremony and stood opposite
the table, talking for about twenty minutes on his feet. Abandoning
my sketch of the Duce sitting down, I boldly pulled my easel behind
the standing visitor, looked over his shoulder, and sketched a life-
size head of Mussolini talking. In about a quarter of an hour I had
quite a good head and what I thought a vivid expression of his flash-
ing eye. I went on working like this until about noon, taking
advantage of his repeating the same position with the same expression,
and adding touches as I could.

There was a brief interval between the interviews with the ministers,
and he came round and looked at the study. "That is splendid,"
he said, "that is the best I have seen ; as soon as I can I will pose
for you." I was quite happy that I had captured his interest. After
the next visitor had gone he said, "Now I can pose for you," and
I pulled his chair near the window. He sat down and in a few
minutes said, "I feel stupid," as a matter of fact he looked stupid.
He is a man of so much vitality that to sit is not characteristic of him.
I had come to realize that I must paint him while he was on the
move.

All the time he was posing for me he wanted me to turn my canvas
so that he could see it, and at ten minutes to one he said, "You must
be terribly tired." I replied that he must be exhausted, for he had
been hard at work the whole morning. "No," he said, "this is
my life. That is the way I keep on all the time. I work for my
country, and I enjoy it." Then he got up and said, "To-morrow at
the same time," and the door behind him opened. There was a
great audience waiting for him on the other side of it, and he was

greeted with a tremendous cheer as the door closed. Thus the curtain fell on the first sitting.

The next morning I went early to the palace again, painting the background to the portrait and filling in details. My studio was like a public highway to Mussolini's room, and I was practically painting in public, generally with an audience crowding round. Official after official begged that I would paint the human side of the Duce. One of the ministers who could speak English expressed his great pleasure with the portrait and said Mussolini really must give up time for it, whereupon I begged him to use his influence.

I had realized the importance of his coming to sit in the room I had prepared as a studio, for it had a beautiful light since I curtained the windows, and, preparing for this, I had a throne made, covered with a fine red velvet. On this throne I placed a Dantesque chair, the antique velvet of the palace wall and the marble pilasters of the doorway forming a stately background. A sitting there would be all I wanted, and I spoke to one of the under-secretaries about it. He was shocked that I should make such a request, and said the Duce never left his own rooms under any circumstances. "You will never get him to do it," he said, but I told him it would cost nothing to try.

So that morning, instead of going into the executive rooms with my canvas and easel, I walked in, linked my arm into Mussolini's as he came round the table to greet me, and said I very much wanted him to come and pose for a short time in the studio I had prepared, as it was impossible for me to satisfy him in his own room. He walked through the long palace with me until we could see the throne with the Dantesque chair, looking very attractive and business-like. He saw at a glance exactly what I wanted, and said, " Oh, yes, I will come and pose for you when I get my work done." In three-quarters of an hour he came back, preceded by his usher and Director of Ceremonies, and said, "I will give you fifty minutes." In fifteen minutes the usher came back and reminded him of his next appointment ; alas, he had meant fifteen instead of fifty !

Later he came and said he was very sorry but he would not be able to pose that day because he had to make an important speech before Parliament ; but he would sit for me the next morning. I expressed my great disappointment at losing a day when I was just getting enthusiastic, and he said, " Oh, well, when it is all over I will come and sit for you at six o'clock." I worked all day to prepare for him, but when he arrived I was horrified to see that he was wearing a soft collar and a light suit, though he nearly always wore a stiff collar and a dark morning braided suit.

He told me during the sitting that he had paid a great tribute to England in his speech to Parliament, comparing England with the Empire of Rome in the zenith of its power ; and he said, " You can do things in England that we cannot do." He asked me what I thought of Rome, and I told him I had not been there for eight years and the transformation was remarkable. I said there was one thing that spoiled Rome, and he quickly asked, " What is that ? " I replied that it was the horns of the motor-cars and taxis that were ceaselessly sounding night and day, and I told him that in England we were going to pass a law prohibiting the use of horns. He said, " Well, we must go slowly here," but I remember that soon afterwards he passed a law prohibiting the sounding of horns.

I got on well with my work, and he was very pleased with the result, promising to give me another sitting next morning at twelve, whereupon I said that at noon I had a private audience with the Pope. " Why the Pope ? Why not me ? " he said, persistently ; but I stuck to my time. I said ten. He said twelve. I said ten, and the next morning he sat at ten. I had won a battle of words with Mussolini ! At this sitting he told me on the previous night he had seen his Minister of Fine Art, who had expressed his delight with the portrait, saying it was one of the best modern portraits he had seen. This was encouraging, and at the end of this sitting Mussolini looked at the portrait and said, " That is beautiful ; that is just the way I feel. I shall not sit again."

On leaving the room, with my mind still on the portrait, I was oblivious of the fact that I was still in the presence of the august Dictator, but as I neared the door I luckily realized that Mussolini was still at the salute, and in full Fascist manner I stood at salute while the curtain fell on a very interesting experience.

After this my wife and I went to the Vatican for a private audience with the Pope. The pomp and ceremony was very impressive. The dignity of art, the genius of Raphael and his school, the colourful robes of the cardinals, all gave beauty and atmosphere to the occasion. Soon after we arrived in the audience chamber the Pope, dressed in a simple white robe, entered with the cardinals, and all present fell to their knees. As he approached us he held out his hand for us to kiss the papal ring, at the same time conferring on each of us a blessing in Latin, " May your noblest ideals be realized."

That afternoon we spent in a final look round Rome, and in the

evening we packed and rolled my canvas up to catch the midnight
train. I finished the portrait at home, and the copy I made was
exhibited at the Royal Academy. The original was sent to Rome
through the Italian Embassy, and I had a courteous letter from the
Duce, with another from King Victor conferring upon me the Order
of Chevalier of the Crown of Italy.

In the autumn of that year I went again to America, and Mr.
Watchorn from California called on me in New York while I had
the Mussolini portrait on the easel. He was much attracted by it,
and told me of his last visit to Rome. He had not been there very
long before he was sent for by the King of Italy, with whom he
talked for an hour. Just before he left the King said to him : " I am
not a collector of stamps or coins or silver, but I am a collector of
thoughts and ideas," and he asked Mr. Watchorn if he could tell him
his thoughts as he entered the palace. Mr. Watchorn said that when
he came into the palace he thought of that passage of Scripture which
says, " Show me a man who is diligent in business, and he shall stand
before kings."

The King asked him how he interpreted the passage, and he replied
by saying that a man who was diligent in business should be rewarded
by being allowed in the presence of kings. " No," said the King
of Italy ; " I think your interpretation is not right. It really means
that you shall stand in advance of kings. Any man who has done
what you have done for my people will hold an honourable position
far ahead of Kings."

Mr. Watchorn had been Customs Officer at the Port of New York
for many years, and many immigrants into America had to pass
through his hands. Often Italians who had sold all their possessions
to seek a living in the New World were faced on arriving at the port
with the bitter news that they would not be allowed to land, and
Mr. Watchorn had interviewed these distracted people, put his hand
on their shoulders, and told them not to be too downhearted. It was
of this great service to Italian emigrants that the King was thinking.

H.R.H. THE PRINCE OF WALES. 1935

FRANKLIN D. ROOSEVELT, PRESIDENT OF THE UNITED STATES (1935).

CHAPTER XVIII

PRESIDENT ROOSEVELT

LONG before he became the Man of the World and the hope of the United Nations it fell to my lot to paint Mr. Roosevelt, an invigorating experience after my sad time with Mr. Hoover. The problem with such men is always to find time for sittings, and I found the President overwhelmed with engagements.

We had arrived at Washington in a blizzard of snow with the taxi skidding all over the road. I went to the White House and Colonel Macintyre showed me into the President's Office, a big room with a semi-circular bay in which were three fine windows. The desk was in the centre of the circle, the Stars and Stripes on the right and the Presidential banner on the left. The President, who was in the middle of his first term of office, arrived at ten o'clock and in half an hour I had my first meeting with this inspiring figure.

With all his genius and power he had a simplicity and grace of manner that made me instantly at home. He said he was extremely busy, but if I could carry on while he was at work he would try and look in the direction I wanted and help me as much as he could. As the next room was filled with men waiting to see him there seemed little chance of his having much spare time for sitting, and I went forward with black and white studies. The next day the President found a quarter-of-an-hour when he was able to pose for me, and during the afternoon when he was dictating and answering letters, I was able to make great headway. On Friday we were interrupted by the famous press conference at which he invited me to be present ; the secretary said I had better clear up every trace of my studio before the fifty journalists came in. The President talked to them and they bombarded him with questions ; it is an extraordinary experience for an Englishman to see the ruler of a nation speaking so frankly and intimately to these newspaper men, many of whom he addressed by their Christian names.

It was impossible at that time to foresee that this man talking in this friendly way to the men of his country's newspapers was to remain at White House for three terms, and to become a unique figure in America's history ; and yet it was easy to see that there was something about him that would not be denied. He had gone home from Europe after the last war and tried to save the League and the good name of President Wilson, making a thousand speeches in twelve weeks in a campaign all over the States, but, as all the world knows, he failed to save the League. And then an enemy attacked him, and this valiant figure, so strong and so beloved, was suddenly stricken with infantile paralysis in the lower half of his body. He was in the midst of a career of the highest promise, and it seemed that his life was thwarted by this evil blow. But the spirit of a long line of ancestors was strong within him, and he was like a fire and would not be put out. He fought this evil thing and conquered it, and to celebrate his victory over it he has given America a national place of healing at Warm Springs in Georgia, where twelve hundred acres have been set aside for sufferers from infantile paralysis, and a national thanksgiving fund of a million dollars has been spent on it.

Now this heroic man who saved himself is saving freedom for us all.

At the time of my visit he was in the first years of his Presidency and he has been at the White House ever since. No American could have predicted it and none would have believed it possible had it been predicted. Yet who knows even now when he will leave this seat of destiny?

In spite of the President's helpfulness the portrait seemed likely to go slowly and uneasily, for the light (the vital factor for an artist), was anything but good. Rarely have I known such difficulties with it, owing to the sun and the snow. One afternoon the President said, "Now I can give you half an hour, but as there was a strong and inescapable beam of sunlight between us, blinding us both, I had to abandon work. It is not easy to turn a President's office into an artist's studio. We tried to get some tissue paper to subdue the light, but there was none to be found in the White House that was of any use.

At the next sitting I had the great pleasure of meeting Mrs. Roosevelt for the first time. She came into the room and the President introduced me, as he did to all his visitors as they came in; they sat in a chair behind my easel so that he could talk to them while I sketched his profile—the right way to paint him, I had thought, and the best way to suggest the strength of his character. After some days I told the President that I felt it impossible to get a fine portrait unless he could give me a concentrated sitting. I asked him if he ever broke the Sabbath, and he laughed, saying that occasionally he did. Then could he sit for me on Sunday ? I asked, explaining that I only worked on Sundays in national emergencies, and we might consider this a national emergency. He said that if I would lunch with him at the White House on Sunday he would give me a quiet sitting and no one should interrupt us.

There were eight of us at lunch, and General Hooker asked the President if he had been to church. Mr. Roosevelt replied that he had, and had heard a most uninteresting long sermon, of which he proceeded to give us the main points. It was, curiously enough, about Christianity having existed in England long before Augustine arrived, and about Joseph of Arimathea arriving in Somerset and planting the Glastonbury thorn. To my great astonishment he remembered all this, and I said. " Mr. President, I bow to you for having been able to give your attention even to an uninteresting sermon, and, what is more to remember it with so many important problems on your mind."

It was a revelation to me of the President's power of concentration and detachment. During his interviews I had observed the way he had turned from one subject to another, and had wondered whether he ever thought about them again, whether they made a very lasting impression on his mind ; but his remembering this sermon proved to me that he never lost a thing. The problem of the World Court was disturbing him in those days, for the Senate had gone against his wishes on that subject. The news was brought to him as he was sitting for me, and he was clearly disappointed. Yet he was the essence of friendliness and courtesy ; never have I had a more delightful sitter.

When we went back to the executive room, which I was using as a studio, all the guests came with us and expressed their opinions of the portrait. Now we set to work again, I having scoured round the White House to find a throne on which the President's chair could be placed. I was wondering very much whether he would be able to mount this, but I was glad to see he had no difficulty at all. It is, indeed, an astounding thing to see how entirely he is master of his infirmity, of which he never speaks because there is so little need to speak. Yet I was anxious about my troubling him with this high throne. Often, as I think of it now, the story of Cardinal Newman and his portrait painter has come running through my head. The artist wanted the aged Cardinal to mount the dais and could hardly find words to encourage this saintly and fragile figure to clamber up so high. At last the critical moment came, the Cardinal was nearly up, and the excited artist burst out, "That's it, that's it, get up, you dear old boy!"

With the President now sitting at leisure I had my great chance, but to my horror the paint on my palette which I had prepared earlier became sticky and dry in the heat of the room, which had kept me in purgatory the whole week. But I completed the head, and he was then wheeled into a position where he could see it. It was a great relief to me when he declared that he was very pleased with it. The President's mother came to see it, and it was a high privilege to meet this noble woman to whom the world owes so much. Fortunately for me she was enthusiastic, and thought it a wonderful likeness of her son. She said that if the portrait went to the Genealogical Society (for which it was being painted) they would have to make her a life member, which they did. The three following days she came back with friends and relatives, saying she liked the portrait so much that she could not bear to leave it. In view of the difficulties all the way through it was an immense satisfaction to have her warm approval.

The President's mother unveiled the portrait at a great reception at the Genealogical Society's Auditorium, Mr. and Mrs. Myron Taylor being host and hostess. The portrait was well received, and as it was the King's Jubilee year it was felt that it would be a happy idea to exhibit it in England. I therefore painted two, and was able to exhibit it at the Royal Academy and in the provinces. I was glad to have the second copy in my studio during these years of crisis, and most happily it has since become a messenger of goodwill between our two countries.

In these tremendous years the President's wonderful speeches, and his unique achievement in leading his nation to a new world-leadership, have inspired us all. His courageous proclaiming of the spiritual ideals have stirred men everywhere, and after his famous broadcast in January 1939, heard so plainly in London in the middle of the night, I felt constrained to send him a cable thanking him for his New Year's message of hope to mankind. I expected no reply, but to my surprise received a delightful letter.

A biographer who was writing the President's life asked if he might reproduce my portrait of him as the frontispiece, the book paying me the compliment of saying that the Salisbury portrait was generally considered the best. This suggested to me that the President's family should possess the portrait, and I raised the question of presenting it through the Foreign Office. Lord Halifax asked the

President if he would accept it, which he was pleased to do, and our ambassador went to the White House and presented it in the summer of 1941, the news coming to me in this letter from the British Embassy at Washington :

MY DEAR MR. SALISBURY,

Your portrait of the President arrived here safely through the foreign office a few days ago, and I arranged for it to be duly taken down to the White House.

There it was unpacked and I formally presented it to the President, who was quite delighted with it, and so is everybody else. The portrait will certainly stand out among the pictures of the White House and the President is immensely pleased with it.

Yours very sincerely,

HALIFAX.

From the White House came this letter from the President :

DEAR MR. SALISBURY,

That was an extremely nice letter you sent me on June Fourth and Mrs. Roosevelt and I are thrilled that we are to have the portrait. We have always felt that it was by far the best one that was ever done of me, and it will make the family very happy to own it.

As you know, we think of you much these days and hope that the day is not too far off when you will be coming back for another visit.

My very best wishes and grateful thanks to you.

Always sincerely,

FRANKLIN D. ROOSEVELT.

On my next visit to America the journalists came round to see me and pounded me with questions, some concerned about foreign artists painting America's public men. I replied that I had nothing to say on such a matter, as I quite understood the reaction, but I added that the arts are universal and know no limiting frontiers. I pointed out that the American artist Edwin A. Abbey was the official painter of Edward the Seventh's Coronation picture, and that the American Sargent was offered the Presidency of the Royal Academy. I received enthusiastic welcome from American artists, especially the portrait painters, and one of my most delightful experiences was when one of these took a bouquet of roses to my wife and asked her if she thought I would accept a little souvenir. The next morning came a beautiful wrist-watch with a touching tribute. The artists of Chicago said they welcomed my visits because the exhibition stirred up an interest in portraiture. People became portrait-minded, and therefore they got busy.

The Government of the United States, like our own, have tried to break down all fiscal barriers in things of art, so that the spiritual influence of culture and beauty should have free interchange between our two great countries and Europe. Original works of art are not taxed on entering the States, though copies are liable to duty. Thus Sargent, Abbey, Shannon, Whistler, and other artists were able to carry on their work unobstructed by tariff walls on both sides of the Atlantic. The fact that most of these artists made their names and received their inspiration on this side, and established their reputations from our island, proves that this broad and wide outlook has been of great benefit to both countries and to the world of art.

Alas, in spite of this, an unexpected wall has arisen like a ghost in the form of double taxation. As taxation in both countries has steadily grown, an artist working on both sides of the Atlantic must pay taxes in both countries, a double taxation which a Lord Chief Justice himself has described to me as an injustice. Surely the country where the work is done, and the money earned, should benefit by the tax, not the country in which the money is spent.

My bank manager in London had told me before I left that he did not think I could afford to go to America and work, owing to this weight of double taxation, which might cost me twenty-one shillings to the pound. In America my accountant told me that I was "working for the other fellow", and that when I got home I should be lucky if I got one-and-sixpence out of the pound. However that may be, I would not for worlds have lost the experience of seeing so much of this unique country, of meeting so many of its remarkable people, of seeing so many enchanting spectacles, and of forming so many deep friendships that not even the end of life itself can break.

CHAPTER XIX

AMERICA AND THE KING

ON all my visits to America I have been greatly impressed by the deep interest of my sitters in British affairs. I found nothing of dislike or even indifference in any city or any community that I visited. Rather was the constant impression one of real affection for the land from which the Pilgrims came, and to which all good Americans rejoice to come themselves.

Public concern for the welfare of the King was very marked in America at the time of His Majesty's illness in 1929. It did not matter what church I entered, whether in Chicago, New York, Washington, or South Carolina, there were always prayers for the King, and in clubs, among men standing round the fire, it was the King's illness that engaged their talk—not the King of England, but just The King. I was so impressed that I wrote to tell Sir Clive (now Lord) Wigram, receiving in return interesting letters to say that the King and Queen had read my letter with much interest, and were greatly touched by the anxious concern of the people of America.

This was Sir Clive Wigram's letter from Buckingham Palace, dated March 27, 1929 :

" I write to thank you for your letter of the 10th March, which has been read with much interest both by the King and the Queen. You may rest assured that their Majesties much appreciate the kind and sympathetic thoughts of Mrs. Salisbury and yourself.

We have received a good many papers from America, and it is wonderful to read the number of spontaneous and affectionate tributes which the King's illness has evoked from all classes across the Atlantic. In fact I think it has done more to bring together the English-speaking peoples than all the Agreements and Treaties which had this object in view.

The King and Queen hope that you and Mrs. Salisbury are having a very enjoyable visit in the United States."

This letter also reached me in reply to mine, from the King's assistant secretary, Sir Alexander Hardinge, writing from Bognor :

" The King has read with interest your letter of March 10th to Sir Clive Wigram and wishes me to thank you very much for the kind sentiments and good wishes which it contains. I should add that the Queen joins in this message also.

What you say about the feeling in the United States about the King's illness only goes to confirm what we have heard from many sources, and it is truly remarkable that a republican country, with whom we have frequent differences of opinion on political matters, should demonstrate in so marked a fashion their fellow-feeling of anxiety for the welfare of the King.

His Majesty is making really good progress now that the weather has become more propitious. It is bound to be a long job, but every day seems to show some slight improvement. This place is exactly what is required, and if there is any sunshine in England we get it here."

The concern of the American public for the King's health was again seen in a few more years, at the time of His Majesty's second serious illness on the approach of his Silver Jubilee. There was an obvious anxiety and concern for his health, deepening as the news became more grave. It seemed as if a new brotherhood was growing up between us. We had fought against each other, but that was long ago, and we had fought at each other's side not so very long ago for our common way of life. Now all the old sores were apparently healed. His Majesty, lying so ill at Buckingham Palace, was to America front page news each morning, a significant thing no artist could put on canvas.

The idea came to me then, as I moved about in America seeing all this, that it would be a friendly thing to present the King's portrait to the American Government. He had sat for me just before his illness, and had written to say that in his opinion it was the best likeness of himself that had ever been done. It was based on the study I made for His Majesty in the Abbey ceremony of the Order of the Bath, which I repainted lifesize, because Queen Mary thought it his best portrait. When I was finishing the portrait it needed final vital touches from a personal sitting, and the King and Queen came to Sarum Chase, His Majesty giving me a short sitting while Queen Mary went over the house and garden with my wife. We were busy when they joined us in the studio. The King was under the dome light and the Queen was in the oriel window, interested in a book on the table, the Life of Andrew Carnegie, which Mrs. Carnegie had just sent us. Her Majesty requested us to send a special message to Mrs. Carnegie and ask for an autographed copy.

King George asked if Mrs. Salisbury liked going to America and I said, " Yes, and the Americans like her, and call her the Arch Critic," which made him laugh. My wife, hearing her name from a distance said, " Be careful there, I can hear all you say," a touch of spontaneity, which greatly amused their Majesties.

The King carefully studied the portrait and, discovering that some of the Orders were not quite right, suggested that he should get his valet to put on the uniform for me to see. I went down to the palace for this the next morning, and while I was making my notes a message came asking me to wait as the King would like to see me. On coming in he said, " The Queen and I enjoyed our visit to your beautiful house very much."

The suggestion that the portrait should go to America was made to the Foreign Office and met with warm approval. Our Ambassador, Sir Ronald Lindsay, made a formal presentation of it to the President, who accepted it on behalf of the nation. It now hangs in the National Gallery at Washington.

The Foreign Office sent me the report of the proceeding by Mr. Stephen Early, and also the President's letter.

From the White House the President wrote on May 25, 1935 :

MY DEAR MR. SALISBURY,

I have received your letter of May 10, 1935, and am happy to tell you that I have requested the Secretary of State to notify the British Ambassador that I shall be pleased to accept on behalf of the American nation your generous gift of a portrait of His Majesty King George the Fifth. The portrait will be hung in our National Gallery.

Your donation, coming as it does at such an appropriate time, will bring a great deal of pleasure and satisfaction to the many visitors to the Gallery. On their behalf and on my own I offer you heartfelt thanks.

Sincerely yours,

FRANKLIN D. ROOSEVELT.

This was the report of the presentation ceremony on July 11 :

Remarks of the Honourable Sir Ronald Lindsay, Ambassador of Great Britain, delivered on the occasion of the presentation to the President of the portrait of His Majesty King George the Fifth :

Mr. President, on behalf of the artist, Mr. Frank Salisbury, and with the consent of the King, I have the honour to-day of offering to your acceptance on behalf of the American people, this portrait of His Majesty King George the Fifth.

As the King's Ambassador in America I have often been impressed by the feelings of affectionate respect which His Majesty's personal qualities have inspired widely in America, and which were so noticeable when he was gravely ill some years ago.   They were again illustrated by the interest with which the American public during this summer has watched the ceremonies of the King's Silver Jubilee.

It is in recognition of these feelings that the artist offers this gift of the King's portrait to yourself for the American people, one of the many important bonds of sympathy between the United States and Great Britain.

In accepting the portrait, the President said :

Mr. Ambassador, I am happy to accept on behalf of the American people this admirable portrait of His Majesty King George the Fifth, which is presented by the artist, Mr. Frank Salisbury.

I have already expressed to Mr. Salisbury my appreciation of his gift, but I should be grateful, Mr. Ambassador, if you would tell him of the particular pleasure with which I have actually to-day received the portrait.

I likewise should be grateful if you would inform His Majesty that the portrait will be hung in the National Gallery, where it will be seen by great numbers of our citizens who come to Washington from all parts of the United States.   It will be a privilege for these citizens to observe the likeness of a monarch whose faithful and steadfast qualities of leadership have aroused so much admiration in this country.   The portrait will be a symbol of the many ties which draw together the peoples of our respective nations.

I thank you, Mr. Ambassador, for your courtesy in coming here personally this morning to present the portrait.

This is the description on the portrait :

HIS MAJESTY KING GEORGE THE FIFTH

PRESENTED TO

PRESIDENT FRANKLIN DELANO ROOSEVELT

FOR THE

AMERICAN NATION

BY THE ARTIST FRANK O. SALISBURY

in commemoration of the valiant service rendered by the Republic of the United States of America and the British Empire on behalf of World Justice and Peace.

May 1935.   JUBILEE YEAR.

During these years the problem of the American Debt was uppermost in many people's minds on both sides of the Atlantic, and I had many awkward questions to answer.   One friend said : " We always looked to England as a model of honour, and I am so disappointed that England has defaulted in payment of the debt." I protested that we had not defaulted, explaining that we had paid year by year until we depleted our gold reserves in the Bank of England to such an extent that we were forced off the gold standard and faced bankruptcy, and could no longer continue paying in gold, while America would not take our goods because of upsetting the home market. A ninety-per cent tariff on imports closing that channel. of repayment, I pointed out that to meet this difficult situation a token payment was offered by the British Government, but the Treasury at Washington would not accept it; it was to be all or nothing. My friend thanked me for this explanation and said he had not understood it in that light. What a pity it is that constant lack of understanding between nations should imperil such a vital world friendship as ours.

The challenge would sometimes come in the form of such a question as, "Why don't you pay us instead of building ships like the Queen Mary?" to which I pointed out that that could not alter the position, the building of ships being purely a domestic question of employment and of restarting industry to enable us to meet our obligations in the future. I also called attention to the fact that the American loans in the war went to help our Allies, and that our debtors had ceased to make any repayment of either interest or capital, so that financially we were losers all round.

On coming home I wrote this letter on the subject to my friend Myron Taylor :

DEAR MYRON,

Thank you very much for so kindly sending me the press cuttings relating to the presentation of the King's portrait to the President. Yes, I am very pleased and gratified. Sir Ronald Lindsay, our Ambassador, arranged it splendidly, and it seems to have been received well by the press on both sides of the Atlantic.

In my last letter I said I would give you a detailed account of conversation on the question of the American debt.

The opportunity for me to speak on this subject came very easily because of the enquiry about my yearly visits to America. The Chancellor of the Exchequer takes the matter quite seriously, and I expressed my view freely that the question of Britain's payment of the debt should not be allowed to drift, as it was very important that there should be no cause for misunderstanding between our nations.

The question of our balancing our own Budget and returning to prosperity came up, and I said there was one snag in that—that we could not enjoy our return to prosperity without facing the problem of payment of the War Debt, and that even if there were no means of paying in gold or in goods it should be met somehow. Although the money had gone straight to the Allies and they had not paid us any interest, yet we were morally obligated, because of the Victory Bonds raised among the populace of America, and the American nation was still paying interest on these. I said that if I owed a debt and had no gold in the bank to meet it I should offer a picture in settlement. The reply was that no British Government would survive any such proposal of giving any possessions to meet that obligation. They would be sent into the wilderness for at least ten years. I think they calculated this on the public reception of the offer of land to Italy for the settlement of the Abyssinian problem.

I gather that the general opinion is 'that the ball is in the hands of America, and it is for them to make the next move. I am not losing any opportunity of doing any ambassadorial work to promote a true understanding between our two great nations. You know my love for America, and I know your love for England, and I think it is only a question of the right man tackling the problem to solve it. Somebody did suggest that a loan would be raised here and the money placed in the bank for the credit of America to be spent in this country, and I believe that had been suggested before and was not favoured.

Kind remembrances.

Yours sincerely,

FRANK O. SALISBURY.

The newspaper cuttings Mr. Taylor had sent me were from the *New York Daily Mirror*, which had a very amusing reaction on the debt problem and the presentation of the King's portrait. I was so amused by it that I sent a copy of it to Mr. Chamberlain, who was then Chancellor of the Exchequer, but he did not feel that the responsibility had been so easily lifted from his shoulders ! This was what the New York paper said :

5,000 MILLION DOLLAR PORTRAIT

It will please you, fill you with pride, to learn that Sir Ronald Lindsay, British Ambassador, has presented to President Roosevelt an admirable portrait of King George painted by Frank Salisbury. The Ambassador presents the portrait " in the hope that it may further strengthen one of the many and important bonds of sympathy between the United States and Great Britain ".

Nothing could be nicer—BUT——

It should be remembered that this portrait cost the taxpayers of the United States about FIVE THOUSAND MILLION DOLLARS. That, plus the other billions lent to Europe and never sent back, plus the billions we spent in that war that was not our own.

Let us hope President Roosevelt will treasure that beautiful oil painting of King George, take good care of it. Let us also hope and pray that this country will never get another like it, at *the same price*.

CHAPTER XX

THE JUBILEE

LIVE as long as we may, none of us is likely to forget the Silver Jubilee. King George had said to the Archbishop that he was himself surprised at the manifestation of national feeling, adding that, after all he was just an ordinary kind of fellow. That was just it, perhaps, for though we held the King in highest honour it was felt by all his people that he was one of them. In no sense was George the Fifth aloof from the rest of us. He was our King, yet surely he would have been in truth our chosen man had the occasion called for it. The Jubilee gave us the opportunity of showing it, and right royally did the nation respond. Never since the end of the war had been witnessed such a pageantry of emotion and thankfulness.

All the New York papers in the spring of 1935 were giving graphic accounts of the preparations for the Jubilee, and much was made of the suggestion of a Pageant on the Thames, the King and Queen to be rowed in the State Barge from Westminster to St. Paul's. The idea stirred the imagination and appealed to me very much as a magnificent subject for a painting.

In my enthusiasm I wrote from New York to Sir Clive Wigram emphasizing the possibilities of a decorative picture which I should like to be allowed to present to their Majesties. I received a reply that the State Barge was not going to be brought out, and adding that when I arrived in England they would decide the subject. On my returning home in April, when the Court was at Windsor, I received a letter from the King asking me to be at St. Paul's for the Thanksgiving Service.

The idea of a crowded St. Paul's in a painting was so full of difficulties that I almost despaired of being able to deal with it, but, confident that all problems can be solved, I attended two rehearsals. There was a great throng in the cathedral right up to five o'clock on rehearsal day, all the services rehearsing their parts—Gentlemen-at-Arms, the ecclesiastical group, the choir, and the organ.

The newspapers had four positions under the dome, kept right back and camouflaged, as the King was strongly opposed to having a camera conspicuous at the Service. As I visualized the procession it seemed to me that there was a chance of a fine picture at the great west door. I found an admirably concealed place for a camera between the double columns to the south and north, immediately right and left of the great door. With a little camouflage and a curtain it was easy to screen this position, and the work could be done in a few minutes. It was necessary even for this to get permission from the Dean and Chapter, the Office of Works, the Lord Chamberlain, and the architect, a slow and complicated process.

At eleven on the second morning there was a full rehearsal of all the officials, and I was able to see exactly what was going to happen. The Lord Mayor was there, holding an umbrella instead of the Sword of State, a fine chance for a caricature. I made notes of the positions of the royal procession, the Bishop of London, the Dean and Chapter, the Garter King-of-Arms, and the four Heralds. It was not until the morning of the actual procession that the Yeomen of the Guard were stationed to line the aisle and the steps, one of the things that even in a rehearsal an artist can hardly foresee. The splash of colour was one of the most important decorative features in the picture.

On Jubilee morning I arrived at the cathedral about a quarter to ten, when a great number of guests had arrived. The Lord Chamberlain had given my wife a beautiful position under the dome. I was armed with small cards which I could get into my pocket and hold inside my Service Paper, so that they were not obvious ; and on these cards I made diagrams of the relative heights and uniforms of the important groups. I took my moving camera, and used this on the steps with great advantage, and inside the cathedral I secured one or two remarkable results which proved very helpful.

It is surprising how, before the arrival of the King and Queen at these ceremonies, the whole space is kept clear, while as soon as they arrive crowds seem to spring from nowhere and make it almost impossible to get a clear view. Policemen, Ambulance and Red Cross men, and even Guards, all begin to crowd the scene. It was a moving sight as the royal procession passed out of the sombre shadow of the stately canopy at the west door and walked slowly down the aisle. The State Trumpeters could be seen at the doorway, and beyond them was a vista of the crowds on Ludgate Hill.

I was standing near the pulpit when the King and Queen arrived in their places, a point of vantage at which I could make small sketches. I was sketching on my Service Paper when Mr. Osgood, Secretary to the Lord Chamberlain, quietly stepped up and said, "You are getting very forward, and will be stranded," a reminder for which

I was thankful, because as soon as they sat down I should have been left high and dry. As it was, it became a little difficult to move about in such a solemn scene.

Some days afterwards I received a telephone message that the King would see me at the Palace. He was pleased with the sketches and decided that the service inside the cathedral should be the official picture. We called it " The Heart of the Empire ", from the opening sentence of the Order of Service, and the title of the Processional picture was " O Enter then His Gates with Praise ". I said I wanted to be allowed the privilege of painting this and presenting it to their Majesties to commemorate the Jubilee. The King said, " Well, that is very good of you. We shall be very pleased to accept it, and I will do all I can to help you."

As I was leaving he asked about my visit to America and the portraits of President Roosevelt and Mussolini. He seemed much distressed at the unhappy trend of modern art.

It was surprising to find the King, in the midst of the overwhelming ceremonies of those days, so calm, and with time and inclination to discuss these things so freely. I had a most enjoyable interview, but how little did I dream that it would be my last.

The King advised me to secure my sittings at once before the departure of the Dominion and Indian visitors. Mr. Bennett, he said, had already returned to Canada. As a solution the High Commissioner for Canada sent me a photograph of Mr. Bennett, who, needless to explain, is now the esteemed and distinguished Viscount Bennett. The photograph was all I had to work from. The remainder of the figures were painted from life, and it struck me as very remarkable that Queen Mary, on studying the portraits in the finished picture, thought they were all good ones—with the exception of Mr. Bennett's. Be sure your weakness, like your sins, will find you out. I hope my friend, Lord Bennett, has forgiven me this small crime, the perpetration of which the circumstances rendered inescapable.

General Hertzog, one of my first sitters, gave me an hour at the Hyde Park Hotel just before he left for South Africa. He seemed then very loyal and devoted to this country, and much moved by his reception as Prime Minister of the Union. It is believed, indeed, that he had at this time a particular warm feeling for England, having been greatly struck by its friendliness in all quarters. One of the things he was most delighted with was the gift by the City of Kruger's old wagon, which he was able to take back with him to the Cape. It was noticed that when the wagon was offered to General Hertzog

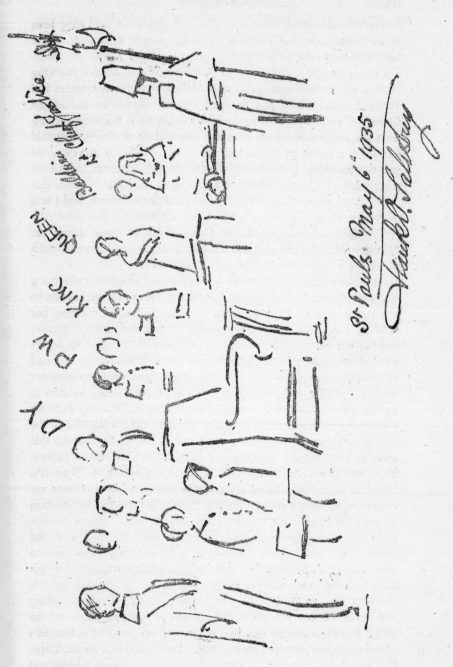

QUEEN

KING

PW

DY

Soldier, Sailor, Jubilee

St Pauls. May 6 1935

Stanley Baldwin

P.P.

he could hardly speak for tears. This old cart was a bit of the soul of the burghers of the Transvaal who had fought against us, and it had been swept out of the land by the tide of war which had swept out Oom Paul too, and doomed him to exile and a foreign grave. Now it was to go home again, to the house where Kruger sat on the verandah with his Bible and his pipe ; and the old man would imagine Oom Paul's stiff figure sitting up under the hood as the wagon jolted over the kopje and spruit, over the lowland to the high veldt. It had left the Transvaal in war ; it was going back home in peace. It was this that filled General Hertzog's heart with tears and moved his rebel spirit to a kind of affection for us in those days.

The royal family all gave me sittings, the Princess Royal, the Prince of Wales, the Duke and Duchess of York and the Princesses, the Duke and Duchess of Kent, the Duke of Gloucester. The Prime Minister (Mr. MacDonald) and the Dominion Prime Ministers, with the Speaker and the Lord Chancellor, were all courteous and patient. Lord Chief Justice Hewart made a wonderful study, and the Judges, Cabinet Ministers, Bishops, and Ambassadors were an extremely interesting collection for an artist.

When the Duke of Kent was sitting for me, and saw the picture nearing completion, he noticed the absence of the Archbishop of Canterbury, and said " There cannot be a Thanksgiving Service without the Archbishop." I felt that he was right, yet at the moment of the picture the Archbishop was in the sanctuary. I took the matter up with the Lord Chamberlain, who assured me that I should be historically right to put the Archbishop where the Bishop of London was, so the Archbishop readily gave me a sitting. He said he was sorry to have to turn the Bishop of London out, but he would have been very disappointed not to have been in the picture. I assured him that that would be all right as the Bishop of London was the central figure in the picture for the Guildhall. It was a simple task to paint the head of the Primate on the figure of the Bishop, though a rather amusing and regrettable thing to have to do. I was glad the Bishop of London saw the humour of it, however, for in a speech soon afterwards he remarked that he was the only bishop who had been beheaded and was yet alive.

It was hard to get Mr. Lloyd George to come, in spite of letters and promises, but when the picture was nearly finished I sent an S O S and the secretary said that if I would go down to Churt Mr. Lloyd George would give me a sitting. I explained that with seventy-five sitters that was almost impossible, and in the end a time was fixed in the studio. The great man arrived with a secretary, and it was astonishing to me to see his quickness of perception. All the world knows that he has a magnetic personality, but it was new to me to find him an art critic—and a good one. When he caught sight of the picture he said, " Come back here ; this is the place to see it ; I can read all the portraits. The best are Mr. MacDonald and Sir John Simon." This was a very clever observation, because these were up to that time the only two who had given me a second sitting for final touches !

Going through all the portraits and summing up the achievements of the people one by one, Mr. Lloyd George suddenly exclaimed, " But you have not got Winston Churchill ! You must get Winston in, for if only for his writing he will go into history." Little could either of us imagine then how much more for his action than for his writing would our great Prime Minister go down to history.

Mr. Churchill was out of office at this time, and, because of his persistent warnings of Germany's growing preparations for war was in the political shadows, a voice crying in the wilderness of a country that would not listen, warning a Government that would not hear. I like to think that in my picture, at any rate, I brought him forward into a front row after Mr. Lloyd George had missed him from the scene.

Mr. Chamberlain, who was then Chancellor of the Exchequer, was very considerate. I had noted his visit in my book as for eleven o'clock, but owing to some confusion he came an hour before the time and said, " I've had a very important Cabinet meeting this morning, but I did not think it fair to put you off, so I asked them if they would carry on until I got back." Consequently I had to make the best use of my hour while the Cabinet waited for the Chancellor.

The chief interest in the Jubilee picture for my twin daughters was the visit of the two princesses. It was a perfect summer day, and the light was streaming into the studio when the royal guests arrived, hand in hand, dressed in the rose pink they wore on Jubilee Day. There could be no prettier sight, and they brought with them the essence of enchanting childhood. For their entertainment my daughter Sylvia brought along her airedale dog and he behaved very well, for as soon as he saw them approaching he sat down and held out his paw. It was his one accomplished trick, and immediately brought a joyous laugh from Princess Margaret. But, alas, my grandson Richard, aged 2, did not behave so well. Princess Elizabeth, who was with my daughter Monica in the garden, came across

Richard sailing his little boat on the lily pond, and, coming forward to him, held out her hand. Richard, now growing up, will read with deep remorse that he immediately turned his back on the princess, for which my daughter most anxiously apologized, saying, " I am so sorry, but he is only a little boy ; he can't even talk yet." Whereupon Richard, to his everlasting shame, looked up smilingly and said, " No, I t'ant."

It was with almost endless trouble that I secured a sitting from the Prince of Wales. Sir Godfrey Thomas was very disappointed that he could not make an appointment. When the Queen of Norway was sitting for me she felt that the only way I could get the Prince to sit was by telling him that he need not be in uniform. With this useful suggestion I again wrote to Sir Godfrey, and received a telephone message to say that the Prince would sit for me at St. James's Palace. I went down to the Palace and arranged the only room available, a dark room with one window, and promptly at three the Prince came in—to my surprise in full dress uniform, which I thought very gracious of him. Then I started to work, and he immediately told his equerry to pull the blind down, as he did not want to be seen. This was truly disconcerting, but, being used to campaigns such as this, I had thought to bring with me an electric light with a standard, and this I quickly fixed up.

Now another difficulty arose. As soon as he realized that I wanted the right side of his face the Prince said, " No, I am not going to be painted on my right side—I want to be painted on my left." I said that if I painted him that way he would be turning his back on the King or leaving the church, and at this he smiled. It is a very curious thing that all the photographs of the Prince appearing in the papers were profiles from the left. Under the circumstances, I had to start working from the left and gradually coax him to pull his head round so that I could see the right side of his face.

Then, on my asking how long the Prince was going to give me, he said, " Ten minutes or a quarter of an hour," and as it was quite impossible to make a satisfactory drawing in so short a time, under so many handicaps, I said that the only thing left for me to do was to make an exposure with my camera, which I had with me. While he was posing for this I asked the Prince to turn his face from left to right, and in this way I was able to get what I was striving for. When the film was developed it proved most satisfactory, and as it was a moving picture I was able to put it on the screen to help me with the portrait.

This was in the middle of November. It was impossible not to feel at that time that there was something wrong; possibly the Prince knew of the King's failing health, and of the seriousness of the situation. Later, when he was King, and Sir John Simon, now Lord Simon, was giving me his final sitting for the picture, Sir John said that now the Prince of Wales was King I ought to invite him to see the picture before it was exhibited. I wrote to Buckingham Palace, but he was too busy to come.

The study I was able to draw from the projection of the film on to the screen was a great help; in fact, for busy artists this would be a very good system to adopt, and no doubt will be in the future. When the Duke of York and the Duke of Kent saw the portrait they both remarked spontaneously, " What a good likeness."

At the private view the portrait study of the Prince was seen by the chairman of the Fine Art Society and Mr. Gustave Tuck, both of whom wanted to reproduce it. Mr. Tuck was so insistent that he secured permission, but later the King forbade its publication, apparently because I had drawn the right side of his face. After the abdication Lord Brownlow, a great friend of the Duke of Windsor, bought it for his collection.

I had some anxiety about the success of this Thanksgiving picture, for the perspective and architecture in so great an interior constituted a real difficulty, especially as under the Dome the formation is octagonal; but I felt that I had made the best of it when Sir Banister Fletcher asked me to allow him to reproduce the painting in his classic book on Architecture.

For the second Jubilee picture, which I told King George the Fifth I should paint for my own pleasure, the Indian Princes made a picturesque group following the royal family, and all gave me sittings. The Maharajah of Patiala, seeing the painting in progress, was very much attracted by it, and asked me to paint the scene for him, which I agreed to do; but when the Lord Mayor (Sir Stephen Killik) came to see the pictures with a number of City officials they felt that the City had first claim, and I cabled to the Maharajah who agreed, asking me still to paint the subject again for him.

When the Maharajah of Patiala visited my studio it was a very hot day in August. He came from Windsor, where he had been accompanying the King at a Jubilee review of the troops, in the uniform of a General, and was feeling the heat terribly; he said it was much more trying than in India. He was quite exhausted, and had to rest before he could dream of sitting for me, but after drinking pint after pint of iced water he recovered. He asked if I would paint him in his robes. I thought he had them with him, but he explained that they were in India, and he could not afford to bring them to London as they were worth six million pounds. He said if I would go to India to paint the portraits he would make it worth while, as he had ten subjects he wanted me to paint. Unfortunately it was impossible for me to go. What a lost chance of splendour for an artist's brush !

Both pictures were fifteen feet long and five feet high, the size of the Queen Eleanor in St. Alban's Abbey, and were done in gold leaf and the simple values of red, gold, and black. The picturesque and historic dress of the Beefeaters made fine figures with their halberds as they stood guard on the Processional Way. The picture was received and unveiled by the next succeeding Lord Mayor (Sir Maurice Jenks) at a very interesting function in the Guildhall Art Gallery.

Alas, the good King George was not to see the completion of the picture in which he had taken so great an interest. When the Duke of York was sitting for me he wondered if it would be possible for it to be sent to Buckingham Palace for the King to see. His Majesty had a chill, and the nation was concerned about his health. When I suggested sending the picture to the Palace, however, the secretary replied to say that the King would not hear of my being put to that trouble, and would come to my studio to see it on December 9. That week the King's sister, Princess Victoria, died, and the visit was postponed until December 18.

The day dawned black and cold with a biting east wind blowing, and I felt sure the King could not face such weather. Later in the day I received a message to say that the King and Queen dare not venture out, but would see the picture on their return from Sandringham after Christmas. Alas, a great shadow was to fall on the hearts of the nation, the empire, and the world, for in a few weeks King George the Beloved had surrendered an imperial for a celestial crown, and passed to his reward. I painted the lying-in-state with Britannia placing her floral wreath of memory, and, knowing how he loved Blake's poem, I painted Blake's chariot of fire in the background.

It also fell to my lot to design the border for Queen Mary's beautiful letter to the nation. On the left I put the State Trumpeters sounding the last watch to the night and the answering stars. On the right was the King's Herald in the rays of the morning sun proclaiming a new era. At the base was the enthroned Goddess of History with the open book of records, the kneeling winged figure of Hope turning the pages of the volume, and the figure of the World bowed with sorrow at her feet.

A week after the funeral Queen Mary came alone to Sarum Chase to view the picture of the Thanksgiving.

It was naturally a touching ordeal for Her Majesty, in view of the deep memories the scene must revive. Princess Alice and the Earl of Athlone accompanied the Queen, and all were wishful that before the picture went to the Palace it should be publicly exhibited, first at the Academy. I repeated my conversation with the King and said I had no desire to see it go, but the President of the Academy wrote and asked if I would send it to the Spring Exhibition, and I replied that the decision must rest with Buckingham Palace. It was decided to exhibit it and the picture was well received.

At this time I had from Dr. Cadman in America, who had seen the painting while sitting to me in London, a letter in which he said, " Do not let your mind be disturbed over the King not being able to see the finished picture, because now, in his spiritual state, he may have avenues of approach we know not of."

The Lord Chamberlain secured the permission of His Majesty for the picture to be exhibited at Liverpool, Kettering, Blackpool, Bournemouth, Lincoln, Eastbourne, and Oldham, and at each of these places a civic ceremony was arranged at which the mayor and aldermen attended in state and I was asked to talk of the picture and its making. *The Times* offered to issue a colour reproduction of " The Heart of the Empire ", and the number of copies thus distributed surpassed all records for those days. The profits were devoted to King George's Jubilee Fund.

My old friend Mr. Lints Smith, the manager of *The Times* in those days, made a great success of this venture, and in addition to the special issue a double-page colour reproduction appeared in the weekly edition of *The Times*, of which seventy-five thousand copies went all over the world.

The picture itself was delivered at Buckingham Palace after its long tour of the country, and I wondered if any other painting had ever been associated with so many dramatic events. In its brief history this scene of a nation's thanksgiving had passed through three reigns. Since it was painted a king had died, a king had abdicated, and a king had been crowned.

CHAPTER XXI

THE CORONATION

WE of this generation have lived through dramatic events perhaps unequalled in any other age, two wars and the shaking of thrones, the disappearance of dynasties and kingdoms, and astounding revolutions of science and thought. Many of us in this country have seen four kings come and three kings go, one coronation postponed and one abandoned, and two filled with joyous splendour. We are not likely to forget the last of these, the crowning of King George the Sixth in an hour of national emotion almost without a parallel.

The events leading up to the accession of King George are passing into oblivion and more and more it is felt that a guiding hand was moving the nation through a bitter experience to some high fulfilment of destiny. It is remarkable to remember that these critical days for the monarchy ended in the triumphant coronation of George the Sixth in the millennial year of the English throne, for King George was crowned in 1937, exactly a thousand years from the crowning of Athelstan, First King of All England.

In the spring of that year, at an afternoon party at Buckingham Palace, the King said he wished me to be at the Coronation Ceremony to make sketches. Soon afterwards I received a telephone message from Mr. Mackenzie King, Prime Minister of Canada, informing me that he had had a conference with Mr. Chamberlain and the Prime Ministers of Australia, New Zealand, and South Africa, and they were anxious to present a coronation picture to their Majesties in the name of all the Dominions. Mr. Mackenzie King added that I had been unanimously chosen to paint it.

This is not the place to dwell on the impressiveness of that great day in the Abbey; to all who were there it was an unforgettable scene, like a page of history being written before our eyes. It was for me to try to put something of it on record.

After the ceremony Mr. King telephoned saying that they left it entirely with me to do something worthy of the occasion, expressing their deep affection, as he said, for " those two dear young people who have consecrated themselves to so difficult a task ". This, he added, would be the greatest picture I had had to paint, and he wished it Godspeed.

I promised to do my best to complete it within twelve months, and he arranged that all details should be settled with the High Commissioners. Mr. Vincent Massey was to get in touch with me as soon as the fact was made public, as Mr. King was leaving for Canada the following day, going home through Germany. I learned afterwards that he called to see Hitler, who was then at his zenith, with Mussolini rattling his sabre to keep him company ; and I am permitted to disclose that Mr. Mackenzie King told the Fuhrer that when he had done with England he had to face the British Empire. How well the Fuhrer knows it now !

In setting to work on this huge canvas I made a model of the dais in the Abbey, with the Coronation Chair, the two thrones, and a complete dressed set of small figures relative in size, so that I could arrange the tableaux to scale. I was able to draw from these groups and arrange the light so that I had the stage set in miniature.

In July I went to Buckingham Palace for an audience with the King, who was pleased with the sketches and told me that he felt the moment for the picture should be where he was crowned with Edward the Confessor's Crown. He showed me a photograph taken from the clerestory of the east end of the Abbey, and as we looked at it the King said, " Where were you on that day ? " Curiously enough I was in this photograph, quite clearly seen sketching, and on my pointing it out the King said, " You are the first I have been able to recognize. Now you must paint your own portrait in the picture and put a note ' This is the artist.' "—I said, " No, Sir ; I will put ' *This is the perpetrator of the crime.*' " The King laughed and went on to say, " I expected to see you on my left ; I looked but could not find you." I thought this very wonderful, and explained I could not be on that side because the cameras were there. I said the bishops had the best position, and the King said, " Oh, you mean my angel choir," adding that they should have made me a bishop for the occasion—which was exactly what I had wanted.

On studying the order of the service at the particular moment the King had referred to, and, realizing how impressive and significant it was, I started a new sketch in oils, which pleased His Majesty, who now went carefully through all the groupings of the figures. On my saying I thought I had everyone of importance in the picture, the King said, " Yes, all except my two brothers the Duke of Gloucester and the Duke of Kent."

It was very disappointing, but from my point of view in the Abbey the dukes were eclipsed by the group around the throne.

I found, however, that with a slight rearrangement I could get them in, and we also decided that it was important that the Dominion Prime Ministers and Mr. Baldwin should all come into the picture, though at that moment they were not within its range. I took the opportunity to explain to His Majesty that I was anxious not to spoil the picture by overcrowding it with portraits, as ceremonial subjects were so often ruined by the mass of miniatures. The King quite agreed, and I managed to complete the scene with only forty-two portraits.

Though too many portraits may ruin a picture, it is to be remembered, on the other hand, that to limit the number of recognizable portraits in a historic painting is to limit the scope of its interest. Most ceremonial pictures which have been considered a success in the past have a multitude of portraits—all potential subscribers to a twenty-guinea mezzotint engraving ! The number of proofs sold of Queen Victoria's Coronation picture realized £120,000 and King Edward the Seventh's, £80,000. I do not know the figures for Bacon's proofs of the Coronation of King George the Fifth, but I question if to-day the numbers sold would balance the cost of the plates and printing. The spirit of the day continually changes, and mezzotint engraving is out of fashion. Colour proofs have taken its place, but as colour printing is more of a mechanical process it has not the same artistic value, and the rush of the age is also a detrimental factor as colour takes a long time. In the old days an artist would take three years to paint such a scene, and the engraver two years, so that it would be five years before the proofs were ready. In these days the interest would be dead in twelve months. The unbounded spirit of hero worship has gone. We worship our heroes, it is true, but keep our worship within bounds. Yet we may be thankful (and certain) that the loyal devotion to the throne remains.

The Queen gave me a delightful interview in which I was able to show her the sketches and explain how the picture was to be painted. Her Majesty arranged that the Princesses should give me a sitting at once. In my rough sketch I had them wearing their coronets, but though the coronets were charming, as the Queen was uncrowned at that moment in the picture, they could not be painted with them. The Queen suggested that I should paint them with the coronets another time.

Having determined on the plan of the picture and the size of the figures, the next task was the collecting of all the material, no light business. The Office of Works supplied me with the tapestry and the gold brocade facings to the royal box ; and I was also able to obtain from them a square of the Chinese gold carpet used in the sanctuary of the Abbey—a touch of genius, and a credit to the man who thought of it for making a simple foil to the rich ceremonial robes. The over-patterned Persian carpets in some of our old coronation pictures have absolutely ruined them. The Office of Works also sent me the King and Queen's red velvet and silk chairs, and, knowing that a coronation chair had been used for the Queen Victoria film of " Sixty Glorious Years ", I managed to trace this chair at the Alexandra Palace and secured the loan of it. It was a perfect copy. The replicas of the royal regalia used at the rehearsals were also put at my disposal, and the Lord Chamberlain's office informed me that I could have the gold plate at the studio when I wanted it. This we thought a great responsibility, but our anxiety was allayed when the Lord Chamberlain later told me that it was never allowed out of the Palace except for coronations, and that Garrards of Albemarle Street would lend me similar plate that would answer my purpose. This they kindly did.

It was no light matter to house all these things. Most of them came under the cover of my ordinary studio insurance, but the royal robes had to be specially insured as long as they were at Sarum Chase. The King's coronation robe of cloth-of-gold, made for George the Fourth, was considered priceless, and we were much relieved when everything had been safely returned without damage.

In notifying all the important people coming into the picture, and asking them for a sitting of two hours, I made up my mind that I would get all these finished and the studies of the interior of the Abbey ready before beginning actual painting, but in the meantime I squared up the canvas (which was fourteen feet by ten) and had a coloured lantern slide made from my original sketch, which could be thus projected on to the canvas actual size. This was a great help, and a considerable saving of time. Drawing the composition in charcoal on the canvas enabled me finally to settle the size of the forty-two figures and determine exactly where my sitters would come, and the poses and grouping in relation to the architecture. Having now drawn out the foundation of the picture, my assistant, Reginald Lewis, carefully fixed and painted in black and white all the architectural details, a very great help to me.

An awkward situation arose when I had secured about half the portraits, for I received a message from the Lord Chamberlain to say that the royal robes had been returned from exhibition at Edinburgh, and as they were to go to the Dominions for exhibition I could have the use of them for three weeks only. This upset all my plans, for it became necessary to begin painting the King and Queen before I had a note or a key of colour in the background. But in three weeks I had painted the robes, my architect nephew Vyvyan and my daughter Monica sitting in the robes for me.

Unfortunately the King was in Scotland and could not sit, but I was able to obtain a sitting of two hours from the Queen in her robes. It was arranged by the Lady-in-Waiting that Her Majesty would come to the studio as I had the setting, lighting, and the robe there in perfect order, but eventually it was found necessary for the sitting to be at the Palace. In these circumstances, and as this was the only chance I should have of seeing the Queen in her full robes, I asked to be allowed to have a photographer there so that I could check it on the canvas when properly drawn out in the studio.

The King sat to me a little later, and for this sitting I sent down to the Palace the replicas of the regalia and the copy of the Coronation Chair, in which His Majesty was most interested. I was glad that I had done so, for the King had sent to the Tower for the Crown jewels, and the crown itself had been brought from the Tower with an escort of guards. On my remarking how splendid it all was he said, " I thought while we were about it we might do the thing properly and well."

As fate would have it we had just started work when a dark yellow fog fell over London and we were driven to use electric light.

I painted a study of the King in oils, but it seemed impossible to do justice to all the beauty of the robes, crown, and sceptre. The sight of them all is so wonderful in colour that any number of sittings could hardly be equal to it. As I had already painted the robe from my model, however, I was able to concentrate in my two hours on essential points. The King gave me three-quarters of an hour with the Confessor's Crown on, and then asked if he could take it off, as it weighs nearly eight pounds, and put on the lighter Imperial Crown, which he often wore at work before the coronation " to get used to it ", as he said it was no good being a king unless you could wear a crown properly !

His Majesty pointed out that the Colobium-Sinbonis, the under-tunic in which he was anointed King, must show in the picture, as it had a great significance, indicating that he was Head of the Church. The garment symbolizes His Majesty's priestly functions and represents our Lord's clothes after they had cast lots for His garments at the Crucifixion. With this in mind we went round the Palace to see the

H.M. Queen Mary.

The Coronation of Their Majesties King George VI and Queen Elizabeth, 1937.

two earlier coronation pictures by Abbey and Bacon, and found that Abbey (at the express wish of Kind Edward, as we learned) had moved the robe of the cloth-of-gold in order to reveal the Order of the Garter, much to the painter's distress because it was too obvious, and is rather an artistic defect. The King pointed out that in the coronation picture of his father Bacon had not shown the Colobium-Sinbonis at all. I found that the King's suggestion was artistically very valuable, as the white made a contrasting foil to the gold robe.

The painting now proceeded quickly. I started work at nine in the morning and worked often until midnight, having a powerful electric light fixed over the painting so that I became independent of daylight. In the Abbey floodlights were fixed in the roof. The picture was therefore painted with almost fifty per cent. of artificial light—perhaps a fortunate thing, for at the World's Fair Exhibition in New York it was illuminated by electric light, and was said to look marvellously well.

Queen Mary enabled me to make one of my best charcoal studies, generously giving me three hours. Her Majesty's crown was brought from the Tower with all the State robes and jewels.

All the time the individual sittings proceeded, but the translating of the studies into the picture was the most difficult work imaginable with so huge a canvas. Often when a close view of the canvas made the likeness seem quite satisfactory, it looked entirely different on climbing down and going to the other end of the studio, wrong in scale, too small or too big, too bright or too dark. Sometimes a study which had taken me only an hour would take three days to put into its final setting ; a single portrait on a forty-by-fifty canvas could be painted with more ease.

Mr. and Mrs. de Laszlo came in one afternoon before I had gone very far, and I was much encouraged by his enthusiasm over my original sketches. He laid special emphasis on the importance of the sparkling high light on the upraised Sword of State held by Lord Zetland, considering it a dramatic effect. I had also made a special emphasis of the sparkle of the jewels in the shadows, which I tried to represent in the picture throughout, taking full advantage of the light falling on the Archbishop's gold crozier, the glitter on the Sword of State, culminating in the brilliancy of light upon the King, his crown, sceptre, and robe of gold.

The Archbishop of Canterbury was very considerate. He gave me three sittings at my studio, one for the study, one for the actual canvas for colour, and one for the finishing touches. Dr. Lang said it was

the best portrait he had had, and this reminds me of a comment made
at the private view of the picture, which shows the Primate raising
his hand in blessing immediately after the crowning.   It is natural
that at such a solemn moment all eyes should be upon the King,
but in fact the eyes of Princess Margaret were just then on the
Archbishop, a truly noble figure as he stood, and, seeing this, a friend
at the private view observed that he noticed that Princess Margaret
was unable to take her eyes off the Primate, and supposed that she was
saying to herself, " I can see Daddy any day."

All the bishops lent me their robes, and I was fortunate to be able
to manage with one sitting from most of them.   Lord Cromer, the
Lord Chamberlain, exceptionally busy throughout this period, was
prevented from sitting until the picture was practically completed,
and I had his robes painted from memory, but gained little by this
because there was so much alteration when he sat.   He and Lady
Cromer came up one afternoon, and he said he never realized how
much diplomacy and work was entailed in painting such a picture.

The Lord Chancellor was unable to sit for me for some time because
he had to go to Bermuda for his health, but he lent me his robe and
the Purse, and as I had taken a good pencil sketch of him at
one of the rehearsals I felt I was safe in going ahead.   When Lord
Hailsham returned, however, and was taking his pose, he said, " Let
me see, I have the train over my arm and hold the Privy Purse up,"
which would make my work of no avail, for in my sketch he was
holding it down.   When I showed him my sketch he said, " Oh,
I must have been resting then."   But as the heraldry of the royal
arms brocaded on the Privy Purse with its rich tassels showed to better
advantage the other way I scraped out and repainted the whole figure,
the only really serious correction I had to make from beginning to
end of the painting.

When the King was studying the composition he enquired if I had
the Dean of Westminster (Dr. Foxley Norris) in, and I told him that
as, unhappily, he had died during the interval, I had not been able
to get a sitting.   The King said, " But you must get the Dean in,"
and, referring to the order of the service at this time, I found that
Dr. Norris was holding the Bible, " the most precious gift this world
affords ", and was taking it back to place on the altar.   I seized on
this moment, and this touch added a significant note to the scene, as
the whole ritual of the service was built up and established on the
sacred word of the Bible.

It was impossible not to be impressed by the way in which the

King had dedicated himself to the high service of the State, for His Majesty pointed out three most salient and important points connected with the whole of this impressive ceremony ; the moment of the Archbishop's Benediction on the King enthroned and crowned, the significance of the anointing surplice, and the presence of the Bible.

In reflecting on all my experiences with this picture I have learned the true spiritual significance of the Throne and Kingship. King George the Fifth always bowed to the National Anthem and King Edward the Seventh would join in the singing of the Anthem, never taking it to himself but regarding it as something beyond personality. What artist could hope to express on canvas an idea with so solemn a meaning ? If it were possible, such a picture should enshrine all the history and tradition of the coronation and should be called, " Greater than I—Long Live the King ".

It was interesting, also, to realize the deep personal interest taken in the event by the notable figures concerned. They were all delightful to deal with, and full of help and encouragement. It was more difficult to get the Maids-of-Honour than most of the other ladies, though four of them did sit for me. Lady Margaret Cavendish Bentinck, Lady Elizabeth Percy, and Lady Elizabeth Paget, were all very helpful. The page boys wrre astonishingly apathetic : this was fortunate as they were so irregular in height, some short, others taller than the King, thus I made them uniform in height and did not trouble about portraits.

One of the most considerate sitters was the Duke of Portland, who held the Queen's crown on a velvet cushion and stood near Her Majesty. When I asked him how long he could give me he replied, " As long as you like : my time is yours, and I do not mind if I am late for dinner."

The Earl Marshal at the moment was nowhere within the range of the picture, but I found a place for him next to the Duke of Portland, for the Garter King-of-Arms was anxious to give up his place in the centre of the composition rather than that the Duke of Norfolk should be left out. The problems of personnel in a scene such as this are very difficult, and it is a thankless task to try to solve them.

In due time my task was accomplished and I had fulfilled my promise to complete the picture within twelve months. I invited the four High Commissioners up to see it, and was gratified to find them delighted with it. The picture was sent down to the Palace, where it was placed at the end of the gallery and presented to their Majesties by the High Commissioners : Mr. Vincent Massey for

Canada, Mr. Bruce for Australia, Mr. W. J. Jordan for New Zealand, and Mr. C. F. te Water for South Africa. The Lord Chamberlain and the King the next afternoon went carefully over it, but fortunately there were no material alterations to be made.

From the Palace the picture went to the Academy, where it was given the place of honour and received an excellent reception, the critic of a famous newspaper saying that it was the finest picture painted during the last hundred years.

At the close of the Academy there was a general wish that the picture should be shown in the provinces to the public free of charge, but the Lord Chamberlain, after consulting the King, felt it would be better to keep it in London, where Dominion visitors could have free access to it. Several places were suggested, St. James's Palace, the National Gallery, and Westminster Hall. What a glorious setting Westminster Hall would be, with its ancient tradition, for this gift of the Dominions to the King !

There seemed some difficulty in relation to each of these places, and, as the European situation was gravely upset, nothing could be decided. Later I was surprised to receive a letter to say that the King had been pleased to lend the picture to America for exhibition at the World's Fair in New York. It therefore happened that on the occasion of the royal visit to New York they saw the picture with the Canadian Prime Minister. After the close of the World's Fair the King allowed the picture to go to Australia and New Zealand, and it was there when the war broke out.

I painted two other pictures of the Coronation pageantry. Lord Wakefield wished to present to the City pictures to commemorate the historic ceremony at Temple Bar and the procession to the Guildhall, and he left it to the committee to select the artist. To my delight a deputation called on me and said it was the committee's unanimous wish that I should do the work. I was given a seat for the presentation of the Keys of the City and the Sword at Temple Bar, and received a roving pass for the banquet. Ultimately when the day arrived it was terribly wet and foggy and the procession had to be abandoned. I therefore concentrated on the banquet.

Solomon J. Solomon had painted the last state reception of George the Fifth and Queen Mary, showing the Lord Mayor walking to the high table and proposing the health of the King. This time there was no presentation of address, no reception, in fact no dramatic moment. I interviewed the Master of Ceremonies to discover if there would be any incident that would make a suitable scene, but

without success, and all I could do at the banquet was to make sketches
and visualize the scene from all points of view. The most interesting
feature of the ceremony was that for the first time in history the Lord
Mayor and Lady Mayoress sat at the high table with royalty.

For days afterwards I struggled to find a suitable moment for the
picture, but almost despaired, and feared it would be impossible to
do anything worth while. Then I boldly resolved to take the chief
guests in perspective, looking down the length of the high table.
The idea worked out splendidly and enabled me to bring in the noble
setting of the interior of the Guildhall itself, and the fine Gothic oak
panelling with the canopy of red and gold over the King and Queen.
The important guests were seen to great advantage, while the focus
came upon the royal group as the Lord Mayor (Sir George Broad-
bridge) was giving the Royal toast. I had unfortunately the backs
of two guests (the Marquess and Marchioness of Carisbrooke) in the
forefront of my view, but the uniform of the marquess and the grace
and beauty of the dress of the marchioness saved the situation.

The other picture I painted was the Coronation Procession for
Lord Milford Haven to present to Lord Louis Mountbatten, chief
aide-de-camp to the King. It was a very exciting task owing to
the great detail and the length of the procession, and made a picture
fourteen feet by three feet. But surely Pall Mall has never in our
generation seen a grander spectacle than when it was filled with horses
on that day. One of my friends who saw it, and has been in many
lands and seen many of our great pageants, told me that he had never
seen a more glorious spectacle than Pall Mall was then. All the
horses at the Royal Mews paraded for me.

On the throne in the studio I had a barrel on legs which acted as
a horse while I was doing this picture, and most of my sitters rode it
well. Lord Cavan, however, sprang into the saddle as if mounting
a restive charger, and I rushed forward only just in time to save the
structure from collapsing. It was an exciting moment, but all was
well. I painted the procession in spirit fresco and gold leaf.

These two pictures occupied the year following the coronation,
and in March 1939, the Lord Mayor and Lord Wakefield wished the
Guildhall picture to be exhibited at the Academy. The President,
Sir Edwin Lutyens, came to see it and invited me to send in both
pictures. The unveiling of the luncheon picture took place at the
Guildhall, where Lord Wakefield made an appropriate speech, and
the Lord Mayor, to my horror, called upon the artist. The Lord
Mayor had pointed out that much of the pomp of national ceremonies

had in the process of time been stripped of its ancient splendour, and this gave me the opportunity of dealing with the difficulties such changes have made for the artist. The Lord Mayor also recalled the fact that this was not the first picture I had painted for Lord Wakefield to present to the City, for I had already painted a Royal Exchange panel of King Alfred rebuilding the walls of London. I could not help following up this reference with a word on Lord Wakefield's own work for strengthening the walls of the City. Lord Wakefield rang me up the next morning and congratulated me, which pleased me greatly, for I was nervous, and while I was speaking he had twice pulled out his watch and put me off my word. Of course I ought to have made play on the incident by calling attention to the way in which Lord Wakefield resented any compliment. What a noble son of London and the Empire he was!

How I delight to recall our last meeting at Wakefield House! Breaking away for a moment from the rush of business, he turned his thoughts to some of the new ideas of transport and flight that he had pioneered, and to life's achievement generally. I seemed to feel an illuminating splendour in contemplating his fearless vision and his great courage, which made failure and disappointment count as nothing in the blazing sunlight of opportunity and high endeavour.

CHAPTER XXII

THE CHALLENGE TO BEAUTY

ART exacts unwearying devotion from its votaries. Supreme beauty, however fleeting its charm, appeals irresistibly to the eye and soul of the artist for permanence of counterfeit existence. Only by untiring effort can that appeal be adequately met. The artist must toil at his subject with unremitting energy before he dare permit himself to hope that the divine afflatus, so long wooed, has been won to his canvas to illuminate his work and crown his artistic endeavour.

Looking back to the days when Lord Leighton would come to inspect our work at the Royal Academy Schools, those happy days of Art seem like another world, and it is impossible not to be conscious of a mighty change that has engulfed us all. In those famous days students still rose when the President came into the lecture-room to take the chair. I remember how we watched with a sort of awe the queues that began to form at nine in the morning outside the doors of Burlington House for the Spring Exhibition, enjoying the crush as the crowd surged round the exhibiting artists, and how we were thrilled with the excitement of Show Sunday. Would that such times could come again, and the days of hero worship that have gone with them.

The interest in art is not the same. Even membership of the Academy means little to-day, nor do the once magic letters R.A. increase the value of a picture. Competition is keener, self-interest is more vital. The craze for plain walls and steel and glass furniture ; the motor-car ; the kinema, wireless, and the colour camera have all played their part in ruining the serenity and threatening the foundations of the Palace of Art. Old traditions and fine quality are derided. Crude incompetency is acclaimed originality. Freaks and short cuts to notoriety are practised to achieve publicity or notoriety. Perhaps it is significant of all this that the noble motto inscribed in letters of gold round the central Rotunda of the Royal Academy has been blotted out :

> The hearts of men, which fondly here admire
> Fair-seeming shows, may lift themselves up higher,
> And learn to love with zealous humble duty
> The Eternal Fountain of that Heavenly Beauty.
>
> SPENSER.

The words have gone and their place is left bare, and we are left wondering why this should be. To some the blank space will seem without significance ; to those who remember, it may seem to say that where there is no vision the people perish.

The Royal Academy is a national institution enjoying endowments and royal patronage for the encouragement of the Arts—painting, sculpture, and architecture ; and it is right that it should be expected to pay homage to all true and faithful endeavour to record in Art the passing life of the generations. Its main interests are traditionally devoted to painting, and it should be the consistent recorder of all true Art, seeking to portray the life and pageantry of its time. No one can object to changing styles in Art, or hope that the walls of the Academy will not reflect them. The striving after a more original expression of ideas and nature, the experimental adventure in form, colour, and composition of modern Art, have made a definite effort to redeem itself from the tame, mediocre chocolate box pictures of the Victorian era. It is not strange that the Academy of 1943 should appear very different from that of 1893. And yet it can hardly be claimed that the changes which indeed have come about are simply the natural changes of time, the result of the growth of feeling and the changed intellectual outlook of mankind. It is only too true that, while all over the world an astounding revolution has changed the life of men and nations, in Art the change has been to a great extent outside the bounds of nature and beyond the range of reason.

It is not a normal evolution that we have seen in Art. It is not the simple progress of time that is registered on the walls of our galleries. It is something artificial and humiliating that has happened in the generation since the war that broke up the old Europe. This seems evidenced at the Tate Gallery, where we see Lord Leighton's great masterpiece, " The Sea Gave Up The Dead Which Were in it ", the only representative work of his in our national collection, ruthlessly torn from the frame designed for it, and a surrounding moulding substituted, and the picture skied in a small corner gallery. One cannot but feel that the Watts masterpiece would have been relegated to the basement did not the deed of gift make such a course illegal.

Let us be frank about it and confess that Art has been passing through a phase that must be called a craze. The Arts should not be subject to crude whims and passing fancies, as if Art were nothing but a fashion plate. There should be some reliable trusteeship, a safeguarding continuity of judgment somewhere, and where if not to start with at the Academy ?

The nearest approach to the securing of recognition for contemporary " outside " artists was to post in the gallery a list of all such exhibitors. Thus when the Spring Exhibition came to be arranged, their work could be speedily considered and placed.

The French Salon shows greater complaisance to artists by according them permanence of recognition. When a gold medal is awarded, the artist, no matter what his nationality, has a right to exhibit yearly one picture, which cannot be rejected.

Very different is the experience now of artists in England. The Academy appears to be dominated by the few in authority who keep abreast of what is politely called Modern Art. Many fine artists find their work unacceptable when judged by such standards of taste. Were a Romney or a Titian to appear to-day he would stand little chance of appreciation.

The great Sir William Richmond told me that, whenever he was elected on the hanging committee, he would send no pictures of his own, as he said he was there to hang other men's paintings, not his, but now it appears to be an accepted principle that a hanger should look after the hanging of his own work, and that of his friends, as compensation for the time he gives up.

There must always be an element of chance, of course, and the work of the Academy is perhaps full of difficulties. The balance of a wall will often give a work of inferior quality a place better than it deserves, or a poor frame may prevent a good picture from securing the position it merits. Many artists have had their pictures rejected one year and the next year hung and purchased by the nation. Whistler, Gainsborough, Romney, and Alfred Stevens were all subject to these strange happenings, and there is on record the case of a painter whose entire works were rejected one year, though the following year he was elected an Academician. Another case was that of an artist who was asked to take his pictures away because it was discovered that they were painted on a photographic basis ; before the next season came round he, too, was one of the chosen few, with the academic letters to his name.

There has been much improvement in the spacing of pictures, which is now far better than in the old days when they were placed from floor to ceiling. The question has always been difficult. Soon after the end of the Great War the Academy introduced some extreme reforms which had the tragic effect of reducing the number of paintings exhibited at the Summer Exhibition by about a thousand, giving only one line of pictures instead of a double line. It happened that nearly forty men of standing, who had always contributed their best, had to suffer for this innovation, and consequently varnishing day was a sorry and pathetic experience for them. There was much feeling in the matter, but as I was well represented by the Unknown Warrior picture, I felt that I could speak without being counted one of the aggrieved, and I wrote a letter to *The Times* from which I give a few extracts.

Never in the history of British Art has the Royal Academy opened its doors under more tragic circumstances than it does to-day, not because its courts of serenity and beauty open upon a world staggered by industrial paralysation, and held under a spell ominous and relentless, but because artists of reputation and distinction, who have continuously exhibited for ten, twenty, or forty years, have been ruthlessly thrown aside. Frequenters of the Spring Exhibition of the Royal Academy will be at a loss to account for the noticeable gaps of distinguished painters.

The result as one looks round the exhibition is not encouraging or inspiring, but most depressing. Art must be in a very bad way if that is the best that can be done. I understand that about one thousand fewer works are hung this year than is usual. That is to say that the Committee prefer one-third of their red distempered walls to some of the fine pictures which I have seen of the rejected. I cannot think that these gentlemen stayed to count the cost and sacrifice.

Do they realize what these artists must suffer to have for the first time in their lives a year's work condemned? They surely know the damage it must mean to their reputation, to say nothing of their pecuniary losses.

To-day the depression and distress in the art world is very serious. The shortage of gallery space for artists to exhibit their works, on account of the high rents and expenses generally, has never been worse, and yet this is the moment selected to launch this reform.

Naturally everyone prefers a space around one's pictures, and, better still, nothing over it. If in order to do this the hangers seriously felt it was their duty to reject so ruthlessly, they might in all fairness have taken more of this sacrifice upon themselves.

The daily papers inform us that a girl of fifteen has two drawings on the line. On varnishing day I noticed a group of young girls going round, and upon enquiry I found they were exhibitors. I now learn that fifteen girl students of the R.A. Schools have one or more pictures exhibited. We all wish to encourage the young aspirants, but why should these students be placed before matured and able painters?

The result was astonishing. Sir Alfred Temple, Curator of the Guildhall Art Gallery, came forward with the Lord Mayor and Corporation and lent the Guildhall galleries for an exhibition which had the support of the President of the Royal Academy himself, Sir Aston Webb, and on the hanging committee there were three Academicians, Sir Luke Fildes, Mr. Henry Wood, and Mr. Julius Olesson. It was, however, not surprising that a number of the artists did not want it to be known that their pictures had been rejected, nevertheless the exhibition was a great success, and £1,500 worth of pictures were sold.

The newspapers took up the matter and some of them called the R.A. exhibition the Flapper Academy. Photographs of the girls at the Royal Academy Schools appeared with my own photograph superimposed with that of Charles Sims, who was then Keeper of the Royal Academy. At the Academy's July soirée, Sims came up to me in a most friendly way and said, " Salisbury, I want you to come along and meet some friends of mine," leading me through the gay crowd that flocked the gallery on such festive occasions. We arrived in the great Rotunda, where the President and Council had just finished receiving the guests, and I wondered who were the friends I was to meet. Imagine my surprise when I was led up to a bevy of girls with everyone looking on. Fortunately my presence-of-mind did not desert me, though I felt that I had been caught in a trap. Sims introduced me to " The Flappers of the Royal Academy ", and I bowed and said that if their work was as beautiful as they were it must be very good indeed, and that the photographers should certainly have been present ; whereupon the little plot ended pleasantly enough.

A few years ago the Art Critic of *The Times* praised the picture of a newly-elected " modernist" member as being the only work in the exhibition that would fifty years hence truly represent British Art. It was an incredible thing. At the private view I was talking to Lord Plender when the President, Sir William Llewellyn, came up. Lord Plender said, " What are you going to do about that outrageous criticism of *The Times*? Are you going to let it go unchallenged ? " The President said he was in an awkward position and could do nothing, but Lord Plender remarked that something must be done. I offered to write to *The Times*, which I did. The editor was fair enough to give it a good place, which was more than fair in view of the contents of the letter :

Sir,—The President of the Royal Academy, at the Banquet on Thursday last, said that art criticism " often is more of a menace than a help ". The first article on the exhibition of the Royal Academy by your Art Critic constitutes a very serious menace to the whole fabric of the art world. Had such a statement appeared in any paper other than *The Times* it would have been considered a jest, or a reckless expression of a disordered judgment.

At a recent exhibition a hopelessly bad picture came up before the Judging Committee, and there was at once a unanimous shout of "out", but the picture was found to be the work of a member and could not be rejected, so it was hung in a dark corner. Imagine the surprise of the Council when the Press proclaimed the picture to be the saving grace of the exhibition !

At the private view (and at the Arts Club on Saturday) artists, connoisseurs, and art collectors alike were appalled and staggered by the article in your paper. The proprietor of an important gallery in Bond Street, referring to the prophesy by your critic that fifty years hence these pictures would be the few works truly to represent British Art, said it would be better if our civilization collapsed at once than that we should be misrepresented by such works. . . .

Too often in these days the art critic places upon the altars of public opinion false gods dedicated to the cult of ugliness and depravity, and bids us all fall down and worship. It is a very serious menace when the ideals of beauty are confused, Nature called commonplace, and good drawing and craftsmanship ignored.

Taxation and death duties may temporarily kill art patronage, but to foster and confuse the real standards of true and reliable judgment, disregarding the traditions of technical accomplishment, is to paralyse all true inspiration, creating a hopeless outlook and a derelict future for the arts.

The next morning I was overwhelmed with letters and telegrams of approval from artists, though I remember with much amusement how, at a public dinner, certain artists were clearly shy of being seen speaking to the man who had criticized the Art Critic of *The Times*, evidently anxious not to get into the black books of the High Oracle.

Sir John Lavery, writing in 1939, remembered this criticism and spoke of the critic's estimate of the representative of British Art in fifty years. He was writing his life, and asked me for the loan of a book on my work written by Aquila Barber, of which 750 volumes waiting at the binder's were burned in the Battle of Britain. I was able to find a copy for Sir John, and it was an inspiration to receive this letter from him :

MY DEAR SALISBURY,

When I saw your amazing record of achievement lying on Lamb's desk in the Royal Academy, I had no conception of what you have done. Certainly no painter in my time has touched such heights. It may be fifty years before it will be realized that you truly represent British Art.

It's an ill wind that blows no good, and had it not been for trouble in my lumber region I might have missed the privilege of seeing this wonderful work, and of sincerely thanking you for your kindness.

Believe me, gratefully,

JOHN LAVERY.

Truly a great and generous heart. I was deeply touched by his nobility of spirit when he came up to me at a private view and congratulated me on having the commission to paint the Coronation. "I am glad I am not to do it," he said; "you are the man."

Sir John's distinguished paintings both here and in America, brought him much success and honour. He was twenty years my senior, a member of the Royal Academy who enjoyed the inestimable privilege of the friendship of Lord Leighton, G. F. Watts, Burne-Jones, Millais, Sargent, Abbey, Shannon, and all the great men of that glorious Victorian era. I cannot but wonder what they would all think of the decadence that has come upon the Art of which they were such masters.

Not long ago some students were debating the question whether the final standard of judgment on a work of art should be aesthetic or moral : is it possible for a work of art to be good when it inspires bad emotions ? Such a question is the result of the modern critic's praise of the worship of ugliness and obscurity, probably due to the fact that the critic is as much bewildered as the public by the craze of the modernist school, and accepts what he is afraid to reject lest there should be some subtle good in it beyond his understanding. At the beginning of my career I was taught never to look twice at an ugly thing, so that it should not register itself on my mind. The good, the beautiful, and the true were the inspiration of all the great masters, from Cimabue and Giotto to Michael Angelo and Sir Joshua. The Greeks maintained that Art revealed the ascendancy or the degeneration of a people. Such was the view accepted universally until the other day. I well remember what Lord Leighton used to say—that whatever depraved the spirit of a man would drag down his work, and whatever noble fire burned in his soul would burn in his work.

Alas, how far we have wandered from that high ideal ! I cannot help thinking that the present decadence is all part of the degeneracy which has produced the German barbarism now overrunning the world. Is it not merely the craze to be different ? Everybody knows that there are always people with more money than understanding, collectors of curious things like nothing else—anything different in this age when the senseless craze for Difference has become a sort of lunacy. So, no doubt, the thing that began as a queer joke grew up into a solemn farce, becoming more and more melancholy and more and more farcical until a poem became an illiterate thing and a picture became a daub.

And the Critics (the people who make the Immortals) still fearing there was something that they could not see, spoke of the marvellous new school of poets and artists arising among us in this twentieth century, the new genius that could make wonderful stuff of what ordinary mortals cannot understand, could make a poem by writing backwards and cutting up the words like a jigsaw, could make a splash of ink or paint which would go down the ages as a master-piece, with Michael Angelo or Raphael or Milton or Keats.

It was an Editor of *Punch* who said one of the wittiest of things about this stuff that masquerades as Art. These people, said Sir Owen Seaman, thought they would better Nature's best, *but Nature knows a thing or two* ! After all, as another artist said, Art is at its best where it seems to be Nature.

One would have thought the great joke had gone far enough (far enough indeed to become a tragedy), but it would seem that nobody can stop it now. If the critics cease their admiration, who will believe them any more ? If the collectors stop buying, what value will their collections have ? And so it goes on. One modern idea is to strip exhibitions of all religious subjects, which are ridiculed as commonplace. A wartime exhibition of recent acquisitions at the National Gallery—save for a few paintings by Sargent, Burne-Jones, and William Blake presented to the nation and not purchased—included examples of the worship of the incompetent and the ugly. A critic had praised certain works so highly that I felt I must not miss so big a treat, but on arriving I could not but feel that the nation had been insulted and the spirit of the Chantrey Trust betrayed. Here exhibit after exhibit was repellent and lacking in craftsmanship and ideas, and an official showing visitors round, when I challenged him, touched his head as if to suggest that it needed a great intellect to understand such work. Never has been known such impudence as this conceit of the daubing school which would have us believe that Art has been all ugly for a thousand years, and that the sacred flame is theirs.

Do these people ever pause to think of the sin they commit against high heaven by teaching our youth that a botch of paint is Art ? Even the Director of the National Gallery has declared that the modernist school is beyond the understanding of the average man, who can never, he declares, be the ultimate authority on Art, but confuses the issue by saying that " Great Art should be non-representational ". Are we then to assume that Art is forever to be aloof from the world, something the people cannot appreciate ? Why, in that case, open our galleries at all ?

No, it is the Art of the Ages that will endure, not the Daub of a Day. Surely what we have seen in this generation is part of the moral breakdown of the last Great War. Is it not the Nazi idea in Art ? It is a generation since Germany tried to destroy the Bible with its higher criticism, but the Bible remains unshaken. Now a quisling spirit appears to be seeking to break down our idealism in Art and set up a pagan school to worship ugliness. The Nazis, after all, have tried to conquer the world by turning all things upside down, and creating a world without a moral idea or a beautiful thing. They scorn the past and all that it has been. Let us leave them alone in their madness, content that they have lost the Future.

CHAPTER XXIII

CANADA

IT has been my good fortune to count among my friends two Prime Ministers of Canada, the popular Viscount Bennett who has settled down among us and delights us with his speeches on our national modesty and our universal Empire ; and Mr. Mackenzie King, the Liberal leader of our first and greatest self-governing Dominion, Prime Minister of a greater area of the American Continent than President Roosevelt has beneath his sway. With Mr. Mackenzie King we had lunch just before the war at Government House, the guests of Lord Tweedsmuir, the brilliant Governor-General whose death has been so grievous a loss to us all. Afterwards we spent the week-end at Kingsmere, the Prime Minister's beautiful country home.

On this visit to Canada I had the precious opportunity of seeing the Canadian sculptor who has enshrined the spirit of the Dominion in Art, for we called on the Allwards at York Mills, Ontario. The last time we had met had been at Vimy Ridge, where Walter Allward was putting the final touches to his great monument to Canada's dead. For fourteen years he had worked in London bringing this wonderful conception into being. Only those who have seen it can realize how magnificent it is, crowning the famous hill round which for so long surged the emotions of two continents. Here Canada's youth died that freedom might live and nobly has Walter Allward immortalized their memory in stone as John McCrae immortalized them in words. He has built tall pylons wrought with figures of valour and courage surmounted by the triumphant figure of Hope gazing into space. What a solace and inspiration to all who behold it ! Never shall I forget the day I stood gazing on it with the great sculptor from whose genius this mighty monument has come into existence. Dark storm-clouds were gathering, and suddenly the sun shone and set the monument in dramatic relief, Nature seeming to crown this majestic wonder with a glory of her own.

It was with the thought of this great tribute to Canada that we left for Ottawa, where we were to be deeply stirred by the Prime Minister's account of the visit of the King and Queen. Never had the Dominion seen such days since she had come into her imperial heritage. What struck me particularly was the scene at the Parliament House, where the King and Queen stood on the steps with the Prime Minister just behind them, the King saluting Canada, and the great crowds cheering themselves hoarse just in front. It was a moment for any painter's brush, and though I had not been there I was fortunately able to obtain a moving picture which gave me all the material I wanted. I had recent studies of the King, the Queen, and the Prime Minister, and was able to sketch the grand archway approach to the Parliament House, with the carved lion and unicorn holding the national flags at the top of the flight of steps. On my return home, therefore, I was able to begin on the picture. The Queen's dress was unfortunately not available, but Her Majesty lent me its beautiful gold train, with pearl embroidery.

I made up my mind to send the painting to Mr. King as a token of my admiration of his work in promoting understanding between the Empire and the United States. Before it could be despatched, however, the Queen asked that she might see it at Buckingham Palace, and while it was there the B.B.C. announced the unexpected arrival of Mr. King in London. This happy circumstance prompted me to spring the surprise upon him while he was here, so two days before he left London, we found him at the Dorchester Hotel, busy preparing the speech he was to deliver at the Mansion House the next day, which so greatly moved the nation when it was broadcast.

It has always astonished me that these public men, on whose shoulders rests such grave responsibility, and whose lives are absorbed by countless engagements, can find time to prepare these great speeches, sometimes epoch-making utterances upon which the world hangs with breathless expectancy. My wife and I found Mr. King surrounded with papers, but he gave us his time as if he had nothing to do, and read us parts of his speech. We went to Buckingham Palace and saw the picture together, and Mr. King then gave me a sitting for his portrait. He was delighted with the painting of the King and Queen and said he could not keep it himself but would give it to Canada, where he would like it sent as soon as possible. The High Commissioner, Mr. Vincent Massey, despatched it to Ottawa, and a few weeks later I received this cablegram from the Prime Minister, who was then home again ;

Your wonderful gift arrived Ottawa safely. It is now at Laurier House, and in perfect condition. It is truly magnificent. I shall, before the year is out, take the appropriate moment to have it hung

in our Houses of Parliament, where you may be sure it will for all
time be a treasured national possession.

                                                    MACKENZIE KING.

When the picture had been placed in position I received this further
cable, dated December 30, 1941 :

Your magnificent painting of their Majesties at the entrance to
Houses of Parliament was hung to-day in the main entrance to the
Hall of Fame, which is the central feature of the interior of the Parliament Buildings. To-day, December 29, is the twentieth anniversary
of the day on which I assumed office for the first time as leader of a
Liberal administration and Prime Minister of Canada. The placing
of the painting in its present position in our Halls of Parliament
will also always be associated with the arrival to-day in the capital
of Canada of the Prime Minister of the United Kingdom, the Right
Honourable Winston Churchill, who to-morrow is to address the
members of both Houses of Parliament in a worldwide broadcast.
To my personal thanks I should now like to add the thanks of the
Government and people of Canada for your memorable historic
gift, which more than ever has become a symbol as well as a bond of
Empire unity.

                                                    MACKENZIE KING.

I still recall with delight my first meeting with Mr. King, who
came for a sitting while he was in London for the Coronation. On
the Sunday morning he rang to ask if he could call with a friend,
and by a happy chance there was with us at the time Mrs. Andrew
Carnegie, a friend he had not seen for years. As we walked into
the studio the mystic words escaped his lips, " Like as the hart desireth
the water brooks ", and our conversation turned on humility, Mr.
King quoting some beautiful lines which I was moved to write
down, these : " True humility always sits on the threshold of power ;
you cannot attain true power till you cross the threshold where
humility sits. If you cross to power any other way it does not last."

The next day I received from him a wonderful letter written as
he was leaving for Canada, in which he described how he had felt
he would like to go to some service on his last Sunday night in England, and, being fond of the old church in the Strand, had gone to
St. Clement Danes. Imagine his surprise when, for the first lesson,
the rector had read Psalm 42, beginning " Like as the hart desireth

the water brooks, so longeth my soul after thee, O God ". The second lesson was from St. Paul's Epistle to the Romans, with its reference to humility, and when the preacher gave out the text it was, " Be ye clothed with humility ". So struck was he with this coincidence that he felt he must write to tell me of it, but the coincidence was not yet complete, for it was to be crowned when next I visited Canada and went with the Prime Minister to church at Ottawa, to hear the opening sentence of the service : " Like as the hart desireth the water brooks . . ."

Could there ever be a finer link of friendship ? I could not but feel that in this realm of time, with the oceans ebbing and flowing between the centres of activity, the timeless tides of the spirit break in mystic sequence, revealing a deep current that for ever links all friendship, defying time and space.

CHAPTER XXIV

A PORTRAIT GALLERY

ONE of the most beautiful portraits Sargent ever painted was that of the Duchess of Portland, who, of course, gave him a wonderful subject. It was delightful to see the picture in its setting at Welbeck Abbey; for vigorous handling and brush work in all its simplicity it must always remain a masterpiece. I was much interested to hear from the duchess how the portrait was painted, and how, after sitting for three weeks, while Sargent had worked hard, she came down one morning and found the canvas wrecked. Sargent was so displeased with it that he had put his foot through it. When she saw what had happened she wept, but Sargent assured her that the time was not lost, for he had learnt how to do it and would start again. This he did, for the perpetual enjoyment of all who see his work. Philip de Laszlo has a room of portraits all to himself at Welbeck, which it was good to see on our visit to that historic house.

De Laszlo was to dine with me at the Glaziers' Company's banquet at the Mansion House, when the Duke of Kent was chief guest, soon after our return, and I called for him at his studio in Fitzjohn's Avenue. Mrs. de Laszlo said, " Do take care of him; he is not at all well." We were rather late, but in his enthusiasm he would insist that I should go into the studio to see his latest portrait of the Duke of Connaught. It was a masterpiece, and I said, " Your last portrait is your best ! " Alas, it was only too true that it was his last, for he never went into his studio again. That night he was taken ill and within a few days he died.

His quick portraits stand unrivalled, and if he had painted only the portrait of the Marquis of Reading he would rank as a great master. Few men have had such unparalleled success, and few have suffered such shameful and unmerited abuse. For his nationality he suffered terribly, especially during the last war; mainly through his open-hearted simplicity. We made a pact to paint each other at work, but, alas, death intervened.

The County of Wiltshire wished to commemorate the great public service rendered to it during forty-five years by the Marquis of Bath, and this pleasant commission, coming during the war in 1941,

FIELD-MARSHAL J. C. SMUTS.

Sir Henry Wood

took me down to the ancestral estate of Longleat, one of the outstanding homes of England for four hundred years, a majestic place eight hundred feet round, with over a thousand lights in its mass of stone windows, and domes, cupolas, and sculptures which make it a memorable spectacle. Longleat is rightly famous, and known to many visitors from far and wide. Here I was to paint the marquis, for his town house had been destroyed and mine was out of action, so we sat with the stately portraits by Holbein, Reynolds, Gainsborough, Godfrey Kneller, Sir William Richmond, G. F. Watts, and Orpen on the walls about us. The County Council wanted a full-length portrait of the marquis in the Robes of the Garter, to hang in a panel designed by the architect on the grand entrance staircase of the beautiful county hall at Trowbridge.

Rarely have I met a man so nobly modest and retiring as the marquis. The idea of being painted in the Garter Robes shocked him beyond measure. I had had a slight indication of this sensitiveness in a letter from him, in which he said that his robes were in London and it might be impossible to obtain them. I was not going to run any risk, so I managed to obtain the loan of a set of Garter Robes, and after making a number of studies in an ordinary suit I at last suggested that the marquis should put on these robes, pointing out that the distinction was the pride of the county, and that it would give me a chance to make a decorative portrait. After much persuasion he donned the robes, I made new sketches, and the portrait came magnificently, so that he agreed that if the committee wished it he would sit like that. We arranged a committee meeting, and it happened, after all, that they preferred a profile sketch of the marquis in a frock coat.

Longleat was at this time in the occupation of the Royal School of Bath, with three hundred girls whose school had been taken over by the Government. Lord Bath kept three rooms for himself, which we shared. Mine was a stately room twenty feet high, with beautiful brocade-velvet walls and a Tudor portrait over the mantelpiece. But it was rather cold weather that autumn and we had no fire. The old marquis (nearly 80) was a veritable spartan, faithful to the stern demands of war, though the fuel economy campaign had not yet been thought of.

One afternoon he took me over the house and into the Long Gallery, which was disarranged and filled with beds. Remembering all the beautiful rooms I have seen in our palaces, and in the great houses of Florence and Venice and Rome, I could recall nothing that gave me more pleasure than the thought of what this noble gallery must look like when in perfect order, with its tapestries and Old Masters on the walls. I said, " I must see this when it is put back," and Lord Bath made a heartbreaking answer. " It will never be put back," he said. " I shall not be able to afford to live here. Taxation makes it impossible. At nineteen and sixpence in the pound I have nothing left, with all my responsibilities and liabilities." It was not possible to resist the tragic pathos of all this, or to avoid the feeling that it seemed a poor reward for a man nearing his seventy-ninth birthday, who had devoted his whole life to the service of the country and the State, and whose son and heir was at that moment at the front in Libya.

Yet no word of complaint came from him. He accepted the situation heroically. On the Sunday we went to the village church together, he reading the lesson, and as we came out an old farmer hobbling along on crutches was trying to get down the steps leading from the church. Lord Bath, seeing him, walked forward with a helping hand, and when the farmer was safely down he turned and said, " When you are like this, Sir, I shall be most pleased to help you." It was pleasant at another time, as we walked in the park, to see the exquisite courtesy of the lord of this great estate.

When the portrait was sufficiently completed it was placed in the Great Hall for all in the house to see. It was no small task to be worthy of that great house with its artistic treasures, and I could not help remembering that, ten years before, Orpen had painted one of his very best portraits of Lord Bath in evening dress, with the sash of the Garter giving a charming slash of colour. Time alone will pass judgment ; all I can be happy about is that on that Sunday my portrait stood the test.

The visitor to Longleat is generally interested in the little chapel which is part of its story. The great house and the little chapel are the sights of the Wiltshire village of Horningsham. When the house was being built, by a company of artisans brought from Scotland, there was no place in England for Nonconformists, and Sir John Thynne, who had married an heiress, rich beyond the dreams of avarice, built the workpeople a chapel with a thatched roof. It stands to-day as it stood then, away from the house and still the Nonconformist chapel for the village folk, the oldest in England, for it was set up twenty years before the Spanish Armada. For nearly four centuries this little chapel has been the scene of worship, and on the walls are still the wooden pegs on which the Puritans must have hung their big hats.

One of the loveliest families imaginable became my little models, the Congleton Group of seven children, Lady Congleton also coming into the picture, with her favourite St. Bernard. It was a great chance, and after I had been down to their beautiful home in the New Forest, and taken sketches in the garden, they all came to the studio for sittings. After serious work we had great romps together, giving one another toboggan rides with a rug over the polished floor.

Mr. John W. Davis, the American Ambassador in London, sat for me for a portrait asked for by the Law Society of New York, but Mrs. Davis liked it so much that she would not part with it, and I had the pleasure of painting another.

An American friend, Mr. George F. Baker, son of the wonderful Mr. Baker whom I had painted eight times in New York, wrote to me and said the portrait I had painted of him was hung in the attic, as neither his friends nor his wife liked it. This was a thorough disappointment to me, after my success with his father, and it was the first I had heard of it. I wrote telling him how sorry I was, and saying that if he would bring the portrait to London I would correct it or paint a new one. I received a cable saying he would be in London the next week, and I cabled him to bring a dark business suit with him. He duly arrived with the portrait and I saw at once that I could not improve on it. What disappointed him was that he was in a lounge suit. I started on a new portrait, and it went splendidly. When I put my palette down he made a remark which much impressed me. He was President of the First National Bank in America, and he said, " You should not be taxed as a business man, as I am. I sit here and come to Europe and my income goes on ; you put your palette down or go for a holiday and work stops, and your income is cut off."

As he was very anxious to have the approval of his brilliant sister, Mrs. St. George, then living at Campden Hill, she came along and saw the two portraits, begging him to give her the one from the New York attic. He was naturally delighted to hear this, and when she said she had not a criticism to make he replied, " If that portrait is good enough for my sister it is good enough for my family," and he took both portraits back at the end of the week. On his return home he sent me a charming letter telling me that all his friends were delighted with the new portrait, and that he was pleased to be thus handed down. It was only just in time, for soon after this he was on a cruise on his yacht in the Pacific when he was taken suddenly ill, and died at sea.

Orpen's portrait of Mrs. St. George is an absolute masterpiece, and in my opinion among the artist's finest achievements. She is wearing a beautiful black and white dress which Frans Hals or Velasquez would have revelled in painting. She was very proud of her wonderful collection of Orpen sketches. Alas, with the battering of Campden Hill the house and treasures are dispersed and she has passed the Rubicon of Time.

I had rather an interesting experiment with a portrait the year following the exhibition of the Jubilee picture at the Academy. The treasurer having told me that the picture had greatly added to the gate-money, I thought they really owed me something, so felt that I might safely send in a picture without much risk of its being rejected. It happened that I was requested by an ambitious business man to paint the portrait of his fashionable wife " for the Academy ", but this I told him I could not do, as the chances were ten to one that it would be rejected if I sent it in. He, however, would not accept a refusal, thinking I was joking, and at last I agreed that if he would take the sporting chance I would send it. The portrait was sent in and I was right ; it came back.

Later in the year I received a lawyer's letter from this man demanding back half the fee as he considered the rejection had depreciated the value of the portrait ! I, of course, determined to ignore him, but my solicitors advised me to risk no trouble with such a man as I was hard at work on the Coronation picture. So, regarding it as the case of an adventurer in search of publicity, I let the matter go and paid up. I have never ceased to regret my surrender to such a vulgar claim. What an amusing day the Law Courts lost by my decision ! The picture would have been put up in court. The beautiful lady would have faced the witness-box, the President of the Royal Academy might have been called as a witness, and my little grandson Richard, aged four, would probably have gone into the witness-box to say that he saw the portrait on the easel, and, stepping back to look at it, said, " I like it ; does she not look a pet ? " It seems a shame that such a comedy should have been lost to the courts.

Mr. Pierpont Morgan sat for me four times, on both sides of the Atlantic. It was a hot summer's day when he came to me in London, and as I had the window open I asked him if he felt a draught. He said that as a banker he was used to drafts, to which I replied

J. PIERPONT MORGAN.

Dr. Nicholas Murray Butler, President of Columbia University.

James Gamble Rogers.

that there is such a thing as an overdraft. Sir Bernard Partridge's sister-in-law, hearing this story, said it should be in *Punch* and sent it to Sir Bernard, who, however, wrote the next morning to say that they had had the joke four years before ! We never know where a bit of humour comes from.

Mr. Morgan was the most punctual of sitters. Each time he arrived on the tick of the appointed hour. His friend, Dr. Murray Butler, was more punctual still, for he once came half an hour early when I was sitting down to a sandwich, an apple, and a glass of milk. The renowned President of Columbia University was shown in, and, seeing my lunch, exclaimed, " An apple and a glass of milk are a passport to immortality ; I always have it." I do not think it is his diet, but his wonderful brain and his solid achievements confirm his passport to immortality.

In one year it fell to my lot to paint two strangely contrasting religious leaders, Cardinal Hayes of New York and General Higgins of the Salvation Army. I painted the cardinal in New York, in the fortieth storey of the Waldorf Tower, looking down on the beautiful architectural structure of St. Patrick's Cathedral and the cardinal's house. It was arranged that I should use the cardinal's reception rooms as a studio, as his time was so occupied. He was a glorious subject in his robe and ermine cape. His chaplain continued the sitting for the robe, which all at once looked so well on him that I begged him not to move even if he turned to stone. For over three hours he nobly sat without disturbing a single fold. I put my palette down once because my hand was numb, but the chaplain sat on like a stoic while I completed the robe.

General Higgins I painted in London for the Salvation Army. I felt that both these men, so vastly different, had spiritual serenity. It seemed to me that they would agree on eighteen points out of twenty on religious questions, but on the last two would probably disagree to the death. How unfathomable is the mystery of the human mind !

Mrs. John Crompton, the beloved survivor of the great master, in her ninety-second year, sat to me in his studio, and nothing could have added to the composition of life's work and endeavour than that this portrait should be numbered by general consent with my best portraits.

CHAPTER XXV

NINETEEN-FORTY

NINETEEN-FORTY, we are all agreed, was our year of supreme emotion, and none of us are likely to forget it. One of the hours I remember in it had nothing to do with the war. It was at one of the City Halls in London, where General Evangeline Booth was attending a farewell reception on her retirement. Lord Willingdon, who had lately returned from Delhi, paid a great tribute to the wonderful work of the Salvation Army among the outcast tribes of India. Lord Simon spoke of her great work, and the General herself made a most moving and eloquent speech. Never have I been among an audience more moved, or listened to a more eloquent peroration.

The occasion was broadcast and, turning to the Master of Ceremonies, she whispered, " How long have I got ? "—" Three minutes," he said, and she threw her notes away and proceeded to describe the passing of her father, whose face was turned towards the setting sun.

She found him one evening in his study, weak and helpless. The window looked out across the open landscape, and there was a beautiful sunset. What a Turner she painted in words in one of those three minutes ! High above the golden glow in the western sky were fleecy white clouds in trailing splendour like a choir of angels, and she called to her father and asked if he could see this glory. " No," he said, " I cannot see," so she held him up and led him nearer to the window. But it was in vain. " No, my dear," he said, " I cannot see the sunset, but I shall see the sunrise ! "

In Sir Giles Scott's fine memorial building at Denmark Hill is a series of portraits of the heads of the Salvation Army, and I felt that in such a year as this they would not dream of commissioning a painting of their retiring General, so I offered to present Evangeline Booth's portrait before she left for America if I could be sure that in doing so I was not taking a commission from another artist. This inspired woman came and gave me sittings the week before she was to sail. She sat holding the Army's marching flag which the women of America had presented to her. Her conversation was most illuminating, and as she stood in the studio she would get more and more engrossed in the story she was telling and gradually move towards the easel, until she realized the situation with a laugh.

The day before she sailed she came for the final sitting, and when it was over she remained quiet for a little while and then said, " Could we have a little prayer ? " The three of us knelt down, and the beauty and inspiration of her prayer I shall never forget. I know now what Jacob meant when he said, " Let us place a stone here, for this is none other than the Gate of Heaven ". Very rare are the approaches to those infinite realms of the spirit that outstrip transitory time.

As the Battle of the Atlantic was becoming more ominous day by day she was not enjoying the prospect of the hazardous crossing. The new General and the Commissioners were allowed to go on board to see her off at Liverpool, and the ordeal was tense and trying in the state-room put at her service. The shipping companies show high honour to these workers for the good of humanity, taking them wherever they wish to go free of all expense. Just before they were to say farewell the little group in the state-room knelt down, she praying for a safe voyage, but adding that if God wished to take her home would he take her in a decent way. The very humour of it was a relief in so tense a moment.

I had already painted a portrait of General Higgins on his retirement, and it was rather curious to be told concerning that portrait that the Salvation Army had obtained a list of painters and said, " Let us apply our test and see if any of these men have ever shown any sympathy with our work." Oddly enough, mine was the only name that responded to the test !

General Carpenter and Commissioner Cunningham, with Mr. Hugh Redwood (who has paid such homage to the Army in his books) called upon me to enquire if I would consider painting a fresco for the entrance hall of the Salvation Army building known as the Goodwill Centre at Hoxton. The subject they suggested was expressed in a chapter in Hugh Redwood's book, God in the Slums, a remarkable story of rescue and sacrifice on the part of these heroic salvation workers. After describing the incident, he says, " In a moment of elevation I saw the footsteps of the Redeemer on the pavement of Westminster." The beauty of this idea, however, could not be translated into a painting.

The only way I could shadow forth their idea for this picture in the slums was to take as the central motive the legend of St. Christopher carrying the infant Christ across the dark river. This I designed

in a vesica of gold symbolical of the presence of Christ, with a reflected
rainbow passing across the group and giving a sense of mystery, while
the form of the Christ Child is seen through the colours of the rainbow. On a scroll designed as a nimbus are the words " Inasmuch
as ye did it unto one of the least of these my brethren, ye did it unto
Me ", and on either side are two groups illustrating the work of
the Salvation Army, one of the rescue of a cripple, the other showing
the reading of the Gospel in the street.

One of the sisters brought to my studio, as East End models,
a poor old woman and an aged cripple. This caused endless trouble
for this noble worker, and I tried to make her some small recom-
pense, but she refused all recognition : so recalling what the Commissioner of the Booth Memorial College told me when speaking
of the new candidates who entered for life work in the Army ; he
had yet to meet the man or the woman who once mentioned the
question of money for their work. In these days life has tragically
proved that neither people nor nations can seek shelter and security
under the cloak of neutrality, or by closing the eyes to suffering,
and above the fresco I wrote the words, " Faith is Equipment, not
Escape ".

During the first months of Hitler's War, as the serious menace
to our shipping developed and our lifeline across the Atlantic was in
such grave danger, shipping was a subject exercising all minds. In
February 1940 the King visited the Chamber of Shipping, the occasion
being the first Council Meeting in their new building. Mr. Robertson
Gibb, the President, with Sir Philip Haldin and Sir Vernon Thomson,
came to arrange for a picture, but it transpired that the whole thing
would be quite informal, the King not coming as an Admiral, as
had been expected. I felt that this would spoil any chance of a good
picture, but they urged me to attend, hoping for the best.

The King simply walked into the hall and one by one all the past
presidents were presented to him. This made an interesting but
not exciting conversation piece, and I saw reasonable possibilities as
my sketches developed. The chief figures all gave me sittings,
Mr. Robertson Gibb, Sir Philip Haldin, Sir Vernon Thomson, Lord
Essendon, Lord Runciman, Lord Rotherwick, Sir Thomas Royden,
Sir Arthur Sutherland, Mr. W. A. Souter, Sir William Currie, and
Mr. Philip Runciman. Sir Philip Haldin, who was President when
the picture was completed, presented it to the Chamber of Shipping
at a full meeting of the Council, and the occasion was interesting in
view of the grave war conditions. It was a historic experience to

HIS EMINENCE CARDINAL HAYES.

THE SIGNATURE OF THE ANGLO-SOVIET TREATY IN LONDON, MAY 26TH, 1942.

meet these men who go down to the sea in ships and do business in great waters. In many talks on vital subjects I was deeply impressed by their mutual respect for each other's accomplishments, heads of the great shipping lines that encircle the world, keen business rivals yet with never a word of disparagement or criticism of one another.

In August of this year there appeared in *The Times* a letter from a young airman to his mother, the beauty of which so impressed me that I felt I should like to paint the youth's portrait as a comfort for the mother. I spoke to Mr. Kent, the manager of *The Times*, to see if there were any photographs available. He was delighted with the idea and managed to secure three snapshots the mother had taken of her boy. They were very anxious not to disclose the name of the airman, as the letter had been quoted in every paper in the land and they wished to protect the mother from any trying publicity.

The writer of the letter became known as the Unknown Airman and on the portrait I painted in a *cartouche* his famous words : " The life of one man can only be justified by the measure of his sacrifice." In the last war the spirit of youth was expressed in immortal poetry by Rupert Brooke ; in this war it is expressed in deathless prose by this young airman.

The day arrived when *The Times* arranged for the mother to come to the studio to see the portrait, a very trying ordeal for her but a moving and privileged experience for me. Happily, she was deeply satisfied with the portrait, which was all that I could wish. I feel that I may give this letter from the mother of such a noble son :

" I have thought long to try and find words to express my thanks and appreciation of your wonderful portrait of Vivian.

Perhaps I cannot do better than say that he really seemed to be in your spiritual house awaiting me. Your divination of a soul of someone you have never seen is genius indeed. I should think you must believe that man is not a body possessing a soul, but a soul possessing a body.

These words are by Dr. Percy Dearmer, and I found them in a small Confirmation Book given to Vivian at school, one of several small treasures that have been returned to me.

For some reason hard to express, that picture has very much comforted me. He seems to be about me again more clearly as I knew him, and I am humbly grateful to you. I think it should be widely seen."

The portrait was exhibited at the Royal Society of Portrait Painters, where it must have been a comfort to the mother to see so many distinguished people drawn towards it. It pleased me also at this exhibition to find Viscount Bennett closely studying my portrait of Dr. Posnett and declaring it one of the best portraits he had ever seen.

All this time the Battle of Britain was raging, and the time came when we had to give up the idea of sleeping in our bedrooms. We arranged to sleep in the strong-room, made nearly perfect with timber reinforcements. This proved to be a good dormitory for servants and all the rest of us, my daughters and their husbands, who had had to retreat from their own homes.

The idea of the dugout room was to have a comfortable time together, reading, knitting, with refreshments and tea, reserves of food, and wet blankets in case of gas. We had two ways of escape, and stirrup pumps, sand, water, and pickaxes all ready. But life like this night after night, week after week, brought only exhaustion. It was a little sleep and then the siren, and an all-night sitting, so that I had finally to issue orders for all to be in bed at ten o'clock. For a few weeks of this nightly bombardment naval guns were stationed outside the house, making sleep impossible, and it became so evident that this could not go on that after one intensely bad and hazardous night we decided to get out of London, and found rooms at Ivinghoe.

At first the men folk divided up, my two sons-in-law, Douglas Crichton and Leonard Norris, staying from Monday until Friday while I took the week-ends. On our worst night flares lit up the house like day and a press man told me the next morning that he was outside and felt sure the enemy were taking photographs, as no bombs were dropped. The next night, however, incendiaries rained all around us, setting fire to three houses. It was a terrible experience, sparks flying all round. My 300-year-old oak trees caught fire and one incendiary fell within six feet of the house, but was soon put out. Then an oil-bomb fell about fifty yards away on the heath.

The fire engines worked constantly and I asked if they could not stop the fire in the trees, for it was terrible to see them burning ; but the houses were the first thing. The hose pipes, however, had a slight crack which sent up a fine fan-shape spray of water into the trees and so cut off the fire from spreading.

One night my brother Edgar was staying with me when the sirens went at ten o'clock, and the guns were going all the time.

We settled down, however, to the order of the night and tried to sleep while the guns made the walls shake and the bombs made the foundations rock. At three in the morning a high explosive fell so near that we thought the house must be struck; the strong-room rocked like a ship on an angry sea. I hardly dared to explore, for I thought there would not be a ceiling or a chimney standing, but we found no dust on the floor, and the doors opened without any obstruction. Going out into the darkness in the dim light I fancied that the chimney stacks had gone, but, by a miracle, no damage was done. We could not discover where the bomb had fallen, but only one pane of glass was broken, and this apparently by a stone shot up from the ground. In the morning we found a huge crater twenty yards from the front door.

A week or so after this a division of the Royal Artillery was stationed on the heath in front of the house. The captain said they were thinking of using the crater as a dump for storing ammunition, as in the fortunes of war a bomb never fell in the same place twice; it was one chance in a million. In three weeks I had an urgent call to say that a time-bomb had fallen in the same hole, and everyone was ordered out of the house. The millionth chance had happened. They fortunately had had time to remove the ammunition. The bomb fell at eight o'clock at night and exploded at eleven the next morning without any damage to the house.

Once, when landmines were dropped destroying the Bull and Bush public-house on the Heath and Jack Straw's Castle of Dick Turpin fame, the concussion and the blast sucked out doors and windows and destroyed the dome light of my studio. On the first occasion I had the damage restored, but as it happened a second time it will now be left until the war is victoriously ended.

One of the last portraits painted at Sarum Chase before the studio was closed from September 1940 for two years, was of that lovable genius, Arthur Mee, who was just celebrating his Jubilee as a journalist. What an accomplishment! What a profound store of knowledge and facts he had accumulated, what a wealth of wisdom it was his to pass on to humanity! He stood a veritable hero to the youth of the world. His own personal books, apart from his educators and encyclopedias, have long since passed the million circulation mark. It has been calculated that he sent out into the world twenty-five thousand million printed pages. I have never met such a worker. His letters to me were often dated Midnight on his Kent hilltop. What treasures he showered upon the world!

His death, most lamentable, occurred while this volume was passing through the press. Deploring his loss, I can but express my confident belief that his great work will endure, and his spirit abide, a lasting light and inspiration.

Ivinghoe, where now we were settled in search of peace, is the place made famous by Sir Walter Scott's romantic novel Ivanhoe. It is a beautiful village under the bleak Chiltern Hills, its thirteenth-century Gothic church standing picturesquely in the heart of it. On the hillside the famous gliding club carried out its exercises in time of peace, and close by is Whipsnade. In the valley the names of the neighbouring walks all suggest history and romance. The bridle-path from our gate led to where the ancient Britons in the time of Boadicea continued their struggles against the Roman invaders. The enemy were encamped and in the darkness of the night the women of Ivinghoe stole out armed with knives and slew the army while they slept.

We found a bungalow with a lovely view across the country looking to Mentmore, Lord Rosebery's home. The bungalow offered me the chance of a studio in a long summerhouse at the end of the garden, a place forty feet long, ten feet wide, and six to eight feet high by the windows, which run the whole length. This I converted into a good workroom, and here, very soon setting to work again, I painted " The Briefing of an Air Squadron ", a picture too big for the space in which it was painted. To turn it round I had to open the door and take it outside. Obviously a great studio is not an actual necessity. I remember that Herkomer painted his masterpiece, " The Last Muster ", in an attic.

The Handley Page Company, wishing to present a portrait to Sir George Nelson, head of the British Electric Company, in recognition of their collaboration in producing Hampden and Halifax bombers, Mr. Nelson wished to have a portrait of his wife, who became my first Ivinghoe sitter. Sir Frederick Handley Page also asked me to paint the portraits of two V.C's, Flight-Lieutenant Learoyd and Sergeant Hannah, as he wished to present them to their squadrons. Both were flying his Hampden bomber planes.

It was arranged that they should sit at the aerodrome, and early one winter morning, just after blackout, I set off for a 120-mile run, driving myself. As I neared Northampton all the cars passing me were covered with snow, warning me what to expect farther north, and, sure enough, I soon came into ice and snow. But with a reliable car I arrived in time to meet Group Captain Walmisley and to set my studio before dark. The studio was a bedroom, the light was very poor, and the weather was bad, but the brave fellows started sitting at nine and went on till seven. The Group Captain asked if I would mind letting the men see the portraits in the mess, and their enthusiasm was gratifying. The officers told me they had not heard one hostile criticism, except that Learoyd should have been painted in his worn-out tunic.

The modesty of these heroic souls was too wonderful for me ; I could not get them to talk of their adventures and achievements. I said to Sergeant Hannah, " I thought your face was badly burnt ? " He said, " All the skin except my forehead is artificial." But I could see no scars. He said he had been treated by a new process, his being only the third experiment, but for three days they feared he would lose his sight and so the treatment was not to be used again. Apart from anything else it was a wonderfully artistic feat, for as far as I could see the expression of the face was not distorted in the least.

It was an interesting experience to join the men in the mess, meeting young men from all parts of the Empire, and joining in their concerts at night. ENSA gave us a fine evening ; some items could not have been better on a first-class London stage.

The Adjutant said I ought to see a Briefing, but each day it was postponed, as the weather was too bad for flying, so eventually they staged a Briefing for me.

They were in their blue uniforms and in full flying rig. Never in so short a time have I collected so much material. I decided to paint a large picture of the subject and present it to the aerodrome to fit the panel over the fireplace in the officer's mess, on a five-feet-by-ten canvas.

One afternoon while I was thinking out the idea a visitor called, and before he went he asked if I had seen a poem by Stephen Spender with these last two lines :

Born of the sun, they travelled a short while towards the sun,
And left the vivid air signed with their honour.

I told him the lines were just what I wanted, so I painted them in a *cartouche* under the R.A.F. Eagle and Crown, to be for ever part of the picture. For the title I proposed to use the Prime Minister's famous words, " Never have so many owed so much to so few ", and when the men of the crew room, looking at my sketch, saw these words, one of them said, " That is what I write home and tell my people, asking them to send a cheque on account ! "

When the picture was formally presented at the aerodrome I reminded them of this bit of wit, and thanked them for enabling me, by this picture, to " send them a cheque on account ". Possibly, as the picture is reproduced in colour for the benefit of the R.A.F. Benevolent Fund, it may give others a chance to help to reduce their overdraft !

It is exhilarating to meet these fine airmen at an operational station, so modest and apparently so care-free. A man feels that vast height and infinite space has entered into their very nature, much as we find with the men of the Navy who sail on boundless tides towards limitless horizons. Do we wonder that the young airman could write to his mother : " The Universe is so vast and ageless that the life of one man is only justified by the measure of his sacrifice."

If I were starting life again as an artist I should want a studio with wings. The men who mount the skies see the vision, see the perfect rainbow in all its beauty ; we on the earth see as through a glass, darkly.

One Sunday morning from an R.A.F. station I heard the Commanding Officer read the wonderful words from the eighth chapter of Romans, that neither height nor depth can separate us from the love and power that control the Universe—so beautifully read by this commander of the skies that he gave the words a new meaning, the compass of which could hardly have been in the mind of St. Paul. Also I came upon this poem by Pilot Officer Magee, which I cannot refrain from giving here :

> High in the sunlit silence, hovering there,
> I've chased the shouting wind along, and flung
> My eager craft through footless halls of air.
>
> Up, up the long delirious burning blue.
> I've topped the windswept heights with easy grace
> Where never lark nor even eagle flies ;
> And, while with silent lifting mind I've trod
> The high untrespassed sanctity of space,
> Put out my hand and touched the Face of God.

Art has, through the immortal Leonardo, a link with the Royal Air Force, for he designed the aeroplane. Seeing an eagle mount in the heights, into the rare atmosphere where it was able to maintain itself, and watching a ship sailing proudly over the waves, he said that man with powerful wings could become Lord of the Winds and conquer space. Thus we all salute the men of the R.A.F. :

> · Masters of the Heights,
> Lords of the Winds,
> Conquerors of Space !

Many of the dear lads who sat for the picture of the Briefing have surrendered their precious lives to the great cause of Freedom since I was at the aerodrome. What a cruel war ! While writing this I received a letter from the wife of an airman in the picture telling me that he had lost his life in an operational flight over Germany, and his little son of six insists on kissing my portrait of his Daddy, saying " Good night, Daddy " as he does so. The little fellow cannot understand why airmen and soldiers do not get leave from heaven, his mother says.

Yes, these valiant crusaders of the skies have by their sacrifice entered the Briefing Room of the eternal ages, where the Master of all great heroes on indestructible wings will set their course anew. They have, in the glowing phrase of Shelley, " Outsoared the shadow of our night ".

CHAPTER XXVI

THE ANGLO-SOVIET TREATY

W E owe it to statesmanship of the loftiest, most imaginative
order that the Allied nations have been associated by
community of ideals and interests in a mighty confedera-
tion of peoples, comrades in arms, the hope and beacon of a distracted and anguished world. Across seas and continents hands
of brotherhood are clasped in steadfast understanding.

On the high seas the Atlantic Charter came into being, a noble
instrument of faith and purpose, charged with potential benefit to
mankind. Here for the advantage of all men of goodwill, whatever
their nationality, is a consummation of Magna Carta, that ancient
testament of the rights and liberties of Englishmen, sons of the Mother
of Freedom.

No more salutary commentary could have attended this new
dedication of ideals than the Anglo-Soviet Treaty of Alliance. His
Majesty's Government decided to signalize the execution of the
famous agreement with Russia, our valiant and stalwart Ally, by a
commemorative picture depicting the signing of the Treaty at the
Foreign Office on May 26, 1942, and on March 12, 1943, I was
officially invited and honoured with instructions to execute this
important picture, with a request that it should be completed
in time to reach Moscow for presentation to Marshal Stalin on
the anniversary date of the ratification of the Treaty. In order
that the picture might be flown to Moscow it had to be finished
by May 31.

Mr. Richard Hare of the Soviet Division of the Ministry of Information, supplied me with all particulars, together with a film of the
proceedings.

This, unfortunately, was less helpful than I could have desired,
seeing that it was taken at a cross-angle. Nevertheless, not having
been a witness of the proceedings, I welcomed this access of data
in which I must otherwise have been deficient. An immediate
disadvantage was the absence of M. Molotof who had been compelled to return to Russia. Fortunately a fine portrait of him was
placed at my disposal, and with that I was fain to content myself
for his inability to give me sittings. I had only six or seven weeks

in which to strive to record the historic occasion, and worthily to represent British Art.

I immediately visited the Foreign Office, where I was delighted beyond measure with the fine setting of the Minister's room, and with the inspiring atmosphere engendered by its outlook on the Admiralty, the War Office, Whitehall, and, in the distance, the stark and mystic figure of Nelson on his column, challengingly watchful ; the whole environment charged with incomparable symbolic significance. I seized at once on this scene and painted it. Then, working out the composition, drew a large cartoon to settle the proportions of the canvas, which measures 12′ 6″ × 6′ 6″. I enjoyed the active interest of M. Maisky, the Russian Ambassador. To secure sittings in so limited a time from all who figured in the tableau was, however, a matter of extreme difficulty.

The historic document was lent to me and I painted Mr. Anthony Eden, the Foreign Secretary, in the act of signing. M. Molotof is reading the duplicate with M. Maisky preparatory to signing ; to his right at the end of the table sits M. Arkadi Sobolev, Minister Plenipotentiary. The Prime Minister, Mr. Winston Churchill, is watching with interest ; next to him around the table are Mr. Attlee, the deputy Prime Minister, Sir Alexander Cadogan, Permanent Secretary to the Foreign Office and Sir Archibald Sinclair, Secretary of State for Air. Standing at the back are the interpreters and secretaries. On the mantelpiece is a bust of William Pitt.

I could not but wish, as the work proceeded, that circumstances had favoured me with costumes and pageantry such as those habitual to Magna Carta days. Eminent as are the gifts and qualities of our statesmen, the sombre sobriety of their garb is hardly a picturesque substitute for the gleaming armour and stately robes which would have lent light and lustre to such a scene in a thirteenth-century setting. My task was to suggest the intense and vivid drama of Atlantic Charter days, with costumes proper to our more prosaic sartorial convention.

However, as the outcome of seven weeks of concentrated work, the picture progressed smoothly to completion. Then a somewhat ludicrous contretemps threatened. Scarcity of materials, revealed in so many of our great shops, is no less oppressive among makers of picture-frames. A London firm to whom I applied informed me that they would require three weeks to secure a licence for the wood for the frame I sought, and an additional eight weeks in which to make it. Happily my man, Fowler, of Harpenden, completed the work in three weeks, and the embarrassment was dissipated.

By that time my task was finished. I had kept my promise as to the date of completion. The painting had to be sent to Russia by air, and so had to be compressed into the smallest possible compass. To this end the canvas, removed from the stretcher, was rolled up, and the frame was reduced to sections. Even so, the scanty limits of aeroplane accommodation necessitated the cutting of the frame in halves, for reassembling on the arrival of the picture in Moscow.

A *cartouche* on the frame, with the supporting arms of the Soviet Union and of Great Britain, bore in letters of gold, in both English and Russian, the following inscription :

Presented by H.M. Government of the United Kingdom to the Government of the Union of Soviet Socialist Republics in commemoration of the signature of the Anglo-Soviet Treaty in London, on May 26, 1942.

Rarely has my interest been so stirred as it was during the execution of this abiding commemoration of one of the most important events in our long history of international intercourse and good fellowship.

In due course the aeroplane safely carried the picture to its destination, for it was announced in the news that the Soviet Union thanked the British Government for the gift.

The conferences in Moscow of the Foreign Secretaries of Great Britain and the United States, with Marshal Stalin and Mr. Molotof, were held in the Kremlin beneath the picture in preparation for that historic meeting in the East of President Roosevelt, Marshal Stalin and Mr. Churchill.

CHAPTER XXVII

THE DAWN OF VICTORY

NO one will ever forget the fateful September Sunday morning on which we were bidden await an important broadcast announcement by Mr. Chamberlain, the Prime Minister. The calamitous sequence of events that followed, with the fall of one nation after another, leaving the British Commonwealth alone on its feet, breast-foremost to the foe, was productive of effects on mind and spirit that can never be obliterated from the memory of those who lived through those extremities of apprehension and peril.

With the unbridled forces of destruction raging relentlessly about us, life suddenly became disorganized. To some of us it was as if Kipling's vision of a world in which the last picture has been painted had actually attained reality, and that we must look for solace and promise of ease to conditions sought in imagination by *His* artist when he says :

We shall rest, and, faith, we shall need it—lie down for an æon or two,
Till the Master of All Good Workmen shall put us to work anew.

But there was one good workman whose heart remained staunch and unshaken, his genius for leadership glowing with ever more luminous flame as the danger waxed and mounted. The hour brought the man ! The towering courage of Mr. Winston Churchill inspired and reanimated us all. He could promise at first nothing but blood and sweat and tears, but from those elements of woe he contrived an elixir of new life and hope and valourous endeavour.

He spoke for the British race that confronted Hitler, with his murderous might, as Pitt spoke for the indomitable Britain that resisted the terrible challenge of Napoleon. Never was a nation more heroically served than by our Prime Minister. His invincible gallantry fired me with a desire to paint his portrait as my personal expression of sincere admiration.

The times were critical in the highest degree, and I realized that it would be impossible for him to give me sittings. But I remembered that many fine portraits by Old Masters had been painted from pencil drawings, and having myself served what might be termed a long apprenticeship to painting portraits from quick studies of busy men, and, in the previous war, posthumous portraits from small snapshot photographs. I felt confident that this experience would stand me in good stead in the performance of the difficult and adventurous task that I now proposed to myself.

I would paint Mr. Churchill in Parliament. The historic chamber of the House of Commons had been destroyed in the course of a recent air raid, and it was in the House of Lords that the Commons continued their deliberations. I was gratified by a sympathetic reception of my project, and it was there, thanks to the courtesy of the Prime Minister's Parliamentary Private Secretary, that I was installed. Seated unobserved near the Speaker's chair, I had ample opportunity of making notes and closely studying the man whom, in those crucial hours, destiny had called to pre-eminent office.

The portrait developed well, and, enamoured of my theme, I resolved to paint not one, but two, each typifying a phase of my eminent subject's manifold activities. The first showed the great Parliamentarian, in the conventional morning dress of the grave statesman, our foremost Commoner addressing the assembly as whose servant it is his habit, with proud humility, to describe himself.

Completed, the canvas was placed on an easel at 10 Downing Street, where, with only one minor suggestion of improvement, it successfully passed its ordeal of inspection.

The portrait was presented to Harrow School, which is proud to number Mr. Churchill among the most illustrious of its Old Boys. The gift was that of Sir Frederick Heaton, who, at the time the picture was painted, had three sons at Harrow.

The second portrait that I painted was symbolic. It shows the Prime Minister in his siren suit, habitually immersed in the vital administration of worldwide strategy and the balancing of conflicting elements, as an exemplar of actual toil and physical effort. This portrait was shown at the Jubilee Exhibition of the Royal Society of Portrait Painters at the Royal Academy in the autumn of 1942. The Devonshire Club wished to secure it, but when they learned that Mrs. Churchill liked it and pronounced it an exact likeness of her husband in those tremendous days, they decided to present it to the Prime Minister.

Accordingly, on June 28, 1943, he was entertained at the Club, where Mr. Ormond A. Blyth, the chairman, personally made the presentation. In the course of his speech he ventured the felicitous suggestion that one of Mr. Churchill's famous phrases, describing the R.A.F. during the Battle of Britain, should be adapted, to run, as applied to the Premier himself, " Never in human history have so many owed so much to one man ". On receiving the gift Mr. Churchill declared that the portrait would be a treasured heirloom in his family.

Inspired by the indomitable leadership of the Prime Minister, the city of London, with all its ancient dignity and rights amidst the battered and war-scarred Guildhall, the Lord Mayor, Sir Samuel Joseph, with representatives of the whole Country and Empire, Church and State, conferred upon Mr. Churchill the honorary Freedom. As it was a general wish that this historic scene should be perpetuated I was requested to paint it, and as I write, that picture is in the throes of creation, so that future generations shall be able to witness the incident of an achievement of individual Freedom being conferred upon one who so valiantly and courageously in supreme leadership, led the fight for the ideal and wider Freedom for Mankind.

By this time the national outlook had undergone a transformation. Inspired and fortified by Mr. Churchill's inflexible valour, the nation, single-handed, had resisted the most appalling concentration of new and novel military might and force by which a people was ever threatened. The great free Commonwealth stood fast, it renewed its strength, it kept inviolate its own shores and the major avenues of liberty. The United States, with its illimitable resources in men and munitions of every kind and character, had, with Russia, with powers of recovery from disaster and of force in heroic, sustained attack inconceivable and incomprehensible to the infamous Axis, come mightily to our aid.

Our hopes were strengthened and our faith rewarded as we beheld the Dome of St. Paul's still proudly dominating the City of London with its battered and scarred ruins all around, that majestic and sacred edifice upon which is focused the veneration of our United Empire. Of the thirty thousand Abbeys, Churches and Chapels damaged or destroyed, St. Paul's Cathedral, although battered and its windows shattered, has miraculously weathered the ordeal and siege of war.

There were still shrewd blows to be sustained, grievous reverses, and bitter aching wounds to be endured. But borne and endured they were, without tremour or trepidation, and slowly but surely the situation was retrieved. To defeat and disaster succeeded victory upon victory, embracing every front. The gloom of our skies became tinged with a happy light of progressive brightness presaging the advent of the Dawn of Victory.

CHAPTER XXVIII

REFLECTIONS

NOW, as we face the immortal dawn, the world has passed through the crucible again. Those who have lived through our two wars will realize the effect of those wars on the arts. In 1914 came a sudden halt, but portraits and paintings were called for, and artists grew busy. " I am the civilization you are fighting for," one of them is reputed to have told the recruiting sergeant. The names of Army commanders became household words, and themselves subjects for the painter's brush.

How different was it in 1939, with every doorstep a battlefront and ruin everywhere about us ; pictures, treasures, household goods, hurried to secret places ; monuments moved from the streets and hidden in country gardens ; great houses closed or handed over to schools or Government departments. Now the peril was grave indeed. In one foul sweep lifelong possessions and cherished art collections were hurtled to destruction. It seemed that the only thing left was personality.

The arts of peace gave way to the arts of war. Destruction was afoot, and creation stood bewildered and benumbed. Everything was in the cauldron, metal, bodies, souls, ideals, anything that could produce power to devastate or kill. There was nothing else to be done and it must be so, but what a bitter world for those who have lived to produce beauty !

It is pathetic to realize the effect of it all on the sensitive spirit of the Arts. The famous Arts Club was totally destroyed, and many studios have been turned to dust, often leaving the artist too broken in health and spirit to start again. Stern and terrible days we lived in. One distinguished water-colour painter, broken and feeble in frame, and looking ten years older than his years, said to me, " You cannot spend three months in a public shelter night after night without paying the penalty." What, we wondered, would be the end of it all ? In such a devastating war the test cannot be the survival of the fittest, for here is no natural process at work, no logical selection, nothing but ruthless terror and destruction. But humanity, in spite of all, rises and rejoices when our great Prime Minister reminds us that we " move in an unfolding purpose ". It is evident that in this purpose Justice still stands athwart the world, with its mighty balances weighing out the evil from the good. Never before has this sifting process been so irrevocable, so unmistakable. Purposes, intrigues, motives, designs, are forced into the scales. The Day of Judgment is at hand

And so, although all our ideals are passing through the fires, the marvellous accomplishments of the ages, the incalculable wealth of the Arts recorded in our great galleries and private collections, their masterly technique and the superb achievements of their creators, cannot be permanently plunged into oblivion. The modern worship of ugliness, which is but another phase of the worship of evil, will vanish, and the world will return to sanity. Art is long and time is fleeting, as Longfellow says, and we may remember the fine little lines of Austin Dobson's translation :

> All passes. Art alone
> Enduring stays to us.
> The Bust outlasts the throne
> The Coin, Tiberius.

It seems part of the destroying onslaught of war that confusion should shatter our faith in all directions, weakening our confidence in all such things as painting, sculpture, music, and literature. The Palace of Art is shaken to its foundations. The Temple of Truth and Beauty is rudely assailed. Words cease to have their old meanings. Hitler cries out " Law and Order " when he means oppression and robbery. Japan proclaims " the heavenly task of developing the Chinese incident " when she means that she will go on murdering the Chinese. It is the same perversity which at home distorts the meaning of words by praising an egregious monstrosity as a work of art. Reason and judgment are stunned, and a baffled intellect falls down and worships at the feet of strange gods.

Yet true art remains. The artist's achievements cannot utterly perish, he seeks to stay the flight of Time and to hold fast something of its fleeting pageantry. With the colours of the rainbow on his palette he tries to capture something of the splendour of the panorama of life around him, the effects of sun, sky, earth, and sea. The writer by his pen, the artist with his brush, the sculptor with his chisel, bring the men and women of bygone days to life again that generation after generation have a visible link in the chain of existence.

In living again through a few pleasant hours recalling the spirits of those I have painted I hear their voices, I watch their movements, and in imagination they are here in the eternal Now. The hour in flight has been arrested. The Past and the Present unite in one reality. There is no dim past, no elusive future ; only the vibrating present. "Thus we overcome the tyranny of time and catch a glimpse of the omnipresence of eternity." Imagination and memory are the oracles in the temple of immortality, the artist is the sentinel, for ever striving to keep open the stately portals. Though the foundations of the earth should crumble, the things of the spirit are indestructible.

INDEX